Praise for the "Kids Love" Guidebook Travel Series

On-Air Personality Comments (Television Interviews)

"The great thing about these books is t  *es these adventures"* – **(WI**

"Very helpful to lots of families when t *'t want to go to same places again!"* – **(WISH-TV, Indianapolis)**

"Dividing the state into many sections, the book has something for everyone…everywhere." – **(WLVT-TV, Pennsylvania)**

"These authors know first-hand that it's important to find hands-on activities that engage your children…" **(WBNS-TV, Columbus)**

"You spent more than 1000 hours doing this research for us, that's really great – we just have to pick up the book and it's done…" **(WTVR-TV, Richmond)**

"A family that's a great source for travel ideas…" **(WBRA-TV, Roanoke)**

"What a great idea…this book needed to be done a long time ago!" **(WKYT-TV, Lexington)**

"A fabulous idea…places to travel that your kids will enjoy" **(WOOD-TV, Grand Rapids)**

"The Zavatskys call it a dream come true, running their own business while keeping the family together. Their goal, encourage other parents to create special family travel memories." - **(WLVT-TV, Pennsylvania)**

"It's a wonderful book, and as someone who has been to a lot of these places…you hit it right on the money!" – **(WKRC-TV, Cincinnati)**

Praise for the "Kids Love" Guidebook Travel Series
Customer Comments (actual letters on file)

"I wanted to tell you how helpful all your books have been to my family of 6. I rarely find books that cater to families with kids. I have your Indiana, Ohio, Kentucky, Michigan, and Pennsylvania books. I don't want to miss any of the new books that come out. Keep up the great ideas. The books are fantastic. I have shown them to tons of my friends. They love them, too." – H.M.

"I bought the Ohio and Indiana books yesterday and what a blessing these are for us!!! We love taking our grandsons on Grammie & Papaw trips thru the year and these books are making it soooo much easier to plan. The info is complete and full of ideas. Even the layout of the book is easy to follow...I just wanted to thank you for all your work in developing these books for us..." – G.K

"I have purchased your book. My grandchildren and I have gone to many of the places listed in your book. They mark them off as we visit them. We are looking forward to seeing many more. It is their favorite thing to look at book when they come over and find new places to explore. Thank you for publishing this book!" - B.A.

"At a retail price of under $15.00, any of the books would be well worth buying even for a one-time only vacation trip. Until now, when the opportunity arose for a day or weekend trip with the kids I was often at a loss to pick a destination that I could be sure was convenient, educational, child-friendly, and above all, fun. Now I have a new problem: How in the world will we ever be able to see and do all the great ideas listed in this book? I'd better get started planning our next trip right away. At least I won't have to worry about where we're going or what to do when we get there!" – VA Homeschool Newsletter

"My family and I used this book this summer to explore our state! We lived here nearly our entire life and yet over half the book we never knew existed. These people really know what kids love! Highly recommended for all parents, grandparents, etc.." – Barnes and Noble website reviewer

KIDS

LOVE

North Carolina

A Family Travel Guide to
Exploring "Kid-Tested" Places
in North Carolina...Year Round!

George & Michele Zavatsky

Dedicated to the Families
of North Carolina

For the latest major updates corresponding to the pages in this book visit our website:

www.KidsLoveTravel.com

REMEMBER: *Museum exhibits change frequently. Check the site's website before you visit to note any changes. Also, HOURS and ADMISSIONS are subject to change at the owner's discretion. If you are tight on time or money, check the attraction's website or call before you visit.*

INTERNET PRECAUTION: *All websites mentioned in KIDS LOVE NORTH CAROLINA have been checked for appropriate content. However, due to the fast-changing nature of the Internet, we strongly urge parents to preview any recommended sites and to always supervise their children when on-line.*

ISBN-13: 978-0-9774434-6-8

KIDS ♥ NORTH CAROLINA ™   Kids Love Publications, LLC

TABLE OF CONTENTS

State Detail Map

(With Major Routes and Cities Marked)

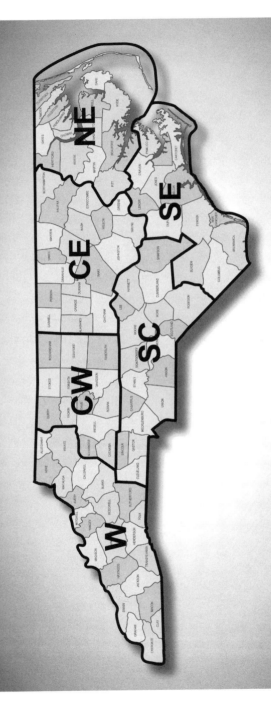

Chapter Area Map

(Chapters arranged alphabetically by chapter name)

CITY INDEX *(Listed by City, Area, Page Numbers)*

CITY INDEX *(Listed by City, Area, Page Numbers)*

Acknowledgements

We are most thankful to be blessed with our parents, Barbara (Darrall) Callahan and George & Catherine Zavatsky who help us every way they can – researching, proofing and baby-sitting. More importantly, they are great sounding boards and offer unconditional support. So many places around North Carolina remind us of family vacations years ago…

We also want to express our thanks to the many Convention & Visitor Bureaus' staff for providing the attention to detail that helps to complete a project. We felt very welcome during our travels in North Carolina and would be proud to call it home!

Our own kids, Jenny and Daniel, were delightful and fun children during our trips across the state. What a joy it is to be their parents…we couldn't do it without them as our "kid-testers"!

We both sincerely thank each other – our partnership has created an even greater business/personal "marriage" with lots of exciting moments, laughs, and new adventures in life woven throughout. Above all, we praise the Lord for His so many blessings through the last few years.

We think North Carolina is a wonderful, friendly area of the country with more activities than you could imagine. Our sincere wish is that this book will help everyone "fall in love" with all of North Carolina.

In a Hundred Years…
It will not matter, The size of my bank account…
The kind of house that I lived in, the kind of car that I drove…
But what will matter is…
That the world may be different
Because I was important in the life of a child.
- *author unknown*

HOW TO USE THIS BOOK

If you are excited about discovering North Carolina, this is the book for you and your family! We've spent over a thousand hours doing all the scouting, collecting and compiling (*and most often visiting!*) so that you could spend less time searching and more time having fun.

Here are a few hints to make your adventures run smoothly:

- ◼ Consider the **child's age** before deciding to take a visit.
- ◼ Know **directions** and parking. Call ahead (or visit the company's website) if you have questions *and* bring this book. Also, don't forget your camera! (*please honor rules regarding use*).
- ◼ **Estimate the duration** of the trip. Bring small surprises (favorite juice boxes) travel books, and toys.
- ◼ Call ahead for **reservations** or details, if necessary.
- ◼ Most listings are **closed major holidays** unless noted.
- ◼ Make a **family "treasure chest"**. Decorate a big box or use an old popcorn tin. Store memorabilia from a fun outing, journals, pictures, brochures and souvenirs. Once a year, look through the "treasure chest" and reminisce. "Kids Love Travel Memories!" is an excellent travel journal & scrapbook that your family can create. (*See www.KidsLoveTravel.com for more details*).
- ◼ Plan **picnics** along the way. Many state history sites and state parks are scattered throughout North Carolina. Allow time for a rural /scenic route to take advantage of these free picnic facilities.
- ◼ Some activities, especially tours, require **groups** of 10 or more. To participate, you may either ask to be part of another tour group or get a group together yourself (neighbors, friends, organizations). If you arrange a group outing, most places offer discounts.
- ◼ For the latest **updates** corresponding to the pages in this book, visit our website: **www.KidsLoveTravel.com**.
- ◼ Each chapter represents an area of the state. Each listing is further identified by city, zip code, and place/event name. Our popular **Activity Index** in the back of the book **lists places by Activity Heading** (i.e. State History, Tours, Outdoors, Museums, etc.).

Mission Statement

At first glance, you may think that this is a book that just lists hundreds of places to travel. While it is true that we've invested thousands of hours of exhaustive research (*and drove over 3000 miles in North Carolina*) to prepare this travel resource...just listing places to travel is <u>not</u> the mission statement of these projects.

As children, Michele and I were able to travel extensively throughout the United States. We consider these family times some of the greatest memories we cherish

today. We, quite frankly, felt that most children had this opportunity to travel with their family as we did. However, as we became adults and started our own family, we found that this wasn't necessarily the case. We continually heard friends express several concerns when deciding how to spend "quality" and "quantity" family time. 1) What to do? 2) Where to do it? 3) How much will it cost? 4) How do I know that my kids will enjoy it?

Interestingly enough, as we compare our experiences with our families when we were kids, many of our fondest memories were not made at an expensive attraction, but rather when it was least expected.

It is our belief and mission statement that if you as a family will study and <u>use</u> the contained information <u>to create family memories</u>, these memories will grow a stronger, tighter family. Our ultimate mission statement is, that your children will develop a love and a passion for quality family experiences that they can pass to another generation of family travelers.

We thank you for purchasing this book, and we hope to see you on the road (*and hear your travel stories!*) God bless your journeys and happy exploring!

George, Michele,
Jenny and Daniel

General State Agency & Recreational Information

Call *(or visit websites)* for the services of interest. Request to be added to their mailing lists.

- ◼ NC Association of Agricultural Fairs. www.ncfairs.com.
- ◼ NC Department of Transportation Ferry Division. Morehead City. (252) 726-6446 or (800) 293-3779 or www.ncferry.org.
- ◼ NC Division of Forest Resources. Raleigh. www.dfr.state.nc.us. or (919) 733-2162.
- ◼ NC Division of Marine Fisheries. Morehead City. (800) 682-2632 or www.ncfisheries.net.
- ◼ NC Division of Tourism, Film and Sports Development. Raleigh. (919) 733-8372 or (800) 847-4862 or www.visitnc.com.
- ◼ NC Historic Sites. Raleigh. (919) 733-7862 or www.ah.dcr.state.nc.us/sections/hs/default.htm.
- ◼ NC Scenic Byways Program. (877) DOT-4YOU or www.ncdot.org/public/publications.
- ◼ NC Wildlife Resources Commission. (919) 733-3391 or www.ncwildlife.org.
- ◼ NC Association of RV Parks & Campgrounds. Garner. www.campinginnorthcarolina.com. or (919) 779-5709.

- ◼ **CE** - DURHAM CVB - (800) 446-8604 or www.durham-nc.com.
- ◼ **CE** - RALEIGH CVB - (800) 849-8499 or www.visitraleigh.com.
- ◼ **CW** - HIGH POINT CVB - (800) 720-5255 or www.highpoint.org.
- ◼ **CW** - GREENSBORO CVB - (800) 344-2282 or www.visitgreensboro.com.
- ◼ **CW** - WINSTON-SALEM CVB - (866) 728-4200 or www.visitwinstonsalem.com.
- ◼ **NE** - OUTER BANKS VISITORS BUREAU - (877) OBX-4FUN or www.outerbanks.org
- ◼ **NE** - CRAVEN COUNTY CVC/ NEW BERN - (800) 437-5767 or www.visitnewbern.com.
- ◼ **SC** - CABARRUS COUNTY CVB - (800) 848-3740 or www.cabarruscvb.com.
- ◼ **SC** - CHARLOTTE CVB - (800) 722-1994 or www.visitcharlotte.org.
- ◼ **SE** - CAPE FEAR COAST CVB - (800) 222-4757 or www.cape-fear.nc.us.
- ◼ **SE** - CRYSTAL COAST TOURISM - (252) 726-8148 or www.sunnync.com.
- ◼ **W** - BOONE CVB - www.visitboonenc.com. or (800) 852-9506.
- ◼ **W** - ASHEVILLE CVB - (800) 257-5583 or www.exploreasheville.com.
- ◼ **W** - CHEROKEE TRIBAL TRAVEL AND PROMOTION - www.cherokee-nc.com.

RECREATION:

- ◼ **SKI RESORTS** - skiing, snowboarding, some w/ outdoor ice skating. www.goskinc.com.
- ◼ **W** - Cataloochee Ski Area - 1080 Ski Lodge Road, Maggie Valley. (800) 768-3588 or www.cataloochee.com. has its own specially-named tubing park: Tube World, featuring five runs.

- ◼ **W** - Appalachian Ski Mountain - Blowing Rock. www.appskimtn.com. (800) 322-2373.
- ◼ **W** - Ski Beech - Beech Mountain. (800) 438-2093 or www.skibeech.com. was the first resort in the South to open a tube run in the 1996-1997 season.
- ◼ **W** - Sugar Mountain - Banner Elk. (800) 784-2768 or www.skisugar.com.
- ◼ **W** - Hawksnest Ski Resort - Banner Elk. (800) 822-4295 or www.hawksnest-resort.com. Hawksnest Resort now also features a terrific snowtubing-only park. In fact, you'll find the longest tubing runs in the southeast here.
- ◼ **W** - Wolf Laurel Ski Resort - Mars Hill, (828) 689-4121. (800) 541-1738. skiwolflaurel.com. Summer activities include mountain biking, whitewater rafting, horseback riding and hiking. On site lodging. Today you can also enjoy a speedy descent down the slopes on a tube at four of nine ski areas.

PARKS & REC

- ◼ North Carolina Division Of Parks & Recreation, Raleigh. (919) 733-4181 or www.ncparks.gov. Junior Ranger Program - The junior ranger program engages youth in learning through participating in park educational programs, completing a junior ranger booklet, and completing a park stewardship project. Youth learn about career opportunities in natural resource conservation and gain an appreciation of their cultural and natural heritage. The parks below currently offer junior ranger programs: *Jordan Lake State Recreation Area, Hammocks Beach State Park, Goose Creek State Park, Hanging Rock State Park, Mount Mitchell State Park, New River State Park.*

AIRPORTS - All children love to visit the airport! Why not take a tour and understand all the jobs it takes to run an airport? Tour the terminal, baggage claim, gates and security / currency exchange. Maybe you'll even get to board a plane.

ANIMAL SHELTERS - Great for the would-be pet owner. Not only will you see many cats and dogs available for adoption, but a guide will show you the clinic and explain the needs of a pet. Be prepared to have the children "fall in love" with one of the animals while they are there!

BANKS - Take a "behind the scenes" look at automated teller machines, bank vaults and drive-thru window chutes. You may want to take this tour and then open a savings account for your child.

CITY HALLS - Halls of Fame, City Council Chambers & Meeting Room, Mayor's Office and famous statues.

ELECTRIC COMPANY / POWER PLANTS - Modern science has created many ways to generate electricity today, but what really goes on with the "flip of a switch". Because coal can be dirty, wear old, comfortable clothes. Coal furnaces heat water, which produces steam, that propels turbines, that drives generators, that make electricity.

FIRE STATIONS - Many Open Houses in October, Fire Prevention Month. Take a look into the life of the firefighters servicing your area and try on their gear. See where they hang out, sleep and eat. Hop aboard a real-life fire engine truck and learn fire safety too.

HOSPITALS - Some Children's Hospitals offer pre-surgery and general tours.

NEWSPAPERS - You'll be amazed at all the new technology. See monster printers and robotics. See samples in the layout department and maybe try to put together your own page. After seeing a newspaper made, most companies give you a free copy (dated that day) as your souvenir. National Newspaper Week is in October.

PETCO - Various stores. Contact each store manager to see if they participate. The Fur, Feathers & Fins™ program allows children to learn about the characteristics and habitats of fish, reptiles, birds, and small animals. At your local Petco, lessons in science, math and geography come to life through this hands-on field trip. As students develop a respect for animals, they will also develop a greater sense of responsibility.

PIZZA HUT & PAPA JOHN'S - Participating locations. Telephone the store manager. Best days are Monday, Tuesday and Wednesday mid-afternoon. Minimum of 10 people. Small charge per person. All children love pizza – especially when they can create their own! As the children tour the kitchen, they learn how to make a pizza, bake it, and then eat it. The admission charge generally includes lots of creatively made pizzas, beverage and coloring book.

KRISPY KREME DONUTS - Participating locations. Get an "inside look" and learn the techniques that make these donuts some of our favorites! Watch the dough being made in "giant" mixers, being formed into donuts and taking a "trip" through the fryer. Seeing them being iced and topped with colorful sprinkles is always a favorite with the kids. Contact your local store manager. They prefer Monday or Tuesday. Free.

SUPERMARKETS - Kids are fascinated to go behind the scenes of the same store where Mom and Dad shop. Usually you will see them grind meat, walk into large freezer rooms, watch cakes and bread bake and receive free samples along the way. Maybe you'll even get to pet a live lobster!

TV / RADIO STATIONS - Studios, newsrooms, Fox kids clubs. Why do weathermen never wear blue/green clothes on TV? What makes a "DJ's" voice sound so deep and smooth?

WATER TREATMENT PLANTS - A giant science experiment! You can watch seven stages of water treatment. The favorite is usually the wall of bright buttons flashing as workers monitor the different processes.

U.S. MAIN POST OFFICES - Did you know Ben Franklin was the first Postmaster General (over 200 years ago)? Most interesting is the high-speed automated mail processing equipment. Learn how to address envelopes so they will be sent quicker (there are secrets). To make your tour more interesting, have your children write a letter to themselves and address it with colorful markers. Mail it earlier that day and they will stay interested trying to locate their letter in all the high-speed machinery.

GEOCACHING AND LETTERBOXING

Geocaching and Letterboxing are the ultimate treasure hunt and can add excitement and fun to your driving, camping and hiking experiences. Geocaching employs the use of a GPS device (global positioning device) to find the cache.

Letterboxing uses clues from one location to the next to find the letterbox; sometimes a compass is needed. Both methods use the Internet advertising the cache, providing basic maps and creating a forum for cache hunters.

GEOCACHING

The object of Geocaching is to find the hidden container filled with a logbook, pencil and sometimes prizes! Where are Caches? Everywhere! But to be safe, be sure you're treading on Public Property. When you find the cache, write your name and the date you found it in the logbook. Larger caches might contain maps, books, toys, even money! When you take something from the cache you are honor-bound to leave something else in its place. Usually cache hunters will report their individual cache experiences on the Internet. (www.geocaching.com)

- ### GPS RECEIVER

  You'll need a GPS receiver that will determine your position on the planet in relation to the cache's "waypoint," its longitude/latitude coordinates. You can buy a decent GPS receiver for around $100. More expensive ones have built-in electronic compasses and topographical maps, but you don't need all the extras to have fun geocaching.

LETTERBOXING

The object is similar to geocaching — find the Letterbox — but instead of just signing and dating the logbook, use a personalized rubber stamp. Most letterboxes include another rubber stamp for your own logbook. The creator of the letterbox provides clues to its location. Finding solutions to clues might require a compass, map and solving puzzles and riddles! This activity is great fun for the entire family! (www.letterboxing.org)

Chapter 1
Central East

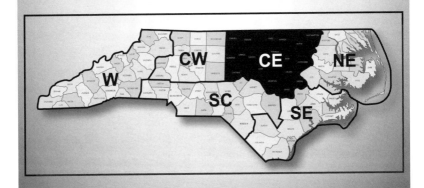

CE Area

A Quick Tour of our Hand-Picked Favorites Around...

Central East North Carolina

Wanna visit the land of the FREE? Head to Raleigh, my friend. With 20 FREE attractions, including the North Carolina Museum of Art, North Carolina Museum of History and the North Carolina Museum of Natural Sciences, it's an affordable escape for parents and children alike!

The **North Carolina Museum of Natural Sciences** in Raleigh is a great free way to spend an afternoon indoors unearthing the natural mysteries of this diverse and beautiful state. "Meet" a giant whale, the Terror of the South, see a dino heart and then admire playful butterflies...all in one fabulous place.

Want a dose of contemporary science? Plan an old-fashioned picnic at **Pullen Park** and then head into the future at the **NC State Solar House** (both sites are on NC State campus in Raleigh). As you ring the doorbell and enter the house – you're now inside a giant science experiment using solar power to generate energy for the whole house. Is it the future?

Some other amazing museums can be found in Durham. Real, very talkative and different lemurs abound at the **Duke Lemur Center**. By appointment, you can walk into a controlled recreation of Madagascar and visit with their adorable leapers! Females rule here, but romeos work hard for your attention.

Rated among the top four family-friendly museums in Southeast, the **Museum of Life and Science** in Durham is a state-of-the-art, engaging indoor/outdoor science-technology center. The key is INDOOR AND OUTDOOR. Rainy days call for physical science experiments indoors. Any day it isn't raining – kids swarm outside along paths leading to so many outdoor exhibits – it's nearly a zoo. Butterflies, bears and lemurs, oh my!

Nearby, you can stand in the spot where the Civil War completely ended. **Bennett Place State Historic Site** is the simple farmhouse where two generals met in 1865, and signed surrender papers for the largest Southern armies to formally end the war.

Spend the night in a real log cabin or historic **Arrowhead Inn** suite for a good nights rest before you go wafting. No, not rafting, wafting. What's the difference? Find out on your group tour in special waft rafts as you go **Wafting the Eno**. No real skill involved, but you must leave your cares at home to truly Waft!

Let's talk about some food joints around here. **Elmo's Diner** is a awesome pick by Rachel Ray's $40.00 a Day. We call this a gourmet diner – parents: try the spicy meatloaf or quiche or hummus – kids: try anything off the $3.00 kids menu. BBQ is all grown up at places like the **Q Shack**. Chili-rubbed sliced brisket, hand-pulled pork and ribs are must orders. Sides are Southern – everyone gets hush puppies. In Durham, you can get both the Eastern North Carolina style (with chopped pork and a clear sauce of vinegar, pepper, and salt) and the Western North Carolina style (with chopped or sliced pork with a red sauce that includes ketchup and sugar along with the other ingredients).

Sites and attractions are listed in order by City, Zip Code, and Name. Symbols indicated represent:

 Festivals   Restaurants   Lodging

Apex

JORDAN LAKE STATE RECREATION AREA

Apex - 280 State Park Road (21 miles southwest of Raleigh off US 64) 27539. Phone: (919) 362-0586.   www.ncparks.gov/Visit/parks/jord/main.php.   Hours: Daily 8:00am- dusk. Admission: $5.00 per car.

A nearly 14,000 acre reservoir, Jordan Lake offers bald eagle watching, boating, camping, education and events, fishing, Heritage Day, hiking, picnicking, swimming. Visitor Center displays allow the visitors to explore the world of water environments and the species that those aquatic environments support. A major feature of the exhibit hall is the life size eagle's nest which allows visitors a bird's eye view of the interior of this massive nest. It is the largest summertime home of the bald eagle in the eastern United States (The observation deck is located five miles south of I-40 on NC 751, 6.5 miles north of US 64). The exhibit hall is open from 8:00 am-5:00pm daily.

Bailey

COUNTRY DOCTOR MUSEUM

Bailey - 6642 Peele Road (from Hwy 264, take the Bailey exit south on SR 581. At the first light, turn right on Hwy 264 Alt. At the first left, turn left) 27807. Phone: (252) 235-4165. www.countrydoctormuseum.org. Hours: Tuesday-Saturday 10:00am-4:00pm. Admission: $3.00-$5.00 per person (ages 3+). Educators: Print off the Scavenger Hunt sheet (found under the Tours icon page online) to use as your trick to keep the kids attentive for "little" things.

Honoring the "old family doctor", this museum consists of the restored offices of two country doctors who practiced from 1857 to 1887. The museum's collections include artifacts relevant to many aspects of health care including nursing, pharmacy, homeopathy, and dentistry. Along with surgical sets and microscopes, the collection now incorporates medicine kits, apothecary equipment, nursing uniforms and memorabilia, and tools that would scare a patient today. You'll read about a lot of home remedies your grandparents may have tried. A medical herb garden located behind the Museum delights visitors throughout the year.

Benson

BENSON MULE DAYS

Benson - Created to celebrate the animal on which the livelihood of this small town once depended, Benson Mule Days has been a Southern tradition for over 50 years. Catch the kickoff concert on Thursday night at the Benson Singing Grove, and stay until the carnival ends on Sunday evening. In between enjoy four days of rodeos, rides, games, barbecue, bluegrass and gospel music, a street dance, a mule pulling contest, arts and crafts, mule and horse rides, and, of course, the annual parade. And there's even camping allowed in celebration of the favorite animal of Benson. (third long weekend in September)

Burlington

ALAMANCE BATTLEGROUND STATE HISTORIC SITE

Burlington - 5803 South NC 62 (Interstate 40/85 in Burlington take NC 62 south, exit 143. Follow the directional signs) 27215. Phone: (336) 227-4785. Hours: Monday-Saturday 9:00am.-5:00pm. www.ah.dcr.state.nc.us/sections/hs/alamance/alamanc.htm Admission: FREE.

"A State Historic Site and a Primary Revolutionary War Site", this historic site is where Royal Governor William Tryon led the North Carolina militia in battle against the Regulators on May 16, 1771. A 1780 log house used by frontier people on the western fringes of the colony is also located on the grounds; the house contains its original furnishings. On the grounds is a three-quarter-mile Outdoor Exploring trail, the James Hunter Monument, and the 1880 granite column commemorating the battle. Colored pennants mark the battle positions and Regulator campsite on the battlefield. An audiovisual presentation of the battle is offered in the visitor center. Best to visit during re-enactment weekend or Colonial Living Week in October.

ANNIVERSARY OF THE BATTLE OF ALAMANCE

Join in commemorative activities featuring a wreath-laying ceremony, picnic, and program. The weekend following is the Century Live-In & Militia Muster. Enjoy a recreation of colonial military and domestic life by costumed interpreters. (May 16th weekend)

CEDAROCK HISTORICAL FARM

Burlington - 4242 Cedarock Historical Park Road 27215. Phone: (336) 570-6760. http://www.alamance-nc.com/Alamance-NC/Departments/Recreation/Parks/Cedarock/ Hours: The farm is open to tour occasional weekends. (see website). Admission: FREE.

The original site of the Garrett farm, this historic farm lies on 414 acres and features beautifully restored buildings, numerous livestock, and demonstrations of farming techniques used at the turn-of-the-century. Livestock on the farm include sheep, goats, dairy and beef cattle, and a team of draft mules.

Chapel Hill

CHAPEL HILL UNIVERSITY OF NORTH CAROLINA

Chapel Hill - Dean E. Smith Center, Home Of The Tar Heels.

The Tar Heel basketball team has produced famous players and garnered numerous championships and awards over the years while playing under the roofs of Carmichael Auditorium and the Dean E. Smith Center, completed in 1986. The structure is only one of 14 facilities that make up the Tar Heel athletics program, comprised of 26 separate sports. www.unc.edu.

JORDAN LAKE EDUCATIONAL STATE FOREST

Chapel Hill - 2832 Big Woods Road (I-40 exit 274, south on SR 751) 27514. Phone: (919) 542-1154. www.ncesf.org/JLESF/home.htm. Hours: Weekdays 9:00am-5:00pm (EST), Weekends 11:00am-5:00pm (EST) and 11:00am-8:00pm (DST). Season is mid-March to Mid-November. Admission: FREE.

Located between the Piedmont and Coastal Plain, this forest showcases a wide variety of pines and hardwoods found in a wetland ecosystem (Wetlands Trails or Forest Trail). At the Forest, visitors can listen to the wind in the trees or they can listen to the trees tell a story (3/4 mile Talking Tree Trail). The Forest is home to a wide variety of wildlife including birds of prey, deer, songbirds, flying squirrels and beavers (Wildlife Trail). Picnic facilities are available, including a shelter to accommodate large groups.

KIDZU CHILDREN'S MUSEUM

Chapel Hill - 105 E. Franklin Street (near intersection of S. Columbia and E. Franklin) 27514. Phone: (919) 933-1455. www.kidzuchildrensmuseum.org. Hours: Tuesday-Saturday 10:00am-5:00pm, Sunday 1:00-5:00pm. Admission: $4.00 person (age 2+).

Kidzu Children's Museum is a hands-on museum in the heart of downtown Chapel Hill where children 0-8 years old and the adults in their lives can safely discover, pretend, and play to their heart's content. Since opening in 2006, they have hosted a series of nationally recognized traveling exhibits, including "Mister Rogers' Neighborhood" and "Where the Wild Things Are." In addition, you'll find a changing Theatre and storytelling crafts each month.

MOREHEAD PLANETARIUM AND SCIENCE CENTER

Chapel Hill - 250 E. Franklin Street (UNC Chapel Hill campus, follow signs) 27599. Phone: (919) 962-1236. www.moreheadplanetarium.org. Hours: Tuesday-Saturday 10:00am-5:00pm, Sunday 1:00-5:00pm. Open from 6:30-8:30pm on Friday and Saturday nights for shows. Admission: $5.00-$6.00 per show. Combo discounts. Online coupons. NASA Digital Theater & Exhibits Admission is FREE.

Visit the facility where American astronauts formerly trained. At Morehead Planetarium and Science Center you can experience dazzling 30-45-minute multimedia star shows (Magic Tree House Space Mission or Laser Show or Solar System Adventure), varied exhibits, and shopping at the Infinity Gift Shop. "Carolina Skies" is one of the oldest shows at the planetarium, but it's never the same twice. The show allows visitors to explore the heavens as they will appear each night above North Carolina. Other programs and events include "Destination: Space," examining the history and future of America's space program, and "Solar System Adventure," a character-driven tour through the cosmos. The Morehead Center's most recent addition is a new digital video theater that shows original science programming produced by world-class film studios.

NORTH CAROLINA BOTANICAL GARDEN

Chapel Hill - Old Mason Farm Road (UNC campus, take Exit 273A, and turn right onto Highway 54 West) 27599. Phone: (919) 962-0522. www.ncbg.unc.edu. Hours: Weekdays 8:00am-5:00pm, Saturday 9:00am-5:00pm, Sunday 1:00-5:00pm. Open until 6:00pm on weekends in the spring/summer. Admission: FREE.

The largest botanical garden in the southeast, established in 1966, consists of nearly 700 acres of preserved land with nature trails, carnivorous plant collections, aquatics and herb gardens, and revolving exhibits of artwork with a horticultural theme. It's like walking across the whole state in one place!

PIEDMONT NATURE TRAILS - provide over two miles of hiking trails through piedmont woodland. The easier Streamside Trail crosses Meeting-of-the-Waters Creek twice as it meanders through the lower sections of this site. The more difficult Oak-Hickory Trail traverses hillier portions.

COASTAL PLAIN AND SANDHILLS HABITATS - reproduce the wide range of ecosystems present in the eastern part of the state, beginning with the rolling sandhills where you see the state tree of North Carolina, the longleaf pine. Soon the terrain becomes flatter, simulating the pocosin and wetland habitats common on the outer coastal plain. In this area grow myrtle and carnivorous plants, such as the Venus flytrap and pitcher plants.

MOUNTAIN HABITAT GARDEN - contains plants and trees that are characteristic of the mountainous areas of the southern Appalachians. Dense shade from canopy trees and abundant moisture create a cove-like environment for these species.

> The University of North Carolina at Chapel Hill is the first state-supported university in America, which was chartered in 1789.

HERB GARDEN - interprets a series of gardens dealing with medicinal, culinary, economic, shade, poison, evergreen and Native American herbs. At the entrance of the Herb Garden, kids will find a booklet that encourages them to take a closer look at the natural world of plants. Children can have fun while discovering the wonderful nature of herbs in the Zoo Garden (dig), a Fairy Find, a Weather Station, Game Boards, and even create their own nature art.

Clayton

CLEMMONS EDUCATIONAL STATE FOREST

Clayton - 2411 Old US 70 West (US 70 east of Raleigh) 27520. Phone: (919) 553-5651. www.ncesf.org/CESF/home.htm.   Hours: Tuesday-Friday   9:00am-5:00pm, Saturday & Sunday 11:00am-5:00pm EST, 11:00am-8:00pm DST (mid-March to mid-November). Admission: FREE. Educators: For great online curriculum visit: www.ncesf.org/tg/tg2_main.htm.

Located between the Piedmont and the Coastal Plain, Clemmons' pine stands and hardwoods are set on rolling terrain highlighted by streams and rock formations. These features are accessible by a series of well-marked trails, accented by exhibits and displays depicting the ecology of the forest. Listen to the "talking" trees and rocks weave tales about the life there; hike the demo trail to see natural resource manager's duties; explore the new exhibit center; picnic, camp or join in on a ranger-conducted environmental education class.

Durham

DUKE UNIVERSITY BLUE DEVILS

Durham - For schedules and ticket info, call (919) 681-2583 (baseball, basketball); (919) 684-4112 (football); NCAA Division 1.

WAFTING THE ENO RIVER

Durham - 5101 N Roxboro Road (US 501 North) (West Point on the Eno City Park) 27701. Phone: (919) 471-3802 trip, (919) 471-1623 park. www.wafter.org. Admission: $13.00 per person. Reservations required. May - September. Miscellaneous:

Inside the park grounds are the reconstructed 1778 working gristmill, the 1880s house, the Museum of Photography, and a recreation of a 19th century blacksmith shop (open 1:00-5:00pm weekends).

Located along a two mile stretch on the scenic Eno River, this city park offers a variety of recreational activities such as picnicking, hiking, canoeing, and especially, rafting.

Wafting - the slowest one wins...
Our kind of adventure!

Guided, natural history float trips are available in inflatable "wafts" (offered daily) on the Eno River led by naturalists "River Dave" and "Rio Josie". So, what is wafting? It begins in a 2 person waft. Don't call it rafting or the "wiver

Something to learn about
around every corner...

cweature" will get mad. As you easily paddle and float the river, River Dave will point out Mommy, Daddy and baby turtles, medicinal plants and historical elm trees. The turn-around point is a wonderful swimming hole where you can swim for awhile. We won't tell you more because you must come for yourself! Come learn lots about nature and the art and leisure of "wafting".

CE Area

CAROLINA BARNSTORMERS

Durham - 4340 East Geer Street (Lake Ridge Aero) 27702. Phone: (919) 680-6642. www.carolinabarnstormers.com.   Admission: $110.00-$200.00   per   ride,   by reservation. Season: September thru the middle of June.

Get a unique, aerial view of Durham during this "flight-seeing" tour aboard the open cockpit of a bi-plane and see sights such as Downtown Durham, the Research Triangle Park, the campuses of Duke and North Carolina Central universities, and Falls Lake. Twenty minute or one hour long tours are available. This is a memory, for sure.

DURHAM BULLS BASEBALL CLUB

Durham - 409 Blackwell Street (home games at Durham Bulls Athletic Park) 27702. Phone: (919) 687-6500. www.durhambulls.com.

Durham residents and visitors set national attendance records for this famous minor-league team. The Bulls are a triple-A farm team for the Tampa Bay Rays. The park captures the brick texture of the historic Bulls Park (a few miles away). Ball Park Corner has Bull's historic memorabilia and most folks bring their kids for the entertaining and goofy seventh-inning stretch antics on the field. The ballpark's most distinctive feature is the Bull that stands tall above the Blue Monster. This Bull was modeled after the bull used in the 1987 film, Bull Durham. The actual Bull from the movie is hung in the concourse level of the DBAP. Wool E. Bull is the lovable mascot of the world famous Durham Bulls and his sidekick is Lucky the Wonder Dog. Special promo nights include $1.00 dogs, fireworks, or running the bases. Good, Americana fun.

MUSEUM OF LIFE & SCIENCE

Durham - 433 Murray Avenue (I-85 exit 176B, Duke Univ. West campus) 27704. Phone: (919) 220-5429. www.ncmls.org. Hours: Monday-Saturday 10:00am-5:00pm, Sunday Noon-5:00pm. Members are admitted to the Museum at 9:00 a.m. Tuesday through Saturday. The Museum is CLOSED on Thanksgiving, Christmas, and New Year's Day. Admission: $10.85 adult, $8.85 senior, $7.85 child (3-12). Educators: Free Field Kits will make your self-guided visit even more meaningful. Kits are available at the Admissions Desk. These pre-designed, 30-minute lessons enhance exhibits in Explore the Wild. Each Field Kit comes complete with directions and materials for six students. They're easy to tote and easy to implement. Printable Wayfinders question sheets are available online, grade level specific. Miscellaneous: Play to Learn area for kids 6 and under. Gift shops. Stroller rentals. Grayson's Café. Train ride $2.00.

The Museum of Life and Science in Durham has a mission to create a center of lifelong learning where people from young child to senior citizen embrace science as a way of knowing about themselves, their community and their world. The museum is an impressive, interactive, indoor/outdoor science-technology center that includes:

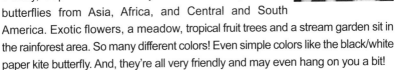

SCIENCE EXHIBITS – about weather and aerospace, and daily science shows. See giant rocket engines or a model of the Apollo 15. Make a giant tornado…taller than Dad!

LIFE'S DEVICES - actual bones to touch, skulls to grind, work ants to watch.

MAGIC WINGS BUTTERFLY HOUSE - The largest museum butterfly house east of the Mississippi. The 3-story, tropical conservatory features rare species of butterflies from Asia, Africa, and Central and South America. Exotic flowers, a meadow, tropical fruit trees and a stream garden sit in the rainforest area. So many different colors! Even simple colors like the black/white paper kite butterfly. And, they're all very friendly and may even hang on you a bit!

FARMYARD & LOBLOLLY PARK - interactive outdoor exhibits include: a barnyard, water play and giant musical drums and bells.

EXPLORE THE WILD - A lush six-acre woodland habitat and thriving wetland site where you can walk in the steps of a wildlife biologist, using field cameras and remote sensing devices to study native black bears, endangered red wolves, and exotic lemurs, baby alligators and owls. Descend a 750-foot boardwalk to a preserved natural setting. Enjoy the ambient sound of waterfalls and streams or explore life in a wetland. Natural observation areas, field cameras, outdoor microscopes, and state-of-the-art technology look into this dynamic natural landscape, its wildlife, plant life, and supporting habitats. You'll feel like a real safari scientist here.

CATCH THE WIND - you can captain a boat in a 5,000-square foot sailboat pond to learn about the invisible power of wind.

BENNETT PLACE STATE HISTORIC SITE

Durham - 4409 Bennett Memorial Road (Interstate 85 north, take exit 170 and follow U.S. 70 to Bennett Memorial Road) 27705. Phone: (919) 383-4345. www.ah.dcr. state.nc.us/sections/hs/bennett/bennett.htm. Hours: Tuesday-Saturday 10:00am-4:00pm. Closed major state holidays. Admission: FREE. Miscellaneous: Be sure to ask for the Activity Book. If they complete it, they get a prize. Reenactment weekends are held about once per month, seasonally. Civil War Cinema movies are shown Saturday nights throughout the year.

Bennett Place State Historic Site (cont.)

This simple farmhouse was situated between Confederate General Johnston's headquarters in Greensboro and Union General Sherman's headquarters in Raleigh, North Carolina. In 1865, the two generals met here, where they signed surrender (largest troops of the War) papers for Southern armies in the Carolinas, Georgia, and Florida. This is where the war completely ended. Why did it take three separate days to compromise? Did the generals follow or disobey orders to compromise further? How did President Lincoln's

assassination affect their agreement? The surrender spared North Carolina the destruction experienced by her neighboring states. Equally important, the economy of the entire state and the development of Durham were boosted when troops in the area were introduced to "bright leaf" tobacco.

The visitor center contains three rooms of exhibits on the Bennett family, the Civil War, and the surrender at the Bennett Place. There is also a model of the Bennett farm showing the arrival of Union and Confederate cavalry troops on April 17, 1865. The fifteen-minute audiovisual program titled "Dawn of Peace" is shown on the hour. Today James Bennett's reconstructed farmhouse, kitchen, and smokehouse give visitors a glimpse into the life-style of an ordinary Southern farmer during the Civil War years.

CIVIL WAR SURRENDER REENACTMENT

This day reenacts the negotiations and surrender between Generals Sherman and Johnston that ended the Civil War. (last Saturday in April)

CHRISTMAS IN THE CAROLINAS DURING THE CIVIL WAR

Visit Bennett Place during the holiday season and witness how Christmas was celebrated in the Piedmont Carolinas. The farm is decorated in a typical Christmas fashion. Music, caroling, and refreshments. (mid-December weekend)

DUKE HOMESTEAD STATE HISTORIC SITE

Durham - 2828 Duke Homestead Road (Interstate 85 in Durham exit on Guess Road (Exit 175). Follow the signs north) 27705. www.nchistoricsites.org/duke/ Phone: (919) 489-3364. Hours: Tuesday-Saturday 10:00am-4:00pm. Admission: FREE.

The patriarch of Duke Homestead was Washington Duke, an Orange County farmer whose chance discovery that Union troops were helping themselves to local Bright Leaf tobacco led him to the fortuitous decision to market this "golden weed." Retrace the beginnings of the modern-day tobacco industry at this National Historic Landmark where Washington Duke started his successful tobacco empire. The Duke family's home site includes authentic barns and original factories, as well as a museum filled with cigarette manufacturing and marketing memorabilia. Living history demonstrations of life on a typical yeoman farm in the 1800's are regularly performed. Keep in mind, this industry flourished and was heavily promoted before the dangers of tobacco use were so widely known.

> **AMERICAN TOBACCO TRAIL**
> www.triangletrails.org/ATT.HTM.
> Downtown to NC 54, eight miles of trails for bicycle, hiking, walking and running.

CHRISTMAS CANDLELIGHT TOURS

Celebrate an 1870 Christmas during evening tours of the Homestead. Period decorations, caroling, hot apple cider, and other goodies. Additional entertainment in visitor center. FREE. (first two Friday nights in December)

DUKE LEMUR CENTER

Durham - 3705 Old Erwin Road at NC Hwy 751 (US 15/501 bypass south to NC 751 to Old Erwin Rd, left on Lemur Lane) 27705. www.lemur.duke.edu. Phone: (919) 489-3364. Admission: $7.00 adult, $5.00 college students, $4.00 senior and child (3-12), $1.00 baby (under 2). **Miscellaneous: During the spring and summer months it is not unusual for all of the tours to be booked up to two weeks in advance so you should make your plans early! Educators: Coloring books, puzzles, species fact sheets & audio of calls, and mazes are found online. Creationists may have to be prepared for comments about evolution.**

CE Area

Duke Lemur Center (cont.)

Encounter the largest population of lemurs outside of their native Madagascar at this research and study center, which is home to 250 prosimian primates. There is an outside walking tour and inside viewing of nocturnal prosimians (like the bizarre aye-aye). Dedicated to the study and understanding of these primates, this center houses many different primates including 233 lemurs encompassing 15 species, along with lorises from India and Southeast Asia and bushbabies from Africa. Some have crowns, some blue eyes and some look like a mouse. Lemurs are pre-monkeys...they are living fossils. Start your tour with an overview video. It explains that the center especially studies the lemurs' personality and use of their hands. What do all those barks, screams and calls mean? Do lemurs heal themselves using chemicals from plants? Girl lemurs may dominate but it's not hard to guess who Romeo is.

> Ruffed lemurs have an elaborate system of alarm calls that alert group members to danger from predators. As many as twelve different calls have been recorded at the Center.

He's big and handsome - and he knows it! Meet the actual "Zaboo" (or a relative) from PBS fame. If these guys grow on you during your wonderfully educational tour, adopt one (not to keep, of course).

ENO RIVER STATE PARK

Durham - 6101 Cole Mill Road (I-85, take exit 173 northwest onto Cole Mill Road, which ends at the park) 27705. www.ncparks.gov/Visit/parks/enri/main.php Phone: (919) 383-1686. Hours: Daily 8:00am-dusk. Admission: FREE.

The Eno River begins in northwest Orange County, flowing eastward approximately 33 miles until, along with the Little and Flat rivers, it forms the Neuse and flows into Falls Lake. The Eno's waters roll through wilderness passing historic mill sites and river bluffs covered with flowering shrubs and fords used by early settlers. Upstream, rapids smash against rocks in the river's path. Further down, the Eno meanders quietly through serene surroundings. This makes for good spots for canoeing and rafting. Hike Cox Mountain Trail for a challenging climb through a scenic hardwood forest. Travel along Bobbitt's Hole Trail to one of the most scenic spots in the park, a place where water rushes around rocks and greenery overhangs stone-lined bluffs. The Eno River has approximately 21 miles of trails where you can enjoy nature at its best. All trails are blazed. See the park map for information on distance and difficulty. Camping and fishing are available at the park, too.

DUKE UNIVERSITY

Durham - (southwest & west central campuses) 27708. Phone: (919) 681-1704. www.duke.edu.

Highlights of the Neo-Gothic campus are:

DUKE UNIVERSITY CHAPEL - This chapel is one of the most popular features in North Carolina and represents one of the last great collegiate Gothic projects in the United States. Features of the chapel include a 5,200 pipe Flentrop Organ, stained glass windows, a 50 bell carillon, and a 210-foot tower. (Chapel Drive, West Campus)

DUKE SPORTS HALL OF FAME - The Hall houses several decades of Duke University athletic history along the northwest side of the famed Cameron Indoor Stadium. The Hall of Fame includes video, audio, a theatre and exhibits that showcase some famous people in Duke sports. (8:00am-5:00pm, school weekdays, Towerview Road, Schwartz-Butters Athletic Center, West Campus)

DUKE GARDENS - Beautiful 55 acre garden that features three major areas including the original Terraces, the Blomquist Garden of Native Plants, and the Sulberson Asiatic Arboretum. Five miles of pathways and hiking trails dotted with waterfalls are located throughout the gardens. (418 Anderson Street, 919-684-3698)

NASHER / DUKE UNIVERSITY MUSEUM OF ART - This museum houses beautiful works that include ancient, modern, Old Master, American, African American, and Russian Contemporary masterpieces. The museum also boasts the Brummer Collection of Medieval & Renaissance Art and a pre-Columbian collection of Central and South America artwork. (North Buchanan Boulevard, Durham, NC 27701, Duke East Campus, 919-684-5135).

STAGVILLE, HISTORIC

Durham - 5825 Old Oxford Highway (I-85 North to exit 177, Roxboro Road North. Go approximately 1.4 miles north. Turn right onto Old Oxford Highway and proceed 7 miles) 27722. www.historicstagvillefoundation.org/. Phone: (919) 620-0120. Hours: Tuesday-Saturday 10:00am-4:00pm. Admission is FREE. Educators: Prep questions and activities are on the Teacher Information page online.

One of the largest pre-Civil War plantations, this historic plantation offers visitors a glimpse into the past and especially the lives of the African American slaves who worked the plantation. By 1860, the family owned almost 30,000 acres and nearly 900 slaves. The American Girl figure, Addy, is loosely based on stories from this place. Two restored historic buildings (slave quarters) and an old barn are on site and self guided tours of the extensive grounds are available. The slave cabins are unusual because they're off the ground (not dirt floors) and several stories high – once housing dozens of people. Historic buildings are only open during hourly guided tours.

JUNE 23 JUNETEENTH CELEBRATION

Juneteenth is a celebration commemorating the end of slavery in the United States. This family-focused event has a jubilant atmosphere, with music, entertainment, period craft vendors and food. To commemorate the history of the site, costumed actors portray actual members of the enslaved community at Stagville. There is also a station with information about the enslaved community and the genealogy project being conducted at the site. Admission is free with a suggested donation of $2.00 for adults and $1.00 for children. (usually sometime the third week of June)

"CHRISTMAS IN THE BIG HOUSE, CHRISTMAS IN THE QUARTERS"

Stagville's holiday celebration includes an 1815 Christmas celebration at the Bennehan House and an 1850's Christmas celebration at the Horton Grove quarter. This living history event focuses on the different ways that Christmas was celebrated on a Southern plantation. Enjoy costumed interpreters, games, crafts, cooking demonstrations and music. Admission is free with a suggested donation of $2.00 for adults and $1.00 for children. (first Saturday in December)

KWANZAAFEST

Durham - downtown Armory. (919) 560-2729. The African-American Dance Ensemble presents an afternoon of entertainment and education. African-styled marketplace, ethnic food, and performances of the last day of the holiday. (January 1st or 2nd)

NATIVE AMERICAN POWWOW

Durham -   North Carolina School of Science and Mathematics. (919) 416-2600 or www.ncssm.edu or www.durham-rtp.com. A full day of traditional Native American dancing, singing, crafts, food and socializing. One of the largest in the Southeast, the Powwow is a family-friendly event emphasizing intertribal brotherhood/sisterhood and education. Typically, 150 dancers and six drums entertain crowds as large as 2,000. In addition to watching dancing, marvel at intricate woodcarving, silverwork, beadwork, and leatherwork. Taste Native American delicacies like fry bread, Indian tacos, buffalo soup, and corn soup. Admission. (third Saturday in February)

PUMPKIN COUNTRY

Durham - Ganyard Hill Farm. (919) 596-8728 or www.pumpkincountry.com. Enjoy feeding farm animals in the barnyard, pumpkin patch (pick your own), hayrides, cotton field, corn field maze, mulch mountain, hay maze (great for young-uns), and general store. Admission. (daily mid-September through October)

ARROWHEAD INN

Durham - (north off Roxboro Road on the Indian Trading Path) Mason Road. Phone: (919) 477-8430 or (800) 528-2207 or www.arrowheadinn.com. Stay in a piece of history! This is a bed and breakfast property (4 star rating), but they are very family-friendly. The home was built in 1775, before the Revolutionary War. They are located on six acres and have swings, a hammock and a horseshoe throw. Owners Phil and Gloria Teber are so comfortable and have a servant's heart. Every morning, they serve a delicious multi-course breakfast. Try Phil's puff pancakes, moist scones, or killer brownies! Kids have a wide selection of coloring, toys and videos to choose from. Parents may want to explore all the history around the house and hear stories from the innkeepers (some history and mystery). For families, they have some large rooms, a log cabin w/ loft, and a cottage (regular rates range from $135-$325). Rollaways and futons are readily available for kid's beds. Ask about non-peak weekday family rates. If you want a special treat, we highly recommend this overnight site! CAMILLA'S: Just a few miles down the road is a great Italian restaurant. Camilla's makes great sauce and daily specials. Wonderful lasagna. Inexpensive kids menu. 5110 North Roxboro Road, (919) 471-0862.

> **LITTLE RIVER REGIONAL PARK & NATURAL AREA.** www.tlc-nc.org Relics from tobacco farmland like barns, houses and sheds have been restored and now serve as picnic shelters and info centers. 15 miles of walking, hiking, mountain-biking, and horseback-riding trails.

ELMO'S DINER

Durham - 776 Ninth St. Ninth Street District. (919) 416-3823 or www.elmosdiner.com. Daily 6:30am-10:00pm or later. Food Network's "$40 a Day" host Rachael Ray proclaims that the diner is an "awesome pick." Though breakfast is served all day, Elmo's whips up splendid lunch and dinner favorites. We call this a gourmet diner. Highly recommend the perfectly seasoned spicy Italian Meatloaf and Hummus dip. There quiches are wonderfully creamy and fresh. Anything on the kids menu is great and under $3.00.

> You know, we feel Durham has some of the most eclectic, yet, family-budget-friendly eateries around! It's exciting to try these places – be sure to begin by trying one of their daily specials.

LAQUINTA INN & SUITES RESEARCH TRIANGLE PARK

Durham - Spending the night? Try LaQuinta Suites at I-40 exit 278, 1910 WestPark Drive, (919) 484-1422 or www.lq.com. For $75-$120 per night you receive a spacious room with a nice outdoor pool and complimentary deluxe breakfast buffet. Fresh breads and pastries were abundant.

Convenient location to base from and unique shopping areas are nearby. One such find is PATTERSON'S MILL COUNTRY STORE. 5109 Farrington Rd between NC 54 & Old Chapel Hill Rd. (919) 493-8149. Open daily except Monday. This turn-of-the-century country store and doctor's office/pharmacy displays mercantile and pharmaceutical Americana. The best part - real Penny Candy! Enjoy a soda and sweet treat while browsing through gobs of crafted art and jewelry mixed with antiques. Something fills every square inch. Fall and Christmastime are good times to visit.

Q SHACK, THE

Durham - 2510 University Drive, (919) 402-4227 or www.theqshack.com. Lunch and dinner, picnic style. Barbecue all grown up. Chili-rubbed sliced brisket (Texas style –  excellent), hand-pulled pork and ribs are must-orders. Sides are Southern. When choosing your sides, don't forget to get a helping of Stanley's organic collard greens, or their signature macaroni and cheese. Those two, along with a bowl of fried okra might just be the ticket for the hungry vegetarian in your crowd! Everyone (even kids size) gets hush puppies. Most BBQ's don't serve salads, but this one does. Try their giant salad greens topped with brisket and blue cheese dressing – yum!

RICK'S DINER

Durham - 4015 University Drive, BB&T Plaza (919) 419-0907 or www.ricksdiner.com. They've consolidated two stores into one. Notice the historical photos from the Durham Herald Sun – fun to look at. Try their Blue Plate specials – salads, seafood and quiches are adult favorites. Secret recipe meatloaf, beef burgers or Carolina pork BBQ are their specialties. No kids menu but just ask for kids portions. Most specialty dishes here are Rick's recipes and some are from Uncle Ray and Mama.

Fremont

GOVERNOR CHARLES B. AYCOCK STATE HISTORIC SITE

Fremont - 264 Governor Aycock Road (I-95 S to Kenly/Fremont exit. Head southeast to south on Rte. 117) 27830. www.ah.dcr.state.nc.us/sections/hs/aycock/aycock.htm. Phone: (919) 242-5581. Hours: Monday-Saturday 9:00am-5:00pm (April-October). Tuesday-Saturday 10:00am-4:00pm (November-March). Admission: FREE. Educators: Teacher Packets are $2.00 each. Purchase at the site or mail a check. Call for dates of regular special events and living history demonstrations.

The Site features the boyhood home of North Carolina's "Educational Governor". Aycock was elected governor in 1900. His ability to rouse people to support education at the local level stimulated the construction of approximately eleven hundred schools-one for every day he was in office. By the end of his term, citizens had seen enrollment increased, school districts consolidated, and teacher training improved. The farmstead home includes a mid-19th century farm, an 1893 one-room schoolhouse and a modern visitors center. The one-room schoolhouse was moved to the site to represent the grassroots educational revival that became statewide after Governor Aycock's election in 1900.

CHRISTMAS CANDLELIGHT TOURS

Celebrate the Holidays of the Past with Primative Baptist Singers, Shadow Play in the One room School House, Open-hearth cooking and more. (first week of December)

Goldsboro

WAYNESBOROUGH HISTORIC VILLAGE

Goldsboro - 801 S. US 117 Bypass 27530. www.wcpl.org/waynesborough.htm
Phone: (919) 731-1653. Hours: Monday-Saturday 11:00am-5:00pm, Sunday
1:00-5:00pm (summer). Monday-Saturday 10:00am-4:00pm, Sunday 1:00-4:00pm
(rest of year). Closed Easter, Thanksgiving, Christmas, and New Years Day.
Admission: FREE.

Founded in 1787 as the first seat of Wayne County, Waynesborough grew
quickly into a bustling town. Its location along the Neuse River promoted
plantation growth and successful river boat businesses. Stage coaches
brought much activity and many passengers to the town. Slip into the nineteenth
century and experience life as it once was in historic Waynesborough. Visit a
family home, a medical office, a one room school, a law office, and a Quaker
Meeting House. Picnic near the General Store. Walk down to the Neuse
River. Listen to the blacksmith beating upon his iron or smell the scents of
herbs drying in the Tuscarora Indian Village. This is a nice place to picnic
amongst the scents of history.

BENTONVILLE BATTLEFIELD STATE HISTORIC SITE

Goldsboro (Four Oaks) - 5466 Harper House Road (I- 40 exit onto U.S. 701 (Exit
343). Follow signs to State Road 1008) 27524. Phone: (910) 594-0789. www.
ah.dcr.state.nc.us/sections/hs/bentonvi/bentonvi.htm. Hours: Monday-Saturday
9:00am-5:00pm, Sunday 1:00-5:00pm (April-October). Tuesday-Saturday 10:00am-
4:00pm, Sunday 1:00-4:00pm (November-March). Closed all major holidays.
Admission: FREE. Miscellaneous: Summer Seasonal Living History Program and
Artillery Demonstrations. On Saturday, costumed living historians from the 1st
/11th NC Troops conduct weapons demonstrations and hold discussions on the
lives of the average Civil War soldier. Highly trained volunteers also demonstrate
the loading and firing of a 3" Ordnance Rifle, a popular Civil War cannon. (one
summer Saturday each month)

The Battle of Bentonville, fought March 19-21, 1865, was the last full-scale
action of the Civil War in which a Confederate army was able to mount a tactical
offensive. Walk on the fields where 80,000 Union and Confederate soldiers
fought. Tour the nearby Harper House (ca. 1855) furnished as a Civil War
field hospital where wounded from both sides received medical treatment.
The upstairs rooms of the Harper House feature period domestic furnishings.
The Harper children remained at home with their parents when the house was

taken over by the Federal XIV Army Corps for use as a field hospital. The site also includes a reconstructed kitchen and slave quarters. The visitor center features a ten-minute audiovisual program explaining the events leading up to the Battle of Bentonville. The center also exhibits artifacts from the battlefield and maps of troop movement during the three days of fighting.

BENTONVILLE BATTLEFIELD ANNIVERSARY

Costumed living historians evoke the lives of the average North Carolina Civil War soldier through infantry and artillery demos. Evening lantern tours. Reenactors portray both surgeons and wounded soldiers in the home. (second weekend in March)

CHRISTMAS OPEN HOUSE

Costumed interpreters decorate the kitchen in festive themes, such as holly and magnolia branches, cotton stalks, various fruits and cranberry and popcorn strands, and serve cookies and hot cider. Also on hand, costumed military interpreters discuss how the common solider spent his time on furlough with friends and family. (first Saturday in December)

GLENWOOD FARMS

Goldsboro (Mount Olive) - 423 NC Highway 403E (Take I40 East to exit 341 in Newton Grove. Follow Highway 55 through Mt.Olive, until it intersects with Highway 403) 28365. Phone: (919) 658-2288. www.glenwoodfarms.net. Hours: Open Monday through Friday for tours by appointment. Saturdays 9:00am to dark, Sundays 1:00pm to dark. Admission: $5.00 per person. $6.00 per person for special events.

Both adults and kids will be entertained and educated at this 100 acre farm that showcases all of the different aspects of North Carolina agriculture (cotton, corn, soybean, strawberry, pumpkin) and helps children learn about seasonal crops. Besides the fields, let the kids enjoy a petting zoo, a corn maze, an aquaculture display in the fish house, duck pond and grazing areas. The two most favorite seasonal crops have to be their pumpkins & strawberries. They grow these on the farm so special tour goers can take part of their experience on a farm home with them. During the early spring & summertime they offer buckets of strawberries and in the fall they provide pumpkins for plucking.

Glenwood Farms (cont.)

CHRISTMAS LIGHT RIDE

'Tis the season for Santa Claus, Christmas trees, and Christmas lights! To celebrate the season, Farmer Glenn puts together a marvelous Christmas light hay ride. Come celebrate by taking a ride through the light show between December 1st & December 23rd, 7:00pm until 9:00pm.

Halifax

HISTORIC HALIFAX STATE HISTORIC SITE & OUTDOOR DRAMA

Halifax - St. David & Dobbs Streets (I-95 take exit 168. Follow the signs south on N.C. 903 to the town of Halifax) 27839. Phone: (252) 583-7191 or (800) 522-4282. www.ah.dcr.state.nc.us/sections/hs/halifax/halifax.htm. Hours: Tuesday-Saturday 9:00am-5:00pm. Admission: FREE. Donations accepted. Miscellaneous: Picnic sites and trails that lead to the Roanoke River overlook.

April 12, 1776, the date commemorated on the North Carolina flag, signifies the Fourth Provincial Congress' adoption of the "Halifax Resolves" during a meeting right here in Halifax. With that action, North Carolina became the first colony to take an official step toward declaring independence from England. The Historic Halifax Visitor's Center offers a thirteen-minute orientation program depicting the history of the first eighty years of Halifax and the surrounding area. A guided walking tour takes you into several authentically restored and furnished buildings. These include the 1760 home of a merchant, the house and law office of a nineteenth-century attorney, and the 1808 home of a wealthy landowner (exhibits and walkways over foundations exposed by the scholar's spade and trowel). The 1833 clerk's office, a jail, Eagle tavern, and a unique archaeological exhibit are also featured on the tour.

HALIFAX DAY

Anniversary of the adoption of the Halifax Resolves. Living history activities, tours, and patriotic observance sponsored by the N.C. Society, Sons of the American Revolution. Halifax Day Parade. FREE. (April 12)

FIRST FOR FREEDOM OUTDOOR DRAMA

The drama traces events leading to the adoption on April 12, 1776, of the Halifax Resolves, which authorized North Carolina delegates to the Continental Congress to vote for independence from Great Britain. The unanimous vote by 83 state delegates at the Fourth Provincial Congress in Halifax was the first official action by a colony that called for independence. Admission. (outdoor evenings beginning late June thru weekend after July 4th)

CHRISTMAS IN HALIFAX

Join the historic site and town of Halifax as they celebrate the Christmas season. Historic buildings exteriors will be decorated with natural arrangements. Visit the local tavern for refreshments, learn about Christmas in colonial times, stroll the streets of Halifax and see the many historic homes and churches, see Christmas wreaths and decorations being created and feel the spirit of a small town Christmas.

Henderson

KERR LAKE STATE RECREATION AREA

Henderson - 6254 Satterwhite Point Road (off I-85 exit 215) 27536. Phone: (252) 438-7791 or (252) 438-7582. www.ncparks.gov/Visit/parks/kela/main.php. Admission: FREE. Fee for camping. Educators: Educational materials about Kerr Lake State Recreation Area have been developed for grades 3-5 and are correlated to North Carolina's competency-based curriculum in science, social studies, mathematics and English/language arts. The Kerr Lake program focuses on environmental stewardship and recycling processes. Accompanying the program is a teacher's booklet and workshop, free of charge to educators.

JULY 4TH CELEBRATIONS
Fireworks and Parade of Lights.

To say Kerr Lake is big is an understatement. Its 850 miles of shoreline stretches across Vance County and the North Carolina / Virginia state line, making it one of the largest lakes in the Southeast. It's also one of the most beautiful. Featuring wooded shores, secluded coves, and tranquil picnic areas. Explore Kerr Lake and enjoy the fishing, camping, boating, skiing, sailing, wind surfing, nature walking, and bird watching. Satterwhite Point has a visitor's center complete with an exhibit hall. An accessible nature trail with an overlook and an amphitheater are nearby. Enjoy the visitors center, yearly sailing regattas, and fishing tournaments throughout the year.

Hillsborough

OCCONEECHEE MOUNTAIN STATE NATURAL AREA

Hillsborough - Virginia Cates Road (I-85, take exit 164) 27705. Phone: (919) 383-1686. www.ncparks.gov/Visit/parks/ocmo/main.php. Admission: FREE.

Rising more than 350 feet from the Eno River, the Occoneechee Mountain summit is the highest point in Orange County. The summit is also reported to be the highest point between Hillsborough, NC, and the Atlantic Ocean. This 124-acre state natural area includes the eastern half of Occoneechee Mountain with an 867-foot-high summit, part of the Eno River. Hiking trails, scenic overlooks and two fishing ponds are popular. Some historic and nature programs are available from park rangers.

OCCANEECHI- SAPONI SPRING CULTURAL FESTIVAL & POW WOW

Hillsborough - (downtown), on the banks of the Eno River. www.occaneechi-saponi.org. (919) 304-3723. Come out for two days of family fun filled American Indian dancing and singing. Native American vendors sell food, arts and crafts. Admission. (first weekend in June)

Hollister

MEDOC MOUNTAIN STATE PARK

Hollister - 1541 Medoc State Park Road (21 miles southwest of Roanoke Rapids on State Road 1002) 27844. www.ils.unc.edu/parkproject/visit/memo/home.html Hours: Daily 8:00am-dusk. Phone: (252) 445-2280. Educators: The Medoc Mountain program introduces students to basic geologic processes and relates them to the Medoc Mountain region. Accompanying the program is a teacher's booklet and workshop, free of charge to educators.

Medoc Mountain is not really a mountain at all. The "mountain" is a granite outcropping with its highest point reaching 325 feet and it is the remains of the core of an ancient mountain range. Most of the trails are easy or moderate in difficulty, and trail scenery includes an artesian well, granite outcroppings and miniature rapids. Winding along Little Fishing Creek, around the high ridge of Medoc Mountain and through the forests, the trails are the best way to appreciate the beauty and diversity of Medoc Mountain. Picnicking, canoeing, nature study, camping and fishing all await you at this North Carolina State Park.

Littleton

LAKE GASTON

Littleton - 2475 Eaton Ferry Road (Eaton Ferry bridge by way of U.S. 158, N.C. 903) 27850. Phone: (252) 586-5711. www.lakegastonchamber.com. Admission: FREE.

Straddling the North Carolina and Virginia border between I-85 and I-95, Lake Gaston has over 20,000 acres of "high quality" water, is 34 miles long, and approximately one and one half miles wide at the lower end of the lake. It has over 350 miles of shoreline offering a wide variety of watersports. Lake Gaston begins at Kerr Dam, a lake built in 1953 for flood control. Lake Gaston is well stocked with game fish which include striped bass or rock fish, large mouth bass, crappie, sunfish and several varieties of catfish. Other species of fish sometimes caught are walleye, yellow perch and chain pickerel. A valid license for either Virginia or North Carolina permits fishing from a boat in either state. No license is required for those under 15.

Mt. Olive

NORTH CAROLINA PICKLE FESTIVAL

Mt. Olive - Crafts, food, rides and concerts – most with pickles. Although the Mt. Olive Pickle Company isn't available for public tours, they welcome a visit and will show a brief video tour of the pickle operation. Corner of Cucumber and Vine. (919) 658-3113 or (800) 672-5041 or www.ncpicklefest.org. (last weekend in April)

Pittsboro

CARNIVORE PRESERVATION TRUST

Pittsboro - 1940 Hanks Chapel Road (Hwy 64 west, crossing Lake Jordan and Haw River. Take the first left at mile marker #387 on to Foxfire Trace, take a Left on Dee Ferrell Rd) 27312. Phone: (919) 542-4684. www.cptigers.org

At a 60 acre reserve in Pittsboro, North Carolina, the Carnivore Preservation Trust cares for a population of over 250 representatives from 16 species. See threatened carnivores from around the world with a special focus on keystone species (species especially important to the ecosystem). The Trust engages

CE Area

in no commercial activity of any kind but is open to the public for guided tours. Come join a guided tour where you will see their collection of exotic species. They will tell you all about the animals you are seeing, from scientific facts about the species, to the story of how different animals came to live with them. You will see up close and personal: Romeo, the 600 lbs. Tiger; Jellybean, their white Bengal tiger; Disney, the friendliest binturong this side of South East Asia, and several more.

Raleigh

MARBLES KIDS MUSEUM

Raleigh - 201 East Hargett Street (corner of Blount Street and Hargett Street, directly opposite of City Market and Moore Square) 27601. Phone: (919) 834-4040. www.marbleskidsmuseum.org. Hours: Tuesday-Saturday 9:00am-5:00pm, Sunday Noon-5:00pm. Admission: $5.00 (age one plus). IMAX tickets alone $6.50-$11.00. Combo tickets to both, generally add $1.00. Miscellaneous: IMAX Theatre has several different shows daily. One show usually has a theme similar to a traveling exhibit on display.

Playspace and Exploris have combined to form a hands-on, interactive museum for children and their families in downtown Raleigh. The museum is geared toward families with children ages birth to twelve and features four indoor galleries, two outdoor escapes and an IMAX theater. Let's explore some of the "landscapes": What do you want to be when you grow up? Try out a few ideas in the Around Town Gallery. You can "pretend play" to be a farmer feeding and caring for animals in their stalls or a Broadway performer putting on shows with costumes and props for an audience. Other exhibits include an ambulance, a fishing boat, a delivery truck, a grocery store, a restaurant, a train, a tree house, a reading area and an underwater crawling area for babies under one. Water and paint activities are a big hit in the Splash Gallery. Two large towers supply a constant water supply to water tables below (full of toys). There is a Liquid Art Lab where children can create and explore with paint and other liquid supplies. A huge wooden pirate ship is where you can find most "kid-pirates" of all ages engaged in swash-buckling fun. Other galleries are geared towards the 8-12 set: Kids can use digital technology to create their own web pages complete with photos or sing and play instruments in a music studio; or, build something large in the Build It Gallery. Adults particularly love the Horizon space that rotates Children of the World exhibits. View life-size photos of children their age from countries all around the world and see what kind of food they eat, what their homes look like and what they did for fun (ex. Russian, Japanese).

NORTH CAROLINA MUSEUM OF ART

Raleigh - 2110 Blue Ridge Road (I-40 to exit 289 onto Wade Ave. to Blue Ridge Rd) 27601. Phone: (919) 839) 6262. www.ncartmuseum.org. Hours: Tuesday-Saturday 9:00am-5:00pm, Sunday 10:00am-5:00pm. Admission: FREE. Miscellaneous: Puppet shows and Kids Summer Camps. The Museum Park Trail is a mile-long paved trail with works of environmental art, which is open to the public during daylight hours for bicycle and pedestrian use only (no motorized vehicles or skateboards). Museum restaurant.

The North Carolina Museum of Art will take you on a voyage through 5,000 years of artistic heritage. Peruse works by American artists as well as collections of African, Oceanic and New World art, Egyptian, Greek and Roman art, 20th-century art and more. 5,000 years of artistic heritage from Egypt to the present is housed at this museum that also offers educational programs, performances, and films. Having trouble making the connection for kids? Good Company offers activities for making connections between art and other, more familiar images—pictures that resemble your own life or those found in popular culture. Bring the kids for other creative activities designed just for them, such as the Museum Cube. And be sure to pick up the simple take-along pocket guide to approaching art museums. Located on the Entrance Level, in the Progress Energy Learning Center.

NORTH CAROLINA MUSEUM OF HISTORY

Raleigh - 5 East Edenton Street (downtown, between the Capitol and the Legislative Building) 27601. Phone: (919) 715-0200. http://ncmuseumofhistory.org. Hours: Tuesday-Saturday 9:00am-5:00pm, Sunday Noon-5:00pm. Admission: FREE. Parking in lots or meters nearby. Miscellaneous: Gallery Backpacks and Times for Tots interactive days. Storytelling.

The North Carolina Museum of History tells the stories of generations of North Carolinians and others who have shaped the state's history. Includes the largest historical flag collection in the United States, a Civil War exhibit, replica of the Wright Brothers' plane, and the North Carolina Sports Hall of Fame. The museum encourages visitors to discover the past, but not get bored with it - so, they change the exhibit spaces quite often. General Exhibits include:

NORTH CAROLINA AND WAR: Uniforms, weapons, flags, and other artifacts enhanced by historical settings, photographs, biographies, and computer interactives. Not only the soldier's life, but home life, too.

North Carolina Museum Of History (cont.)

NORTH CAROLINA SPORTS HALL OF FAME: Audio, video, and interactive biographies, plus Richard Petty's stock car, Meadowlark Lemon's uniform, and other sports artifacts. Our favorite area, by the way.

INVENTORS: A whimsical "construction" site with dioramas of famous inventions. The area includes a Moving and Shaping activity guide for kids. How do you move a lighthouse? Who invented guns?

COMMUNITY & CULTURE: Famous Tar Heel racing or transportation; American Indian practices; Decorative arts from decoys to clothes; and notable music.

NORTH CAROLINA MUSEUM OF NATURAL SCIENCE

Raleigh - 11 West Jones Street (on Bicentennial Plaza in downtown Raleigh between the Capitol and the Legislature Building, at the corner of Jones and Salisbury streets) 27601. www.naturalsciences.org. Phone: (919) 733-7450 or (877) 462-8724. Hours: Monday-Saturday 9:00am-5:00pm, Sunday Noon-5:00pm. Note: The Discovery Room, Naturalist Center, and Living Conservatory are closed Mondays. Admission: FREE. Miscellaneous: Acro Café (with family-friendly offerings and pricing). Educators: Kids page with coloring pages, Nature Notebook sheets and web links.

A science museum that houses four floors of exhibits. You're greeted by a giant shark's jaw. Check out the Brown Pelican (remember Nemo's friend?) as

he scoops his neck down in the water, his balloon pouch expanding and "scooping" up the meal (fish). Take a relaxing stroll along a Carolina salt marsh and shoreline before passing cautiously under the 65-foot prehistoric blue whale fossil that welcomes you. The auditorium ahead is your introduction on a 17-minute journey through "Wilderness North Carolina."

A "Jaw Dropping" Prehistoric Blue Whale Skeleton... Hear the rushing waterfalls and mountain scenes as you enter the second floor.

Now head to the third floor. Lightning flashes and thunder rumbles as the gaping dagger-toothed jaws of an Acrocanthosaurus (Acro-can-tho-saur-us)

lunge for a sauropod dinner. You've just met the "Terror of the South!" Other features of the museum include a Fossil Lab (paleontologists work here), Willo - the dino with a heart (the first dinosaur discovered with a fossilized heart), and an Arthropod Zoo and Living Conservatory buzzing and

A fossilized Dino Heart...

crawling with giant creatures from butterflies to tarantulas. The Discovery Room is a special place where you can engage your senses by touching fossils, feeling bird wings, smelling tropical scents, watching the beehive, and more. Try on costumes, play with puppets, and find hidden animals in a dead tree critter hotel. A lot of things here are giant! Look up, a whale named "Trouble" may be watching. Some items are small - a venus fly trap or baby sea turtles. "Oh, Look!" comments from kids throughout. We like that they focus more on habitats (dioramas) vs. specimens under glass. Best Natural Science museum we've ever seen...and it's free!

Daniel...the Bug Boy!

BUG FEST

Attracting more than 15,000 spectators, visitors may delve deeply into the insect world at this fun, wacky event. Enjoy food prepared at Café Insecta, cheer during the roach races and meet exotic insects from around the world. FREE (mid-September Saturday)

NORTH CAROLINA STATE CAPITOL

Raleigh - 1 East Edenton Street (Capitol Square) 27601. Phone: (919) 733-4994. www.ah.dcr.state.nc.us/sections/hs/capitol/   Hours: Monday-Friday 8:00am-5:00pm, Saturday 10:00am-4:00pm, Sunday 1:00-4:00pm. Admission: FREE Miscellaneous: While you're on Union Square, take time to observe the many bronze statues. You'll see North Carolina's three native sons who later became United States presidents — Andrew Jackson, James K. Polk, and Andrew Johnson — as well as memorials to our many fallen soldiers. Zebulon B. Vance and Charles B. Aycock are the only two governors to have statues here — Vance because he was the state's Civil War governor and Aycock because he was a significant figure in public education.

Originally housing the Governor's office, cabinet offices, legislative chambers, the state library, and state geologist's office, this National Historic Landmark building has been beautifully restored to its original appearance and is one of the best preserved examples of Greek Revival style architecture in a civic building. You'll be amazed by how worn the steps are from so many years of use. It's hard to believe that legislators used this building until 1963. The Governor and Lieutenant Governor currently maintain offices on the first floor. Peek in and say hello. Kids like the fancy "trimmings" on the doors and walls. Is a soldier still lurking the hallways? Did spies use "secret rooms" in the Capitol during the Civil War?

STATE CAPITOL HOLIDAY OPEN HOUSE & CIVIL WAR CHRISTMAS ENCAMPMENT

The Capitol is decorated for the holidays by the Raleigh Garden Club. Decorations feature the "North Carolina Tree," which is trimmed by the Junior Woman's Club of Raleigh with ornaments from all 100 counties. Re-enactors demonstrate how to make period Christmas ornaments, dip candles, and train children to participate in Civil War drill routines. Local performing groups. FREE. (second week of December)

NORTH CAROLINA SYMPHONY

Raleigh - 2 East South Street (performances in Meymandi Concert Hall) 27601. Phone: (919) 733-2750. www.ncsymphony.org.

Based in Raleigh, the North Carolina Symphony (a full-time, professional orchestra with 65 members) performs approximately 170 times each year… with international guest artists appearing frequently. For guests interested in attending a performance, the world-class design, near-perfect acoustics and intimate atmosphere of the Meymandi Concert Hall redefines the concert experience. Also, Music Education concerts for students.

NORTH CAROLINA THEATRE, THE

Raleigh - 1 East South Street 27601. Phone: (919) 831-6950. www.nctheatre.com.
Admission: $20.00-$65.00

The only professional, not-for-profit theatre in the state that specializes in the production of large-scale, classic Broadway musicals (example: "My Fair Lady" or the "King and I").

PULLEN PARK

Raleigh - 520 Ashe Avenue 27601. Phone: (919) 831-6468. www.raleighnc.gov. (parks and facilities) Hours: Monday-Thursday 10:30am-6:30pm, Friday-Saturday 10:30am-8:00pm, Sunday 1:00-8:00pm (summer). Hours vary at other times of the year. Admission: FREE. Small fee for amusement rides.

One of the city's oldest and most loved parks, this beautiful park offers recreational opportunities for everyone and includes a 1911 Gustave A. Dentzel Menagerie Carousel, a C.P. Huntington train ride, a community center, boat rentals, an arts center, ballfields, tennis courts, picnic shelters, a children's playground, and a concession stand. Home of the TV Land "Andy & Opie" statue!

RALEIGH CITY MUSEUM

Raleigh - 220 Fayetteville Street (historic Briggs Bldg., downtown) 27601. Phone: (919) 832-3775. www.raleighcitymuseum.org. Hours: Tuesday-Friday 10:00am-4:00pm, Saturday 1:00-4:00pm. Admission: FREE.

Housed in an 1874 building that was the city's first "skyscraper", this museum aims at a better understanding of present day Raleigh through an exploration and understanding of its past history. Exhibits on display include the tracing of Raleigh's evolving architectural styles, a look at the businesses that built Raleigh, the history of North Carolina's State flag, and the history of the Civil Rights movement. Best if toured as an add-on to another historical tour or for a special event.

WAKE COUNTY SPEEDWAY

Raleigh - 2109 Simpkins Road 27601. www.wakecountyspeedway.com. Phone: (919) 779-2171.

Wake County Speedway was built as a 1/4 mile clay oval in 1962 by members of the Simpkins family. The track has passed through various management arrangements over the years, but continues with Simpkins ownership. The track was paved between the 1986 and 1987 seasons. Hosting stock car

CE Area

racing from April through late September, this speedway runs every Friday night with the 600 Racing Legends cars running several special events.

LEGENDS OF HARLEY DRAG RACING MUSEUM

Raleigh - 1126 S. Saunders Street (off I-440 / I-40 (Raleigh Beltline) at the South Saunders Street Exit (Hwy 401 / Hwy 70 North) 27603. Phone: (919) 832-2261. www.rayprice.com. Hours: Monday-Friday 7:00am-6:00pm, Saturday 8:00am-4:00pm, Sunday Noon-4:00pm. Admission: FREE

This journey goes down memory lane—down the hundreds of quarter-mile and eighth-mile tracks. You'll meet some of the drag racers who have smoked the tires, made a perfect launch, got a great reaction time and set a new record. More than six decades of American motorcycle history are on display, with Harley bikes representing each era from 1936 to the present, both in original and restored condition. The ground floor contains a showroom with dozens of shiny motorcycles on display alongside countless racks of jeans, boots, leathers, jewelry and even children's "Harley" clothing. Price's racing team is headquartered here. Price himself is an inductee of the National Motorcycle Hall of Fame.

CAROLINA BALLET

Raleigh - 3401-131 Atlantic Avenue (BTI Center for the Performing Arts) 27604. Phone: (919) 719-0900. www.carolinaballet.com. Admission: starts at $10.00.

This company presents a full range of ballet from the finest classics to fresh, contemporary works, infused with new energy and excitement. The Triangle's pro ballet company features collaborations with the North Carolina Symphony to provide a variety of ballet performances from the classics to modern such as Romeo & Juliet or Cinderella.

NUTCRACKER BALLET

A grand production of the holiday classic, performed by Carolina Ballet and the North Carolina Symphony. Magnificent costumes and sets plus dazzling special effects delight audiences of all ages in this production. Admission. (mid-November through December)

CAROLINA HURRICANES

Raleigh - 1400 Edwards Mill Road (home games played at RBC Center) 27604. Phone: (919) 467-7825 or (888) NHL-TIX1. www.carolinahurricanes.com. Admission: $12.00-$85.00.

Enjoy hard-hitting, fun-filled hockey games by this National Hockey League team that plays from October to April.

JOEL LANE MUSEUM HOUSE

Raleigh - 728 West Hargett Street (corner of Saint Mary's, near downtown) 27605. Phone: (919) 833-3431.   www.nscda.org/museums/northcarolina.htm#JOEL. Hours: Tuesday-Friday 10:00am-2:00pm, Saturday 1:00-4:00pm (March-mid-December). Admission: $3.00 adult, $1.00 senior/student.

The home of Joel Lane was built on a knoll overlooking the future city of Raleigh. The little house was the center of many historic gatherings. Lane introduced the bill in the Legislature for the creation of Wake County in 1770 and sold 11,000 acres to the State in 1792 for the creation of the capital city of Raleigh; hence he is known as the "Father of Wake County." Costumed docents take you through the oldest home and dependencies in Raleigh.

CHRISTMAS TOUR AT JOEL LANE MUSEUM HOUSE

Decorated in traditional colonial greenery and fruit, the Joel Lane Museum House, circa 1770, showcases ways in which our colonial ancestors celebrated the holiday season. Raleigh's oldest home is now fully restored to its appearance when it served as the residence of Joel Lane, a prominent statesman and patriot. FREE. (first weekend of December)

HISTORIC OAK VIEW COUNTY PARK

Raleigh - 4028 Carya Drive (I-440, Poole Road exit 15 east, 4 miles east of downtown) 27610. Phone: (919) 250-1013. www.wakegov.com/locations/oakview.htm Hours: Daily 8:30am-5:00pm. Closed major holidays. Admission: FREE. Miscellaneous: Occasional spring tea parties are a fun way to visit the past.

The Greek Revival Farmhouse at Historic Oak View County Park was built by Benton S.D. Williams in 1855. The Greek Revival style is typified by the front columns and the double portico porch. Completed in 1997, the Farm History Center is the newest building on the site. It is dedicated to telling the story of North Carolina's agricultural development from colonial times to the present through programs and interactive exhibits. This Antebellum farmstead

CE Area

features the 1855 Greek Revival house, a detached plank kitchen, a cotton gin museum, an herb garden, picnic facilities, a barn, and a large Farm History Center. Look out to the 17-acre pecan grove nearby.

HISTORIC OAKVIEW CHRISTMAS OPEN HOUSE & CANDLELIGHT TOUR

This antebellum farmstead is lit with luminaries for the holiday open-house. Guests can tour the 1855 Greek Revival house and visit with Santa in the living room, devour freshly baked cookies in the plank kitchen, and explore the cotton gin house museum, 1870s gazebo, and a Farm History Center. Sleigh rides are given around the pecan grove, snow or shine. FREE. (second Saturday in December)

MORDECAI HISTORIC PARK / PRESIDENT ANDREW JOHNSON'S BIRTHPLACE

Raleigh - 1 Mimosa Street (corner of Mimosa St and Wake Forest Road) 27611. Phone: (919) 834-4844. www.raleighnc.gov. (Parks and Facilities) Hours: Tuesday-Saturday 10:00am-4:00pm, Sunday 1:00-4:00pm. Admission: $6.00 adult, $4.00 student (7-17).

Andrew Johnson was born in Raleigh, North Carolina in 1808, and like the previous North Carolina born presidents, Andrew Jackson and James K. Polk, he was elected to office from Tennessee. Although a native of the South, Johnson was a firm supporter of the Union. This beautiful historic park includes an Antebellum mansion that was home to a very influential Raleigh family. Students will learn about the Mordecai Family and examine how families and life in North Carolina have changed over time. The surrounding plantation offers exhibits that detail plantation life as it was in its heyday plus features a small wooden house that was the birthplace of President Andrew Johnson (did you know he was born in a kitchen?). Slaves performed virtually all tasks on the plantation. Many continued traditional African farming practices, crafts, cooking and music. After the Civil War, some former slaves remained on the plantation, including Chaney, a cook, and Ananias, a gardener.

MORDECAI HISTORIC PARK HOLIDAY TOURS

Visitors experience the sights and sounds of Christmas past when they tour the historic Mordecai plantation house and grounds, all decked out for the holidays in period decorations including evergreens and fruit displays. Admission. (tours will run in December, on dates to be determined)

RALEIGH SYMPHONY ORCHESTRA

Raleigh - 2 East South St 27611. Phone: (919) 546-9755. www.raleighsymphony.com

With the belief that "music has the power to affect the lives of all people," this symphony orchestra regularly presents classical, family and pops concerts plus offers educational programs. The Family Series four productions (some interactive) are great for families. Most concerts at Holly Springs Cultural Center.

RALEIGH TROLLEY TOURS

Raleigh - 1 Mimosa Street (begin at Mordecai Historic Park or City Market) 27611. Phone: (919) 834-4844. www.raleighnc.gov/mordecai. Admission: $8.00 adult, $6.00 student (7-17). Miscellaneous: Catch the Historic Trolley Tour at any of the following locations: Mordecai Historic Park, State Capitol, Joel Lane House, Capital Area Visitors Center, City Market.

See Raleigh's 200-year history from an old point of view on the Raleigh Trolley! Travel through the historic heart of the Capital City on this historic trolley that offers a narrated tour with six stops. Visit historic sites, art galleries, museums, shops and restaurants. Learn about the city's history, hear stories about Sir Walter Raleigh and other local personalities and notice some unique architecture. Start the tour looking at beautiful Victorian homes. Some homes are occupied, some left empty, some completely gone. Interesting stories at every stop. The Governor's Home was built (brick by brick, literally) by prisoners. Kids, look for the prisoners' signatures on the bricks. The Trolley departs from Mordecai Historic Park on the hour, but can be boarded at any stop.

W. B. UMSTEAD STATE PARK

Raleigh - 8801 Glenwood Avenue 27612. Phone: (919) 571-4170. www.ncparks. gov/Visit/parks/wium/main.php. Hours: Daily 8:00am-dusk. Visitor Center 8:00am-5:00pm. Admission: FREE. Canoe and cabin rental fees apply. Miscellaneous: Campsite, rowboat and canoe rentals are available.

Divided into two sections, Crabtree Creek and Reedy Creek, this 5,439-acre park is easily accessible from Interstate 40 and US 70. Visitor Center Exhibits include: "This Old Farmland Has Stories to Tell" which uses oral histories of past residents to describe daily life on what was once hardscrabble farmland. "Mills and the Community" depicts a replica of one of several gristmills found in the park. "The Kingdom Game" is a computer interactive exhibit that invites visitors to consider the effects of development and preservation. Another series of exhibits describes the natural history of the land including stories of weather, soil and wildlife habitats. Twenty miles of hiking trails provide access to most of Umstead State Park. Visitors may choose between a short stroll along a nature trail or a more extensive hike into the woods. For people who prefer horseback, approximately 11 miles of bridle trails travel through some of the most scenic and secluded parts of the park. Signs mark the equestrian trails. The mountain-bike trails follow the same roads as the bridle trails and are entered at the same points.

RALEIGH LITTLE THEATRE

Raleigh - 301 Pogue Street 27650. Phone: (919) 821-4579. www.raleighlittletheatre.org Admission: $8.00-$25.00

Named "Best Children's Theatre Program", the theatre showcases a mix of high stepping musicals, outrageous comedy, serious dramas and family favorites such as *Cinderella* or *Miss Nelson is Missing*. Opened in 1936, Raleigh Little Theatre is one of the oldest continuously operating community theatres in the country and no other theatre in North Carolina produces as many shows.

SOLAR HOUSE, NCSU

Raleigh - North Carolina State Univ. campus, next to McKimmon Bldg. (corner of Western Blvd & Gorman Street, I-440 exit 2) 27695. www.ncsc.ncsu.edu. Phone: (919) 515-3799. Hours: Monday-Friday 9:00am-5:00pm, Sunday 1:00-5:00pm (except holiday weekends). Admission: FREE. Educators: Ask for worksheets on solar projects.

Constructed by the College of Engineering, this solar house serves as a demonstration and research facility and is the longest ongoing solar experiment open to the public in the United States. The roof of the garage powers their utility truck. Every major room is connected to the sunspace by an operable door or window. The basement/family room is full of experiments. Kids can actually make electricity from sunlight in a circuit. What if your hand blocks the light (ex. Clouds, trees)? - No power? How is energy stored when the sun doesn't shine? Ask about solar model car racing.

NORTH CAROLINA RENAISSANCE FAIRE

Raleigh - www.ncrenfaire.com. North Carolina State Fairgrounds. Have a jolly time in the court of Medieval England, from the time of King Arthur through Queen Elizabeth I. The celebration includes a feast of crafts, entertainment, jugglers, musicians, exotic food and drink, plus brave knights competing in full-contact jousts. Admission. (last weekend in March and first weekend in April)

CAPITOL EASTER SUNRISE SERVICE

Raleigh - NC State Capitol Square. (919) 733-4994. A non-denominational service with musical performances takes place on the east grounds. FREE. (6:30am on Easter Sunday)

AMISTAD SAGA: REFLECTIONS

Raleigh - African American Cultural Complex, 119 Sunnybrook Road. (919) 250-9336 or www.aaccmuseum.org. The "Amistad" outdoor drama tells in song, dance and oratory presentation the famous story of mutiny at sea aboard the famous slave ship. The compelling outdoor drama reenacts the mutiny scene of Joseph Cinque and African hostages designed to preserve the history of African-Americans. This event marked the beginning of the end of slavery in the U.S. The drama brings to life events through powerful speeches, song and dance. Admission. (last two weekends in July)

JULY 4TH CELEBRATION

Raleigh - Capitol Square. www.dcr.state.nc.us. Celebrate with a bang as you watch live bands, eat some good home-cooking and view craft demos. FREE.

NORTH CAROLINA STATE FAIR

Raleigh - NC State Fairgrounds, 1025 Blue Ridge Road. www.ncstatefair.org. (919) 733-2145. With over 700,000 people attending each year, the 10-day extravaganza features livestock, agriculture, arts and cultural exhibitions, an amusement midway and nightly nationally acclaimed musical performances. Admission. (begins mid-October for 10 days)

CELEBRATION OF LIGHTS

Raleigh - Pavilion at Walnut Creek. (919) 831-6666. A spectacular array of lights and animated characters including jumping reindeer, swimming swans, waving snowmen and a tunnel of snowflakes. A 2-mile vehicle drive-thru. $15.00 per vehicle. (evenings, weekends and holidays, weekend before Thanksgiving through weekend after New Years)

CE Area

INTERNATIONAL FEST

Raleigh - Downtown. www.internationalfestival.org. A dazzling mosaic of world tastes, sights and sounds featuring international foods, cultural exhibits, a world bazaar, ethnic dancing, and music. Admission. (first weekend in November)

A CHRISTMAS CAROL

Raleigh - Raleigh's Theatre in the Park, Memorial Auditorium. (919) 831-6058, www.theatreinthepark.com. Production of the Charles Dickens classic, "A Christmas Carol." This wildly popular production, starring Ira David Wood III, is updated each year to include crowd-pleasing humor without losing the spirit of the original play. Tickets range from $12-$58. (one week in early to mid-December)

NEW HOPE VALLEY RAILWAY & NC RAILROAD MUSEUM

Raleigh (Bonsal / New Hill) - P. O. Box 40 (Take US 1 south to Exit #89 at New Hill to Bonsal Road) 27562. Phone: (919) 362-5416. www.nhvry.org. Admission: FREE to walk around and peek in museum. Rides run: $9.00 adult, $6.00 child (1-12).

The line that the New Hope Valley Railway scenic railroad takes was originally called the Durham & South Carolina Railroad and ran 31 miles from Bonsal to Durham. This line connected with the Seaboard Airline Railroad at Bonsal and was used to haul, among other things, tobacco to Durham for processing and finished cigarettes to market. A collection of antique trains including classic steam and diesel locomotives, as well as other train cars, are on display. This museum is open for self-guided tours on weekends. On the first Sunday of each month (May-December), visitors may take an eight-mile, round-trip train ride in open or enclosed cars and cabooses. Nice forest scenery along the way. At the New Hill Yard Limit, the engine is decoupled and switched to a siding. It then passes the cars to travel to another switch, gets back on the main track, and is recoupled with the cars to haul you back to Bonsal. This is the highlight of the trip. Santa Train first two weekends in December.

BIG ED'S CITY MARKET

Raleigh (City Market) - Fuel up with southern food (Breakfast, Lunch) at Big Ed's City Market just blocks walk away from the museums in downtown Raleigh. Big Ed (in red-checked shirt, denim overalls and a big smile) oversees the operations saying "I'm gonna fill your belly". Choose from 8 fresh meats and 12 fresh vegies for lunch. Ed uses ancestral recipes to create authentic traditional Southern staples like hot cakes (made from a pound cake recipe!), biscuits, chicken and dumplings, collard greens and country cured ham. If Ed Watkins isn't available to offer a firsthand story about his rural heritage, the restaurant itself provides a healthy dose of Americana, with Big Ed's own collection of antique farm implements, baskets, tin signs and other nostalgia items on display. Big, inexpensive breakfasts, too. After lunch, stroll along the cobblestone streets and browse the specialty shops. Tour Artspace (FREE), where artists work in open-to-the-public studios.

FALL HARVEST & PUMPKIN FESTIVAL

Raleigh (Youngsville) - Hill Ridge Farms, 703 Tarboro Road. www.hillridgefarms.com. (800) 358-4170. Fall hayrides where you choose a pumpkin from the patch out in the fields. Pony rides, train rides, gem stone panning, live music, food, a petting barn, fish feeding dock and a kids' playland are all available. Admission. (mid-September thru October weekends)

CAROLINA MUDCATS

Raleigh (Zebulon) - 1501 NC Hwy 39 (home games played at Five County Stadium) 27597. Phone: (919) 269-CATS. www.gomudcats.com.

A member of the Class AA Southern League, this farm team for the Florida Marlins baseball team offers family recreation from April to September. Don't miss Friday Night Fireworks, "pig" out on hot dogs on Tuesday's Dollar Dog Days and quench your thirst with $1 beverages on Thirsty Thursdays. Picnic tables down first baseline provide a great view of the game while you enjoy ball park fare. But heads up, because you are in prime foul ball territory - you may have the opportunity to take one home as a souvenir.

Roanoke Rapids

ROANOKE RIVER MUSEUM & CANAL TRAIL

Roanoke Rapids - Highway 158   27870. www.roanokeriver.com. Phone: (252) 537-2769.   Museum Hours: Tuesday-Saturday 10:00am-4:00pm.

ROANOKE RIVER FALLS PARK - This safe still water harbor offers easy access to the Roanoke River and the overlook offers an excellent view of the river's picturesque rapids. Canoeing and fishing are among the most popular activities along the river banks. The park has a picnic area with grills and is an entry point to the Roanoke Canal Trail. Located just off Hwy 301 in Weldon.

CE Area

Roanoke River Museum & Canal Trail (cont.)

ROANOKE CANAL TRAIL - This trail contains some of the most impressive and best preserved early nineteenth century canal construction in the nation. Begun before 1819, and completed in 1823, the Roanoke Canal was built as the North Carolina segment of the ambitious Roanoke Navigation System. It was designed to connect the Blue Ridge Mountains of Virginia with Norfolk, over a distance of 400 miles. Today you can experience the seven-mile trail along the old Canal in Roanoke Rapids.

ROANOKE RIVER MUSEUM - The museum tells the fascinating story of transportation and navigation on the Roanoke River and the history of the Roanoke Canal. The storyline weaves together the navigational history of the Roanoke River, the beginning of the railroad, transportation during the Civil War, and the coming of hydro-electric power with the river and the canal as common threads.

Rocky Mount

ROCKY MOUNT CHILDREN'S MUSEUM & SCIENCE CENTER

Rocky Mount - 270 Gay Street (Imperial Centre for the Arts and Sciences) 27804. Phone: (252) 972-1167. www.rockymountnc.gov/museum/ Hours: Tuesday-Saturday 10:00am-5:00pm, Sunday 1:00-5:00pm. Closed Thanksgiving and Christmas Day. Admission: $3.00-$4.00 per person (age 3+). Planetarium $3.50. Wonderful Wednesdays (2pm-5pm) - FREE for everyone! Miscellaneous: In town (Sunset Avenue on River Drive) is Sunset Park - mini-train, historic carousel, sport courts, and swimming pool (252-972-1151).

The Children's Museum and Science Center brings the stars out in Rocky Mount everyday with North Carolina's first digital planetarium. It is housed in the oldest of the factory buildings which also includes permanent and rotating exhibits, a puppet theater, live animal habitats and a NC coastal "living marsh." For example - Bears, In North Carolina? - NC Black Bears are very misunderstood animals. Visit this display and learn the real facts about one of North Carolina's largest land mammals. The state-of-the-art digital SciDome planetarium features live and recorded sky tours, laser light concert shows and exhibits - Discover the secrets of the stars, moons, and planets in this fascinating astronomical exhibit. In Microbes, visitors can technologically interact with viruses and bacteria - ugh! Leading edge technology also allows visitors to see crystallography of a variety of deadly viruses represented as "virtual" 3-D photography. Through high-tech video games, visitors can combat bacteria with antibiotics, use virtual reality, help microbes gobble up oil spills and participate in a microbes "quiz show."

Selma

AMERICAN MUSIC JUBILEE THEATRE

Selma - 300 N. Raiford Street (Rudy Theatre) 27576. Phone: (919) 202-9927 or (877) 843-7839. www.amjubilee.com.

A little bit of Branson, a little bit of Myrtle Beach entertainment style. Their student matinee show includes comedy and songs about self-discipline, responsibility, patriotism, loyalty, respect and much more. Shows now begin at either 10:30am or 11:30am depending on the date. Please check the Schedule for start times. Admission is only $8.00 each. All teachers and school employees admitted Free of Charge. FREE Pepsi and popcorn (one each) to everyone.

Seven Springs

CLIFFS OF THE NEUSE STATE PARK

Seven Springs - 345A Park Entrance Road (I-40 east, take US 70 east through Goldsboro. Turn right onto NC 111) 28578. www.ncparks.gov/Visit/parks/clne/main.php. Phone: (919) 778-6234. Hours: Daily 8:00am to sunset. Admission: FREE. Fee for camping, swimming and rowboat rental.

At the turn of the century visitors flocked to the area. They drank mineral water from local springs to cure their ills and they took riverboat excursions to the cliffs. Things have changed since then. Witness the effects of erosion that carved cliffs in the south bank of the Neuse River. The cliffs extend 600 yards and rise 90 feet above the water. The cliff's face is multi-colored, adding to the beauty. Follow the cliffs' edge for lovely views of the river below. A path bordered by a rail fence leads along the riverbank. The park offers three 1/2 mile hiking trails, seasonal swimming lake, and canoeing on the river. Creative dioramas and audio-visuals in the museum depict the unique geology and natural history of the area.

CE Area

Snow Camp

SNOW CAMP HISTORICAL DRAMAS

Snow Camp - Greensboro Chapel Hill Road (I-40 west to Burlington, I-85 exit 145, turn left onto NC 49, go 13 miles) 27349. Phone: (336) 376-6948 or (800) 726-5115. www.snowcampdrama.com. Shows: Thursday-Saturday evening starting at 8:00pm (July - mid-August). See schedule for alternating plays. Admission: $14.00 adult, $12.00 senior (60+), $6.00 child (under 11). Children's Theater (Saturday mornings) $5.00. Miscellaneous: Be sure to show up early for some Country Cooking at "Ye Old Country Kitchen" located on the grounds. Children's Show each Saturday Morning @ 10:00AM ($5.00).

THE SWORD OF PEACE - is a dramatic portrayal of the American Revolution. It enlightens the audience about the struggles the peaceful Quakers must face in a time of war. General Nathanael Greene, second in command under General George Washington, is about to meet Lord Cornwallis, Commander of the British Forces in America, at the battle of Guilford Courthouse. Simon Dixon, a Quaker miller, is faced with an important decision like that of his neighbors…take up arms and fight or remain true to his faith. Simon and other historical characters reveal their heart-torn decisions as you witness this exciting, action-packed dramatic tribute to the Quakers.

PATHWAY TO FREEDOM - tells the story of how anti-slavery North Carolinians and freed African-Americans helped hundreds of escaped slaves flee to the North. This play is an exciting account of the struggles and heroism of the 1840's and 1850's along the "Underground Railroad" from North Carolina to Indiana. Both individuals and some organized religions fought slavery in the legislature and on the farms, while some, like Levi and Katie Coffin of Guilford County, led volunteers and free slaves in amazing efforts to help escaping slaves to freedom. The play centers on George Vestal, son of a slave-owning family, and how and why he became a worker for the "Underground Railroad". Both plays help to explain our past and shine a light to the future. Parents: History and character development all in one entertaining evening.

Wake Forest

FALLS LAKE STATE RECREATION AREA

Wake Forest - 13304 Creedmoor Road (US 1 north to NC 98 west to NC 50. Turn right on NC 50 and travel north one mile) 27587. www.ncparks.gov/Visit/parks/fala/main.php Phone: (919) 676-1027. Hours: Daily 8:00am-dusk. Admission: $5.00 per vehicle. Educators: Rangers hold regularly scheduled educational and interpretive programs about Falls Lake and its aquatic environment. The Falls Lake program focuses on the food chain. Accompanying the program is a teacher's booklet and workshop, free of charge to educators.

A total of 13 miles of trails through a variety of terrain are open for single-track mountain biking. Located in the Beaverdam area, the park offers three loop trails totaling a distance of 6.5 miles of easy/intermediate riding. For hikers, Falls Lake Trail will eventually travel the entire south shore of the lake. A portion of the Mountains-to-Sea Trail, the trail will connect two recreational areas and provide camping for backpackers. Sandling Beach, Rolling View and Beaverdam provide sandy swim beaches with nearby restrooms and changing facilities. Holly Point offers swimming for campers only. US 1 north to NC 98 at the town of Wake Forest.

Wilson

IMAGINATION STATION

Wilson - 224 East Nash Street (Hwy 264 East to Wilson. Take Exit 36B onto Alternate 264 East) 27893. Phone: (252) 291-5113. www.imaginescience.org. Hours: Monday-Saturday 9:00am-5:00pm. Admission: $4.00-$5.00 (age 4+).

Located in the historic Wilson Federal Courthouse that was built in 1928, this hands-on science and technology center features over 200 exhibits that are related to the environment, space, and health. All of the exhibits at Imagination Station are hands-on. They want you to push, pull and handle everything. Exotic animals from around the state are a favorite but the best part is the up-close science experiments and demonstrations. Can you: Generate your own electricity? Look in a mirror and see yourself floating in air? Or, race against a bat, bear and a cheetah?

WHIRLIGIGS

Wilson (Lucama) - Wiggins Mill Road (I-95 exit 107 north to town. Turn left at light at Clints Korner, go to Wiggins Mill Road. Turn left approx. 4 miles) 27542. Phone: (800) 497-7398. Hours: Who knows. Best to stop by the Wilson County Visitors Center just off the freeway for daily schedules. Daylight hours preferred. This is someone's home so respect his privacy and follow any instructions. Admission: FREE.

Vollis Simpson's Windmill Farm is a remarkable collection of elaborate "whirligigs" produced by local folk artist Vollis Simpson. The works incorporate complex movement and sound as an integral part of the more than 30 GIANT works erected on Simpson's property. Simpson's welded and painted constructions are large in scale and have been exhibited at noted art museums and are featured in downtown Raleigh. Vollis can often be seen at the front of his shop, working non-stop. He's happy to talk to you, but he doesn't ever interrupt his work. Inside, the shop is filled with over a hundred smaller whirlygigs, all completely finished and painted.

45

Chapter 2
Central West

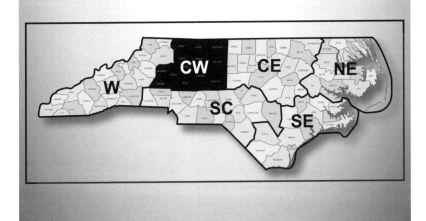

A Quick Tour of our Hand-Picked Favorites Around...

Central West North Carolina

Let's start at a castle! Actually, several "castles." **Castle McCulloch Gold Mill** (off I-85 south in Jamestown) has a true medieval feeling with thick walls, a drawbridge, a moat, and a 70-foot tower. Even a knight in shining armor greets you. If you take I-40 east of Winston-Salem just a bit, your kids won't want to miss the "strangest house in the world" at **Korner's Folly** in Kernersville. Kids are surprised by all the many hidden nooks and crannies. This home is quirky but so full of whimsy!

Still in the mood for some strange stuff? Wake Forest University **Museum of Anthropology**'s permanent exhibits consist of cultural objects from the Americas, Africa, Asia and the Pacific. The kimonos and masks are big hits with the kids. Learn how to make a Kimono (w/paper). Play a painted gourd or sleep on a wooden head rest. What's that? Find out when you visit.

Deeply rooted in a pre-Revolutionary War history, folks in the Piedmont region needed to clear wilderness to begin a colony. The town of Winston-Salem has built a reputation for a connection to the arts that ties back to the pioneering Protestant group of Moravians that founded the original settlement called "Salem." Head to **Old Salem** and take your time to enjoy the historic museums here. In addition to a collection of antique toys and the playful **Children's Museum** (dress up), you can walk through this restored community dating back to 1766. Families seem to gravitate to the church and the old schools. The wafting smell of ginger from the bakery draws them in by the dozens to this cozy little space to purchase a bag of goodies to snack on.

Now that you're hooked on that bakery smell, **Mrs. Hanes Moravian Cookies Tour** is a must on your itinerary after lunch. Guess what, you get to be taste-testers! A sample of one of the 6 different flavors is given at each "station" along the tour. They make around 10 million Moravian cookies, each cut out one by one using a cookie cutter!

With your cookies as your "trail" snack, let's head east to Greensboro to visit favorite museums. Diversity is the best way to describe the **Natural Science Center** - so many different things - no signs of boredom here... inside and outside. Look up, look down, look all around. We notice they only have a handful of exhibits in each theme room, but they have the things kids really love.

Children can learn as they explore the PROCESS of art at **ArtQuest**. Travel on an art expedition where you can dig in the clay garden or construct a house of fabric. Then, weave on a giant 7-foot loom or crawl into Pablo's Place of puppets. Make a story quilt or create a mosaic postcard. The best part - you get to take most everything home!

The **World's Largest Chest of Drawers** is a building shaped like a chest of drawers built in 1926 to call attention to High Point as the "Home Furnishings Capital of the World." The **World's Largest Chair** is a similar oddity in Thomasville. It's one of those odd side trips you just have to say you've seen. Explore the history of High Point and many of its inhabitants as you tour the **High Point Museum & Historical Park**. You will be introduced to the Native Americans who first settled the land; to the development of the town from a small Quaker village; and then through the establishment of the furniture and textile industries. The awesome exhibits of the Furniture Discovery Center should be on display in the future.

Although all of North Carolina is race country, the Piedmont I-85 or I-77 corridor is full of racing headquarters. For a favorite tour of both a Nextel Cup teams' shop and a Craftsman Truck teams' shop – all roads lead to **Bill Davis Racing** (High Point). Stop by to see the cars being built and to get a true behind-the-scenes glimpse of what it takes to compete in the NASCAR Series.

For a big dose of the outdoors, try two zoos – one you WALK through, the other you DRIVE through. What a treat to have a drive-thru safari right in the middle of North Carolina! The **Lazy 5 Ranch** in Mooresville is now home to over 750 animals from 6 continents, this place is anything but lazy. Still haven't got your fill of animals? The **North Carolina Zoo** (Asheboro) was America's first zoo designed around the natural habitat philosophy and contains over 1,100 animals.

Step back to a simpler time when you visit Mount Airy. Actor Andy Griffith grew up here, and it's no coincidence that a stroll down Mount Airy's Main Street reminds people of the town of **Mayberry** from The Andy Griffith Show. Fans of the show can visit Floyd's City Barber Shop, Opie's Candy Store,

Wally's Service Station, Mayberry Soda Fountain, Mayberry Courthouse, the Old City Jail, Snappy Lunch, and take a ride in a Squad Car Tour. You may even want to stay overnight in his childhood home (**Andy Griffith's Home & Town**). On a clear day you can see **Pilot Mountain** (Mount Pilot in the series). Take an adventure hike towards the top!

Sites and attractions are listed in order by City, Zip Code, and Name. Symbols indicated represent:

 Festivals    Restaurants   Lodging

Asheboro

AMERICAN CLASSIC MOTORCYCLE MUSEUM

Asheboro - 1170 US Highway 64 W (Intersection of Hwy 220 and Hwy 64/49) 27205. Phone: (336)629-9564. www.american-classic-motorcycle.com/. Hours: Monday 6:00am- 2:00pm, Tuesday - Friday 6:00am - 5:30pm; Saturday 6:00am - 4:00pm. Admission: Donations suggested. Miscellaneous: Restaurant on site.

One of the South's finest collections of antique and classic Harley Davidson motorcycles. Over 30 bikes dating from 1936 through 1972 and an authentic 1948 Harley dealership / repair shop.

NORTH CAROLINA AVIATION MUSEUM

Asheboro - 2109 Pilots View Road (Hwy 49 south, go two miles and turn left on Tot Hill Farm Road) 27205. Phone: (336) 625-0170. www.ncairmuseum.org. Hours: Monday-Saturday 10:00am-5:00pm, Sunday 1:00-5:00pm. Admission: $5.00 adult, $3.00 student (over age 6).

In this Museum you will see many examples of America's greatest warplanes from WWII through Vietnam, all flyable, except for one. Surrounding the aircraft, you will find collections of authentic military uniforms and memorabilia. You might read a newspaper headline and then look up and see the same aircraft that made those headlines. Kids like the fun names of War Birds. New planes are often from recent commands - even a Homeland Security Condor. Come and learn about a time, a generation and the machinery that preserved our freedom.

CW Area

NORTH CAROLINA ZOO

Asheboro - (US 220 south) 27205. Phone: (800) 488-0444. www.nczoo.org. Hours: Daily 9:00am-4:00pm. Open until 5:00pm (April - September). Only closed Christmas Day. Admission: $10.00 adult, $8.00 senior & student, $6.00 child (2-12). Miscellaneous: Free parking. Picnic sites, restaurants and gift shop. Educators & Scouts: Kids scavenger games and teacher lesson plans are on the Education icon.

This was America's first zoo designed around the natural habitat philosophy. You'll see more than 800 wild, African animals living in large, natural habitats in the rolling Uwharrie Mountains. In the African Pavilion, watch colobus monkeys and meerkats or herds of

> If you walk the whole zoo - it's 5 miles! This place is so large and spread out, you may want to ride the tram around so you don't "tucker out".

antelope leaping and running across the large re-created African Plains. The North America exhibit has everything from arid deserts, to grassland prairies, to dense swamps to cold northern coasts. See alligators bask in the sun while polar bears wade in the cold water. In the indoor desert, look for cactus, roadrunners and rattlesnakes. Another indoor exhibit is the Forest Aviary. Scores of birds swoop and call noisily from their overhead roosts. The scarlet ibis and the Chilean flamingo are only a couple of the interesting species you'll encounter. But, to what are kids looking the most forward? - the western lowland gorilla. This chest-thumping primate routinely scares the willies right out of you with his noisy charges at the glass enclosure.

NORTH CAROLINA POTTERY CENTER

Asheboro (Seagrove) - 250 East Avenue 27341. www.ncpotterycenter.com . Phone: (336) 873-8430. Hours: Tuesday-Saturday 10:00am-4:00pm. Closed Good Friday, the 4th of July, thanksgiving, and Christmas through New Years. Admission: $1.00-$2.00 (9th grade and up). Note: If your time is limited, definitely visit the Seagrove Pottery Gallery, which represents about 45 local and regional potters. It houses a remarkable diversity of pottery styles, colors, glazing methods, shapes and functions, and it is a good way to get a feel for the diversity available in the region.

At the lone stoplight in Seagrove where South and North Broad crosses East and West Main streets, small street signs point in two directions toward "America's Pottery Highway." See exhibits of North Carolina pottery and related activities from prehistoric Native American times to the present at this pottery center that promotes awareness of the techniques, history and technology of pottery making in the state. The museum is a great introduction to Seagrove - the oldest and largest community of working potters in the U.S. Maps help you locate more than 100 potters in town and across the state. Found your favorite styles? Now, go out and meet the potters at their studios nearby. Visitors to Seagrove are often confounded by the notion that tucked in amongst the farms and fields are some of the best-known pottery families in the country.

Danbury

HANGING ROCK STATE PARK

Danbury - P.O. Box 278, Hanging Rock Road (I-40, take US 52 north. Take the Germanton/NC 8 exit, and turn left, following NC 8 for 25 miles through town. Follow signs) 27016. http://ncparks.gov/Visit/parks/haro/main.php. Phone: (336) 593-8480. Hours: 8:00am-dusk. Admission: FREE. Boat rentals, swimming (small), camping and cabin fees apply.

For the adventuresome, there's Hanging Rock State Park, located just north of Winston-Salem near Danbury. The area is composed of sheer cliffs and peaks of bare rock, quiet forests and cascading waterfalls, and views of the piedmont plateau that stretch for miles. A hall in the visitor's center offers a variety of interactive exhibits. Open panels of a dead tree to see what's inside. Or, watch a video about the people who formed the park. Learn about geology, bend a rock, or try to build a wall out of stone. Enjoy dioramas of the plants and animals that live on rocky cliffs and near creeks. Hike one of the eleven trails of Hanging Rock State Park. An easy adventure for smaller children is Upper Cascade Falls. Older children will find their efforts rewarded with two beautiful waterfalls, Window Falls and Hidden Falls, within a short distance of each other. Rent a vacation cabin or camp. Join an interpretive program and discover something new about nature's bounty. Nestled in the hills is the cool Sauratown Mountains with a lake that beckons to swimmers, canoers and fishermen.

Gold Hill

VILLAGE OF GOLD HILL

Gold Hill - St. Stephen's Church Road 28071. www.historicgoldhill.com. Phone: (704) 209-3280. Hours: Wednesday-Sunday 11:00am-5:00pm. Extended holiday hours. Admission: FREE. Miscellaneous: Ms. Ruby's restaurant, the Gold Hill Bakery & and many old-fashioned gift stores are now open in the village.

"The richest mining property east of the Mississippi." This was the message sent to England in the mid-1800s after gold was discovered here in 1824. Once a thriving, rough and rowdy mining town in the eastern part of Rowan County, the village is coming to life again with the restoration of area homes

and stores. Visit the Rock Jail, Mauney's 1840 Store and Museum, and the E.H. Montgomery General Store. Gold Hill Mines Historic Park has a walking trail extending from the barn to the amphitheater. It crosses the bridge and joins the Gold Hill Rail Trail. Picnic and playground area in the park.

Greensboro

ARTQUEST!

Greensboro - 200 North Davie Street (corner of Friendly and Davie) 27401. Phone: (336) 333-7460. www.greenhillcenter.org Hours: Tuesday-Saturday 12:30-5:00pm. Open for pre-scheduled group tours only during weekday morning hours. Closed holidays. Admission: $5.00 per person (age 2+). FREE admission Wednesday 5:00-7:00pm for Family Night.

This upscale visual arts center and gallery features changing exhibitions by North Carolina artists and offers a variety of educational programs for children and adults. You may want to first take a look at the FREE galleries including original works in glass, fiber and wood, as well as pottery, jewelry

Clay Sculpting Fun

and paintings. Now, apply those visual mediums to the hands-on children's gallery of creative fun in ArtQuest. Travel on an art expedition where you can

dig in the clay garden (using North Carolina clay) or Claytown; construct a house of fabric in the Architecture Corner; weave on a giant 7-foot loom; or crawl into Pablo's Place of puppets. Make a story quilt or create a mosaic postcard. The best part - you get to take most everything home! No trouble engaging here - a great "creative" stop!

GREENSBORO BALLET

Greensboro - 200 North Davie Street, Box 12 (performances at the War Memorial Coliseum) 27401. Phone: (336) 333-7480. www.greensboroballet.com. Admission: $12.00-$25.00.

Performances given by this professional ballet company include fairy tale classics, exciting contemporary works, comedic ballets, and the holiday favorite, "The Nutcracker." "Dance in the Schools" school and community outreach programs, too. The Ballet for a Buck program is an introduction to the art of classical ballet where the audience will enjoy a fun and informative demonstration and even some audience participation (All performances in STUDIO 301 on the third floor of the Greensboro Cultural Center - $1 / Ticket. Reservations strongly suggested).

GREENSBORO CHILDREN'S MUSEUM

Greensboro - 220 North Church Street (downtown Greensboro) 27401. Phone: (336) 574-2898. www.gcmuseum.com. Hours: Tuesday-Saturday 9:00am-5:00pm, Fridays until 8:00pm, Sunday 1:00-5:00pm. Admission: $6.00 general, $5.00 senior, Family Friday Fun (evenings) and Sunday afternoons $3.00. Miscellaneous: Tot Spot Early Childhood Area. Play Lot. Creation Station arts and crafts area. Great museum for age 10 and under.

This museum is designed around an "Our Town" theme. Since adults go to work in a town, children can learn their roles in the community in their version inside the museum. Children can shop, scan and buy pretend groceries, use a real ATM to get "kid cash", hop into a real US Postal jeep or climb the steps to a real DC-9 jet cockpit, slither through the window of a real Petty NASCAR Pontiac, scramble into the driver's seat of a real Greensboro Fire Department tanker, hit the lights and siren inside a real patrol car, and stand inside a hug bubble. They even make music or direct a symphony or play in a huge sandbox full of buried treasure. Finally, the kids see how North Carolina streams create electricity and how high and low tides affect the intracoastal waterway. Our favorite, most educational area: the Media Room where you can choose to be a newscaster, sports, weather, traffic or even the producer (best set we've seen). They provide scripts to keep things together. Nice layout.

GREENSBORO HISTORICAL MUSEUM

Greensboro - 130 Summit Avenue (downtown, near the Children's Museum) 27401. Phone: (336) 373-2043. www.greensborohistory.org. Hours: Tuesday-Saturday 10:00am-5:00pm, Sunday 2:00-5:00pm. Closed City holidays except Fourth of July. Admission: FREE.

Discover the history of the area and the Piedmont people at this museum that features twelve exhibit spaces and two American History restored homes. Among the 10,000 artifacts housed in the museum, have the kids see who can first find: the churns and sewing machines; a dagger found on the battlefield at Guilford Courthouse; a letter from the great short-story writer O. Henry to his sweetheart; Dolley Madison's, wife of the fourth president of the United States, snuff box; and phonograph records from the 1920s. Visit in an old-fashioned general store, doctor's office or schoolhouse. Learn about the Woolworth sit-ins that helped launch a national civil rights movement.

BARN DINNER THEATRE

Greensboro - 120 Stage Coach Trail (I-40 to Guilford College Rd/Jamestown Exit 213) 27405. Phone: (336) 292-2211 or 800-668-1764. www.barndinner.com. Shows: Evening performances begin at 8:00pm. Dinner is served from 6:00pm-7:30pm. Sunday, Tuesday, Wednesday Matinee buffet seating begins at 1:00pm. Admission: Dinner/Lunch Theatre: $35.00-$40.00 adult, about half-price child (12 & under). Children under the age of 5 are not recommended for dinner theatre.

The oldest dinner theatre in continuous operation in the United States, this entertaining theatre allows visitors to enjoy a popular Broadway style play, such as musicals, comedies, and mysteries, after sampling a wonderful traditional buffet. Playtime Theatre shows are shorter and don't include a meal. Special, spectacular Christmas shows - often several different themes to choose from.

BOG GARDEN & BICENTENNIAL GARDEN

Greensboro - Hobbs Road (just north of Friendly Avenue, corner of Hobbs Road & Starmount Drive) 27405. Phone: (336) 373-2199. www.greensborobeautiful.org. Hours: Daily, sunrise to sunset. Admission: FREE. Miscellaneous: Drive over to the nearby Greensboro Arboretum and discover the area's newest treasure. The 17-acre arboretum includes nine permanent plant collections of various species that provide appeal throughout the year. Special displays and features include a hosta and wildflower trail, gazebo, rhododendron garden, vine covered overlook and arbor, a butterfly garden and a lighted fountain.

Arrive at the Bicentennial Gardens and David Caldwell Historic Park. Enjoy seven gardens offering an exotic experience in sight, smell and touch. The Garden of Fragrance is very popular because of its unique scents and the bronze sculpture, "The Student," commemorating the David Caldwell Log College. Stroll across the street and visit Bog Garden, a "swamp-like" park featuring a half-mile elevated wood walkway that provides easy and safe access through the bog. You'll have a rare chance to go inside a bog and see unusual trees, wildflowers and ferns. We especially liked the boardwalk trail, the bamboo garden, and the many beautiful ducks and geese. Neat nature!

GREENSBORO SPORTS

GREENSBORO GRASSHOPPERS BASEBALL - Cheer for a professional Class-A farm club for the Florida Marlins and enjoy America's favorite pastime with a variety of foods and beverages. Games played at First Horizon Park, located at the corner of Bellemeade and N. Eugene Streets, run from April to September and offer family sections and picnic specials. Call (336) 268-BALL for tickets.

CAROLINA DYNAMO PROFESSIONAL SOCCER CLUB - Enjoy action packed soccer at Macpherson Stadium, Bryan Park. May through August. Call (336) 316-1266 for tickets. www.carolinadynamo.com.

GREENSBORO SYMPHONY ORCHESTRA

Greensboro - 200 North Davies Street, Suite 328 (performances at the War Memorial Coliseum) 27405. Phone: (336) 335-5456. www.greensborosymphony.org. Admission: $15.00-$32.00. Students with I.D. $5.00.

Hear masterworks and pops concerts (featuring guest artists from around the world) presented by this symphony orchestra that also offers an array of educational programs. Their programs in the schools are specific to each grade level and offer a wonderful exposure to music. Season runs September-May.

GUILFORD COURTHOUSE NATIONAL MILITARY PARK

Greensboro - 2332 New Garden Road (US 220, Battleground Avenue) 27405. Phone: (336) 288-1776. www.nps.gov/guco. Hours: Daily 8:30am-5:00pm. Closed New Year's Day, Thanksgiving and Christmas Day. Admission: FREE.

March 15, 1781 was the battle of Guilford Courthouse - one of the last battles of the Revolutionary War. Cornwallis held the field after an intense, two-hour fight, but he lost 1/4 of his army...leading to the eventual defeat at Yorktown months later. Today, the park's wooded grounds can be seen by taking a 2 1/2 mile auto or bicycle tour, or by walking along three miles of trails. Along the way, visitors can see 28 monuments commemorating the heroes of the battle. The Visitor's center offers a 30-minute, live-action film (shown on the hour); an animated battle map program; and informational exhibits featuring original Revolutionary War Weaponry and artifacts. Exhibits include: sample firing of muskets, scavenger hunts with stamping stations, and silhouettes of soldiers on the field. Be sure to allow time to see the mini-movie - they take the perspective of interviews of soldiers throughout the movie - it personalizes it.

WET N' WILD EMERALD POINTE WATER PARK

Greensboro - 3910 S. Holden Road (I-85 exit 121) 27405. Phone: (336) 852-9721 or (800) 555-5900. www.emeraldpointe.com. Hours: Call for seasonal hours of operation (May-September). Admission: Day Tickets $25.99 regular, $18.99 junior (under 48"), FREE (age 2 and under). Save with presale Good Any Day Price tickets. Discounts after 4:00pm. Snack bar food extra. All Day Splash Regular - $25.99 (48" tall and over). All Day Splash Under 48" - $18.99.

The largest waterpark in the Carolinas offers more than 35 rides and attractions. Thunder Bay, one of only four tsunami (giant wave) pools in the country, makes massive, perfect waves. Enclosed slides, drop slides, tube rides and cable glides provide thrills for all ages and sizes. Try the Dragon's Den in the dark - if you dare. Two great children's areas and a drifting lazee river. Water just brings out the fun in people - even parents.

TANNENBAUM HISTORIC PARK

Greensboro - 2200 New Garden Road 27410. Phone: (336) 545-5315. Admission: FREE. www.greensboro-nc.gov/Departments/Parks/facilities/tannenbaum/ Hours: Tuesday-Saturday 9:00am-5:00pm. In winter, park closes one-half hour early. Miscellaneous: Picnic area. Museum store.

Operated by the local Parks & Recreation Department, this park was the 18th-century farmstead of Joseph Hoskins (the town sheriff). During the Battle of Guilford Courthouse, Hoskins' land served as a staging area for British troops. The Colonial Heritage Center offers exhibits depicting life in colonial Guilford County. Plan to tour the Colonial Heritage Center - it's both informative and fun! The hands-on displays are a favorite. Best to visit for Living History Weekends.

BATTLE OF GUILFORD COURTHOUSE REENACTMENT

On the anniversary date of the March, 1781 battle, hundreds of re-enactors portray British and American soldiers who fought in the American Revolution. www.nps.gov/guco. (weekend closest to March 15)

NATURAL SCIENCE CENTER OF GREENSBORO

Greensboro - 4301 Lawndale Drive (I-40 exit Wendover Ave. East. Take Benjamin Pkwy. N exit, adjacent to Country Park) 27455. www.natsci.org. Phone: (336) 288-3769. Hours: Monday-Saturday 9:00am-5:00pm, Sunday 12:30-5:00pm. Admission: $8.00 adult, $7.00 senior (65+) or child (2-13). City of Greensboro residents receive a $1.00 discount. Miscellaneous: Adjacent to Country Park, the site also offers outdoor picnic facilities, a modern playground, two small lakes and nature trails. Kids Alley for young ones. Educators: Previsit curriculum sheets online.

This hands-on museum features a zoo, an aquarium, a planetarium, educational programs and a gift shop. Visitors can roam through a Dinosaur Gallery (hands-on rubbings to take home), learn about gems and minerals (how about that giant geode and the emeralds and gold found in North Carolina!), see snakes and amphibians in the Herpetarium, and enjoy a petting zoo. Visit with lemurs and enjoy touch labs. The new Animal Discovery zoological park features tigers, gibbons, wallabies, alligators and many other unique animals. Public shows include: "Indiana Bones and the T-Rex of Doom" and "Meal or No Meal" programs - each teaching nature and science, interactively with a live audience. So popular and funny! Be sure to plan on seeing one of these shows each visit. Diversity is the name of this place - so many different things - no signs of boredom here…inside and outside. Look up, look down, look all around. We noticed that they only have a handful of exhibits in each theme room, but they have the things kids really love.

POW WOW, GUILFORD NATIVE AMERICAN ASSOCIATION

Greensboro - Country Park. (336) 273-8686. www.guilfordnative.org. A cultural celebration of America's first inhabitants. American Indians share traditional dancing, singing, arts and crafts and social customs. Admission. (third Saturday of September)

STAMEY'S BARBEQUE

Greensboro - On your way back towards the interstate, drive-thru Stamey's Barbeque for Carolina pork and slaw. (I-40 exit 217, across from Coliseum). Inexpensive and with regional flavor (tangy).

WINGATE INN

Greensboro - www.wingategso.com. Landmark Center, I-40 exit 214, Wendover Avenue (336) 854-8610. At about $109/night, this is a value. The larger than average guest rooms have separate work and sleep areas plus FREE internet and expanded continental breakfast (even fresh tropical fruit). Outdoor pool and a micro/frig in every room.

TRIAD HIGHLAND GAMES

Greensboro (Browns Summit) - Come celebrate Scottish culture and heritage at the Triad Annual Highland Games. This wonderful family event features traditional Scottish heavy athletics, music, dancing, food, border collie demonstrations, bagpipes, entertainment, children's events, music jam tent, sword fighting, tea tent, fly casting competition, shortbread competition, and much more! www.triadhighlandgames.org. Admission. (first weekend in May)

PIEDMONT DRAGWAY

Greensboro (Julian) - 6750 Holt's Store Road 27283. www.piedmontdragway.com. Phone: (336) 449-7411. Smell the scorched rubber and hear the roar of a high performance engine at this popular drag strip that offers racing excitement from March through December.

CHARLOTTE HAWKINS BROWN MEMORIAL STATE HISTORIC SITE

Greensboro (Sedalia) - 6136 Burlington Road (I-85 exit 135, 10 miles east of town) 27342. Phone: (336) 449-4846. www.ah.dcr.state.nc.us/sections/hs/chb/chb.htm. Hours: Monday-Saturday 9:00am-5:00pm. Admission: FREE.

The museum is a historic site at the former Palmer Memorial Institute, a preparatory school established in 1902 by Charlotte Hawkins Brown, a noted African American educator and national civic leader. This is the first state historic site honoring the contributions of African Americans and a woman. The visitor's center has exhibits and a video is shown. Here's a quote that best sums up her passion: "I must sing my song. There may be other songs more beautiful than mine, but I must sing the song God gave me to sing, and I must sing it until death." —C. H. Brown

Charlotte Hawkins Brown Memorial State Historic Site (cont.)

CHRISTMAS OPEN HOUSE

The museum and campus will be open to visitors to celebrate the season. Dr. Brown's home, Canary Cottage, is decorated as it would have been for Christmas in the 1940's. Local choirs and musicians will perform throughout the afternoon. Fun and surprises for the entire family.

Hickory

CATAWBA VALLEY ARTS & SCIENCE CENTER

Hickory - 243 Third Avenue Northeast 28602. www.catawbascience.org. Phone: (828) 322-8169. Hours: Tuesday-Friday 10:00am-5:00pm, Saturday 10:00am-4:00pm, Sunday 1:00-4:00pm. Admission: $3.00-$5.00 (age 3+).

Discover the fun of science while experiencing the trembling of an earthquake, meeting live animals, making a cloud, being a puppeteer, and much more at this hands-on science center. Visitors of all ages can learn about the natural and physical sciences through participatory exhibits. Discover science North Carolina style - Try climbing the mountain wall, check out the Piedmont tree house and experiment with sound. Touch live Nurse Sharks, Cownose and Southern Stingrays in this truly hands-on, aquatic habitat. You can even search for fossils at the end of the brook or walk into a butterfly cage. Modest, not over-stimulating, facility.

MURRAY'S MILL HISTORIC COMPLEX

Hickory (Catawba) - 1489 Murray's Mill Road (near Hickory, N.C. and is easily accessible from interstates 40 & 77 and state highways 10) 28609. Phone: (828) 241-4299. www.catawbahistory.org/historic_murrays_mill.php. Hours: Thursday-Saturday 9:00am-4:00pm, Sunday 1:30-4:30pm (March-December 21). Closed Easter & Thanksgiving holidays. Admission: $3.00 adult, $2.00 child (under 12).

Nestled in the rolling hills along Balls Creek in rural Catawba County, this site is a historic complex, with four restored buildings that allow you to both see and experience life as it was generations ago. During your visit you will learn how grain was transported between buildings and the four levels of the mill. The large gears will turn and the original millstones (which weigh over a ton) often grind local corn. The Murray & Minges General Store, which dates back to 1890, has provided merchandise for barter/sale for several generations of mill patrons. Today it is restored and open for business, selling anything from old-time candy and yo-yos to pickles and pottery. Refreshments include delicious ice cream and ice-cold drinks. The old wheat granary, three stories high, now displays locally made folk art. John Murray's millwright home is fully restored and provides groups an opportunity to see how earlier generations lived.

High Point

BILL DAVIS RACING

High Point - 300 Old Thomasville Road (I-85 business south to Old Thomasville Road, turn right) 27260. Phone: (336) 887-2222. www.billdavisracing.com. Admission: FREE. Miscellaneous: Lots of inexpensive toys to buy in the gift shop.

Visit the home of the 2002 Daytona 500 Champions. Both the Nextel Cup teams' shop and the Craftsman Truck teams' shop are open for public tours.

Stop by to see the cars being built and to get a true behind-the-scenes glimpse of what it takes to compete in the NASCAR Series. Race fans can actually walk through this hi-tech facility and see new cars in development! Look inside the trailers. So organized - the mechanics claim this is the secret to a successful team. In the trailer, the cars "sleep" on

See winning cars up close!

top while the team naps, eats and preps for the race below on the first floor.

They have at least a dozen different models of the same car they build from nearly scratch - one for each of the different style tracks. Find the most up to date information on the Winston Cup circuit and the Busch Series. Talk easily with the crew. Most stay home, only a few handfuls travel to the races.

MILLIS REGIONAL HEALTH EDUCATION CENTER

High Point - 600 North Elm Street (Route 311 towards High Point. Follow 311 for approximately 10 miles and take 311 Business/Main Street exit. See website for more details) 27260. www.millishealth.com. Phone: (336) 878-6713. Hours: Monday-Friday 8:30am-5:00pm. By reservation. Admission: $2.00-$4.00 per person.

A very unique interactive health education center where you can ride a bike with Mr. Bones, the bicycling skeleton, or measure your height against a life-size Michael Jordan. You can also get health tips from TAM, a talking, transparent mannequin. We absolutely love their programs here. Initially,

begin with a classroom orientation. Start with models of brains (works at 200 mph); then, on to the heart (60-100 beats/minute); lungs; and finally, the digestive system (food to waste and everything in between). The demos are fantastic. Individuals learn about the human body and how to eat right and keep themselves healthy. Touch-screen computers and two specialized learning theaters round out this space...best designed for group academic program visits.

Learning how the digestive system works...

PIEDMONT ENVIRONMENTAL CENTER

High Point - 1220 Penny Road (off I85 Business) 27260. www.piedmontenvironmental.com. Phone: (336) 883-8531. Hours: Monday-Saturday 9:00am-5:00pm, Sunday 1:00-5:00pm. Trails open sunrise to sunset. Admission: FREE, donations accepted.

Take a part of a unique, interactive ecotourism experience at this environment center that is situated on 376 natural acres and includes hiking trails, a visitor's center, a nature preserve, a nature store, small animal exhibits, and access to the six mile Greenway Trail. Eleven miles of relaxing hiking trails wind along creek beds and

Walking on North Carolina...

lake shore, through hardwood and pine forests and in a fragrant wildflower meadow on the Center's North and South Preserves. The most unique part of the site: The walk-on map of North Carolina geography. Six different vertical scales are used to render the highly variable topography of each region. It's pretty cool to "walk across" the state.

WORLD'S LARGEST CHEST OF DRAWERS

High Point - 508 North Hamilton Street (corner of Hamilton & Westwood, downtown. Ask Visitor Info for directions) 27260. www. roadsideamerica.com/attract/NCHIGbureau.html. Phone: (336) 884-5255 or (800) 720-5255. The "Home Furnishings Capital of the World" is crowded with furniture manufacturing operations and bargain hunters. There is a 32 feet tall Chest of Drawers containing the headquarters of the High Point Jaycees... offering a unique photo opportunity. Built in 1925, it stood as the "bureau of information".

It has been restored as an 18th century dresser, now twice as tall, with a new

Furnitureland South, way out near the interstate, built their own chest of drawers -- over 80-feet tall. It's not freestanding, and is an attachment to a big furniture store, but... it's twice as big!

façade. A human can only reach as high as the top of the chest's legs. The restored chest commemorates High Point's role as a significant furniture manufacturing center. Two gigantic socks dangle from a drawer, officially symbolizing "the city's hosiery industry."

HIGH POINT MUSEUM & HISTORICAL PARK

High Point - 1859 East Lexington Avenue I-85 to Hwy 311 north to College Drive. Right onto College Drive. Go approximately 4 miles. Right on Lexington Avenue) 27261. Phone: (336) 885-1859. www.high-point.net/museum/. Hours: Tuesday-Saturday 10:00am-4:30pm, Sunday 1:00-4:30pm. Admission: FREE

Explore the history of High Point and many of its inhabitants as you tour the museum. You will be introduced to the Native Americans who first settled the land; to the development of the town from a small Quaker village; through the establishment of the furniture and textile industries. Did you know that many of the yellow school buses used around the country are made here? Or that the furniture industry evolved from the manufacture of spokes, handles and

CW Area

shuttle blocks? Or, that the hosiery industry (thus, the socks dangling from the Chest of Drawers), from socks to stockings, flourished here? You can also step back in time with costumed guides to tour the historical 1754 Hoggatt House (demonstrates colonial chores) and the 1786 Haley House (lifestyles of wealthy Quaker household).

In the future, the Museum will be opening the FURNITURE DISCOVERY CENTER. How is furniture designed? How is furniture assembled? What goes into making a sofa? Learn answers to these questions on a self-guided tour. The unique, interactive center simulates a modern furniture factory. Follow the flow of production or design your own furniture. Tell the kids to pretend they're building their own chest or chair. Start with design and the type of wood. Now, what carvings? Will you use your hands, a multi-spindle carver, or lathe cutter head? Now, sand, sand, sand and assemble. Most everything is hands-on. Try tools at each station…even power tools! The whole family will have fun learning everything you ever wanted to know about furniture and how it is made.

PETERSON DOLL & MINIATURE MUSEUM

High Point - 101 West Green Drive (downtown) 27261. Phone: (336) 885-3655. Hours: Tuesday-Saturday 10:00am-4:00pm, Sunday 1:00-4:00pm. Admission: $5.00 adult, $4.00 senior, $2.50 child (6-15).

One of the largest doll museums in the South, this museum contains over 2,200 dolls, dollhouses, costumes, miniature displays, and unusual artifacts, as well as special exhibits including over 115 Shirley Temple dolls, a nativity scene with 50 rare creche dolls, 17 African-American Personality dolls, and other rotating doll and miniature exhibits. Look for the Duke and NC State Special Edition Barbies. The Middle East room has dolls that are life-size. We liked the Portrait Dolls of Famous People - can you guess who they all are? Fun looking for girls AND boys. "oh, this looks so cute!" exclaims Jenny.

NORTH CAROLINA SHAKESPEARE FESTIVAL COMPANY

High Point - 1014 Mill Street (performances at Spirit Center) 27262. Phone: (336) 887-3001. www.ncshakes.org. Miscellaneous: NCSF does not recommend bringing children under the age of eight to its productions (including A Christmas Carol). Babies in arms are kindly discouraged.

This professional theatre company presents three major classic and contemporary productions each season from August to October. They also perform "A Christmas Carol" each holiday season and offer educational and outreach programs. Schoolfest (10:00am for $14.00 per person) shows combine explanation with acting and are shorter and easier for the kids to relate to modern times.

MAIZE ADVENTURE

High Point - 1615 Kersey Valley Road (I-85 exit 113, Hwy 62, head west). (336) 431-1700 or www.maizeadventure.com. This ten acre cornfield maze is filled with miles of twisting, turning pathways. Picnic areas are on site and catered lunches are available. Admission $7.00 (age 5+). (September-October Friday evening and weekends)

Jamestown

CASTLE MCCULLOCH GOLD MILL

Jamestown - 3925 Kivett Drive (I-85 business south to Kivett Drive exit, follow signs) 27282. Phone: (336) 887-2206. www.castlemcculloch.com. Hours: Sundays from 11:00am-5:00pm to the public (April-October) Admission: Fee for some activities.

It all started from an old lady's whisper! Ask them about this old, relic castle built during the gold rush in North Carolina. This restored gold refinery is constructed like an authentic medieval castle, complete with three-foot thick walls, a drawbridge, a moat, and a 70-foot tower. The castle used to be a gold refinery factory. Begin by a greeting from a knight in shining armor and then move to the Queen's chamber to watch a video about the gold mines of the state. The castle also offers daily activities, including gold and gem panning, a visit to a modern rock quarry (looks like a high-tech Flintstones set) and historic gold mill tours.

Let's explore the old stone "castle" in the middle of the woods

Maybe enjoy lunch in one of the scenic picnic areas or tour a few rooms (Great Hall with huge chandelier or the Queen's Chamber). They are constantly expanding their mineral museum - many stones are very unusual. A unique castle plus a gold mill - a must see attraction...especially with a tour!

Castle McCulloch Gold Mill (cont.)

CHRISTMAS CASTLE

Enjoy the old world beauty of this magnificent Castle adorned with timeless Christmas treasures. Santa and Christmas Castle, Specialty Crafters, A Family Food Court, 1 hour inside and outside walk-thru show, 40 live singers/actors from around the world, Santa Photos, Elfland and more than 15 acres of lights, a 22ft. singing Christmas Tree. Mrs. Claus, The Grinch and oh so much more. Sunday evenings are designated as Family, Stroller and Walking-Impaired Nights, when the trail will be slightly altered to make a smoother walk/ride for those who may need a slightly easier trail. Admission. (last long weekend in November)

MENDENHALL PLANTATION

Jamestown - 603 West Main Street 27282. www.mendenhallplantation.org. Phone: (336) 454-3819.   Hours: Tuesday-Friday 11:00am-3:00pm, Saturday 1:00-4:00pm, Sunday 2:00-4:00pm. Admission: $1.00-$2.00

A beautiful early 19th century Quaker plantation includes a school house, medicine school, as well as a museum and one of two existing false-bottom wagons used to transport runaway slaves during the time of the Underground Railroad (clever, how did they do that? Find out the secret). Enter "The Other South" of 19th century dissenters, see how they lived, and learn of their anti-slavery and pacifist views, their respect for education, honesty, plain living, and self-reliance. Notice the half door (master bedroom) used to bring in furniture hoisted up on the outside since furniture could not be brought up the winding staircase. Touch and feel cotton, flax, wool and silk. Notice the use of the word "Thy" (why?) and the tremendous simplicity.

Mooresville

DALE EARNHARDT INC.

Mooresville - 1675 Coddle Creek Highway (I-77 north to Hwy 150, exit 36. Turn right on Iredell that turns into Earnhardt Hwy 3) 28115. Phone: (877) DEI ZONE. www.daleearnhardtinc.com   Hours: Monday-Friday 9:00am-5:00pm, Saturday 10:00am-4:00pm. Admission: FREE

You may just be greeted by Dale's relatives, if you're lucky! This racing facility was created by Earnhardt and today houses three top Winston Cup race teams. The public showroom honors the incredible career of the late Dale Earnhardt with mementos from his public and private life. Other displays focus on Junior and other racing heroes. Most fans can't resist heavily shopping in the gift shop.

LAZY 5 RANCH

Mooresville - 15100 Highway 150E (I-77 exit 36 on NC 150 for 10 miles east) 28115. Phone: (704) 663-5100. www.lazy5ranch.com. Hours: Monday-Saturday 9:00am until one hour before sunset. Sunday 1:00pm until one hour before sunset. Admission: $8.50 adult (plus $5.00 for wagon ride), $5.50 senior and child (2-11) (plus $3.00 for wagon ride). Don't accept Debit or Credit cards. Miscellaneous: Petting areas, a blacksmith shop, gift store, horse barn, playground and picnic areas. Please bring any inhalers or allergy medication with you on your wagon ride.

What a treat to have a drive-thru safari right in the middle of North Carolina! Now home to over 750 animals from 6 continents, this place is anything but lazy. The animals can be viewed everyday of the year from a horse drawn wagon or from your vehicle while traveling along a 3.5 mile safari ride. The Ranch constantly changes the variety of animals and adds new exhibits. Its purpose is to educate while entertaining; and to provide a suitable habitat for safety and reproduction

of species of several endangered animals. The Grevy Zebra, Scimitar Horned Oryz, and Ring-Tailed Lemur are just three threatened species making their home on the Lazy 5. The best part is petting and feeding the big and small animals - use Daddy to help feed the giraffe. So you get animal slobber all over your car and your bucket of feed…everything will wash up later. Spring and Summer is Baby Time. How cute!

QUEEN'S LANDING

Mooresville - 1459 River Hwy 704 (Lake Norman) 28115. Phone: (704) 663-2628. www.queenslanding.com. Hours: Daily 10:00am-dark. Admission: Amusements average $6.00-$8.00 per attraction.

Want a fun family stop for your day on the lake? This place offers everything from miniature golf and bumper boats to lunch and sightseeing cruises on the Catawba Queen or Lady of the Lake paddlewheelers. The show boats glide you over Lake Norman. Several restaurants and snack cafes line the docks for a meal with a view.

NORTH CAROLINA AUTO RACING HALL OF FAME

Mooresville - 119 Knob Hill Road (I-77 exit 36 to Lakeside Park) 28117. Phone: (704) 663-5331. www.ncarhof.com. Hours: Monday-Friday 10:00am-5:00pm, Saturday-Sunday 10:00am-3:00pm. Admission: $5.00 adult, $3.00 senior (55+) and child (6-12).

The museum, dedicated to all types of racing, features over 35+ race cars on display. Relive racing's greatest moments in the Goodyear Mini-Theater now featuring "NASCAR's Greatest Drivers". You can simply stroll the hallways and floor car exhibits at your leisure. Some old cars are neat to see especially since they look so different from current models.

Mount Airy

ANDY'S HOMEPLACE BED & BREAKFAST

Mount Airy - 711 East Haymore Street (US 52 E bypass into town. Hampton Inn (check in) is a right on Rockford, the house is left on Rockford, right on Haymore). Phone: (336)

789-9569. www.andyshomeplace.us. (800) 565-5249. Enjoy Mayberry while staying in Andy Griffith's childhood home. Now open to the public, this house was home to Andy until the time he left to attend the UNC at Chapel Hill. This lovely home is filled with period style furnishings and offers two double beds, a private bath, and a full-size kitchen with a coffee maker, stove, microwave, and refrigerator. Host your own Andy Griffith rerun marathon with the

Andy's kitchen...we kept looking for Aunt Bea...it looks like she just left!

videos/VCR provided. Test your knowledge of the show by playing the trivia game. Before turning in, "sit a spell" on the porch swing and see how stars are supposed to look. Bring your guitar and gather everyone together for a family sing-along. Comments like "so cute" and "I can't believe we're here!" prevail! From dated curtains to printed cupboards or the skinny closet doors to the dips in the floors - this is a special treat! It even smells like grandma's house. $150.00-$175.00 per night, including access to the facilities at the Hampton Inn nearby (includes complimentary continental breakfast, pool). Reservations please.

Andy's boyhood bedroom

MAYBERRY & ANDY GRIFFITH MUSEUM

Mount Airy - 218 Rockford Street, downtown (US 52, follow the signs for Andy Griffith Playhouse) 27030. www.visitmayberry.com. Phone: (336) 789-4636 or (800) 576-0231. Hours: Monday-Friday 8:30am-5:00pm. Town open Monday-Saturday during business hours. Admission: FREE. Miscellaneous: One of a few remaining drive-in movie theatres is in town. The Bright Leaf Drive-In is open year round.

Located in a beautiful, historic home that was built in 1910, this museum and visitors center contains the largest collection of Andy Griffith memorabilia in the country including everything from a Matlock suit to a chair he was rocked in as a baby. Artifacts: the suit he wore playing a lawyer for nine years on Matlock (Griffith donated this item himself) and the white-and-orange plastic wrapper that was once the casing for an Andy Griffith Whole Hog Sausage, part of a line of food products that the actor lent his name to back in the '60s. Andy loves his hot dogs!

Hanging out with Andy...

MAYBERRY AROUND TOWN: Now venture over to the OLD CITY JAIL (215 City Hall Street) and peek at a recreation of the "Courthouse" seen in so many episodes of the "Andy Griffith Show". Come on inside and see what it feels like to sit behind Andy's desk. Or maybe you'd like to go see Otis' favorite cell. This building was Mt. Airy's real jail for many years and features a vintage 1962 Ford Galaxie squad car sitting out front. The new TVLand Opie & Andy statue sits on the lawn out front of the ANDY GRIFFITH PLAYHOUSE. Stop by FLOYD'S BARBER SHOP

Stopping for a haircut at Floyd's Barber Shop...

for a pic and a cut. What kid can resist OPIE'S CANDY SHOP or MAYBERRY SODA SHOP. A tour of this town is to step back in time!

MAYBERRY DAYS

Mount Airy - Each year, the three-day festival includes a golf tournament, bowling tournament, horseshoe tournament, apple peel-off, concerts, the Mayberry Days Parade (Saturday morning) and "Colonel Tim's Talent Time" (Saturday night). Other repeating events are a Mayberry trivia contest, a pie-eating contest, free walking tours, children's games with the Ernest T. Bass rock throwing contest (Mount Airy granite – of course!), a pickle toss, and live Bluegrass music - Darling-style, of course. Mayberry Days look-alikes can be found throughout the festival. Every year, an actual star from the hit show is the special guest. www. mayberrydays.org. (last weekend in September)

MOUNT AIRY MUSEUM OF REGIONAL HISTORY

Mount Airy - 301 North Main Street 27030. www.northcarolinamuseum.org. Phone: (336) 786-4478. Hours; Tuesday-Friday 10:00am-4:00pm, Saturday 10:00am-4:00pm (April-October) and 10:00am-2:00pm (November-March). Admission: $4.00 adult, $3.00 senior, $2.00 student.

The desire for independence was the driving force of those who came to the back country and settled in "The Hollows" at the foot of the Blue Ridge Mountains. This area is referred to as "The Hollows" because the entire Mount Airy region rests in a saucer-like depression circled by mountains. The panoramic view from the museum's observation tower captures the beauty of this mountainous circle. Look for dioramas of native animals and native Saura Indians around their Bark House and dugout canoe. Visit the General Store scene to hear the latest news or view a miniature of early Eastern Wagon Roads. See the Hill Log Cabin and a display of tools used in early farming. Later, see life improved during the Victorian era and the "Age of Innocence". This area is also famous for Andy Griffith, Siamese Twins, a famous fiddler named Tommy, and granite quarries.

> Mount Airy or "The Granite City" is home to the largest open-face granite quarry in the world.

SNAPPY LUNCH

Mount Airy - Downtown on Main Street. (breakfast and lunch Monday-Saturday), home of the famous Pork Chop Sandwich (ask for everything on it - sloppy, but fun!), or if you prefer, a big breakfast. Stroll next door for a haircut at Floyd's City Barber Shop or walk off a few more calories checking out the "Mayberry" stores and museums.

SQUAD CAR TOURS

Mount Airy - 625 S. Main Street (tours leave from Wally's Service Station) 27030. Phone: (336) 789-OPIE. www.tourmayberry.com. Admission: $25.00 a carload.

Where else can you ride in Barney's car except Mayberry? Start off at the famous Wally's Service Station, then take a ride down main street and check out all the sites and then swing by Andy's original homeplace (also a B&B, see separate listing) and finally the rock quarry. Cruise in Mayberry style down Main Street past Floyd's Barber Shop and Snappy Lunch. You'll cruise by other Mayberry attractions like The Andy Griffith Playhouse (new home to the Andy Griffith Museum), The Old Jail and the Visitors Center. You will also view the world's largest open faced granite quarry and the statue of Andy and Opie going to the fishin' hole. While at Wally's Fillin' Station, don't miss the best photo opportunity of the day - your photo in front of the Squad Car-or Gomer and Goober's tow truck.

HORNE CREEK LIVING HISTORICAL FARM

Mount Airy (Pinnacle) - 308 Horne Creek Farm Road (From Interstate 74/U.S. 52, take the Pinnacle exit (129) 27043. www.ah.dcr.state.nc.us/sections/hs/horne/horne.htm. Phone: (336) 325-2298. Hours: Tuesday-Saturday 10:00am-4:00pm. Admission: Varies with event. General visit is by donation. Miscellaneous: Horne Creek Walking-Nature Trail (moderate, approximately one-quarter mile) starts at the temporary visitor center and runs through the historic area past the family cemetery, along Horne Creek, and through a beautiful wooded ridge, returning to the visitor center parking lot.

Nestled among the gently rolling hills of Surry County in the northwestern Piedmont of North Carolina stands Horne Creek Living Historical Farm. Costumed guides interpret everyday life as it was during the early Twentieth Century, when Thomas and Charlotte Hauser raised their 12 children at the Pinnacle community farm. The days follow one another much as they did on any middle-class North Carolina farm during the early 1900s. Visitors may encounter farm animals of all but vanished breeds once kept on the Farm or savor old-fashioned apple varieties grown in Horne Creek's heritage apple orchard. You can try your hand at cutting grass with a scythe or listen to a talk on how to cook on a wood stove. You can almost see the Hauser family caught up in their annual cycle of everyday chores, farm labor, and festive celebrations.

CW Area

HERITAGE DAY

Daily activities seen on a farm during the spring season. Music and food of the era will also be featured. Fee charged for food. (first Saturday in May)

ICE CREAM SOCIAL

"Ice Cream Social." Help the site's staff and volunteers make some "melt-in-your-mouth" ice cream using a hand-cranked ice cream freezer. Then, sit back and enjoy some great old-time music. Fee charged for food, drinks, and ice cream.

CORNSHUCKING FROLIC

Traditional rural activity featuring harvesting, shucking, shelling, and grinding of corn. Visitors enjoy cider making, craft demos, quilting, cooking, woodworking, wagon rides, and traditional music. Small admission. (mid-October Saturday)

CHRISTMAS BY LAMPLIGHT

Experience the warmth of a rural turn-of-the-century Christmas. Enjoy music and food of the era, tour the Hauser Farmhouse and enjoy holiday decorations. Reservations and Admission. (first weekend in December)

PILOT MOUNTAIN STATE PARK

Mount Airy (Pinnacle) - 1792 Pilot Knob Park Road (From US 52, take the Pilot Mountain State Park exit and travel west) 27043. www. ils.unc.edu/parkproject/visit/pimo/home.html Phone: (336) 325-2355. Hours: Daily 8:00am-dusk. Admission: $5.00 a day per vehicle. Fee for camping.

The view from near the top !

Does the title of this park sound familiar? Pilot Mountain or "Mount Pilot" is nearby Mount Airy. The Indians called it "Jomeokee," meaning "Great Guide" or "Pilot." Early white settlers called it

Mount Ararat for the mountain where Noah's Ark came to rest after the Flood. Andy Griffith referred to it as "Mount Pilot" in numerous episodes of The Andy Griffith Show. A switch on words, but near Andy's home town and worth a stop on your way south of Mayberry (Mount Airy). Approach from any direction and see Pilot Mountain rising more than 1,400 feet above the rolling countryside of the upper Piedmont plateau. This solitary peak is the centerpiece of Pilot Mountain State Park. The park is divided into two sections with 1,000 acres located on the Yadkin River. Little Pinnacle Overlook offers hikers a close-up view of Big Pinnacle and distant views of the valley below. Try to hook up with a ranger lead hike as they tell you "secrets" of nature and folklore along the path. Treat yourself to a horseback ride through the woods or challenge the river from raft or canoe. They have hiking trails, scenic overlooks, picnicking, and family and group camping.

You can't miss "Mt. Pilot" ... It reminded us of a castle on top of a mountain...

Randleman

RICHARD PETTY MUSEUM

Randleman - 142 West Academy Street   27317. www.pettyracing.com. Phone: (336) 495-11143.   Hours: Monday-Saturday 9:00am-5:00pm. Admission: $5.00 adult, $3.00 student (age 6+).

Honoring the seven-time Winston Cup Series champion, this unique museum highlights Petty's 35 year career and includes awards, photos, more than 800 dolls, belt buckles, a movie, race cards and a Winston #1 showcar display and NASCAR history from the "dirt days" to recent competition. A gift shop is on site, too.

Salisbury

DAN NICHOLAS PARK

Salisbury - 6800 Bringle Ferry Road (I-85 exit 76A or 79, follow signs) 28145. Phone: (704) 636-2089. www.dannicholas.net. Hours: 8:00am until sunset. Some activities only have business hours. Admission: FREE. Small fee for Gemstone Mining, petting zoo, mini-train or carousel. Miscellaneous: If there's enough time before nightfall, you might want to take a hike at the Eagle's Nest Nature Preserve. Continue past Dan Nicholas Park and across High Rock Lake (about 3 miles). After the lake crossing, continue about another 3 miles to the second paved left which is Black Road. Turn left onto Black Road. Road dead ends after 3/4 mile at the entrance to Eagle Point Preserve. Currently a little over two miles of trails including a self interpretive tree and plant identification loop, a high water canoe access to High Rock Lake, and an additional hiking trail leading to beautiful isolated coves are open to the hiker and nature lover.

Begin the day by packing a picnic lunch and heading to Dan Nicholas Park which is situated in the scenic countryside. Spend the morning playing a round of putt-putt, riding the little train and Haden's carousel, feeding the ducks, paddling the paddleboats around the lake, and panning for beautiful gems at the gem mine. This park enjoys its own lake complete with paddleboat rentals (in season), a walking path loop trail which covers over a mile and a half, a miniature golf course, sport courts, horseshoe pits and ball fields. "Nicks Playground" is the park's latest addition, a specially designed and equipped playground for all children of every skill level. The Nature Center and Petting Zoo are free and open to the public and boast a collection of slithering snakes and native wildlife from bears to owls, many up close. For a small donation, you are able to get face-to-face with a calf, pig or goat.

EASTER EGG HUNT

Special events by age group. See "Nutty the Squirrel" and "Cosmos the Bear". Free. (weekend before Easter)

SALISBURY / SPENCER TROLLEY WORKS

Salisbury - 204 East Innes Street (downtown, departs from the Visitor Center near Depot Street) 28145. www.visitsalisburync.com. Phone: (704) 638-3100 or (800) 332-2343. Admission: $5.00 to ride all day and go on guided tour. $11.00 to ride all day, go on guided tour, plus admission to several historic homes.

A great way to experience 250 years of Salisbury history is on a guided trolley tour. Enjoy a leisurely ride through several national Historic Districts and stop along the way to visit some historic homes (best for older ones). Entertaining guides will give you a personal glimpse into preservation efforts and the famous and infamous personalities that made this town. Or, take a trolley to the Transportation Museum as an appropriate way to arrive and depart the large complex in Spencer.

TROLLEY TREAT TOUR

The Salisbury/Spencer Trolley will run downtown with carolers and special treats on board from 10:00am - Noon. Horse and carriage rides will be available for a small fee. (second Saturday in December)

OLD CHRISTMAS AT THE OLD STONE HOUSE

Salisbury - (704) 633-5946. Colonial Christmas celebration with German traditions. Tours of a 1766 house and enhancement of colonial family's Christmas celebration, including guides in period costume, customs, crafts, musket firing, woodworking, weaving, music, games, dancing, open fire cooking, candlemaking and such. (first weekend in January)

LORD SALISBURY FESTIVAL

Salisbury - www.thelordsalisburyfestival.com. Downtown attractions. Live music, plays, Waterworks Visual Arts Center theme activities; Paint Lord Salisbury ties; create theme costume materials; Movie-Off-The-Wall - Come dressed to impress in your favorite movie character and enjoy the movie with friends and family; and the Annual OctoberTour™ Historic House Tour. FREE (second weekend in October)

Spencer

NORTH CAROLINA TRANSPORTATION MUSEUM

Spencer - 411 South Salisbury Avenue (I-85 exit 79, follow signs for 2 miles) 28159. Phone: (704) 636-2889 or (877) NCTM-FUN. http://nctrans.org. Hours: Monday-Saturday 9:00am-5:00pm, Sunday 1:00-5:00pm (April-Labor Day). Tuesday-Saturday 10:00am-4:00pm, Sunday 1:00-4:00pm (early September-March). Admission: FREE. Small charge for train rides ($5.00-$6.00 per person).

CW Area

Diesel Cab Rides (ride with the engineer) are $10.00 per person. Miscellaneous: Download and print several activity sheets (before you ride) to color and complete while riding the train ("For Kids" icon).

Get your tickets at Barber Junction for train rides around the site and pick up information about tours and exhibits. The exhibit "Wagons, Wheels, and Wings" touches on transportation from a dugout canoe to a 1922 fire engine. There are videos and interactive exhibits along with shop areas at which locomotives are still worked on today. It looks like a giant "Thomas the Tank Engine" episode. One of the largest roundhouses remaining in the country houses more than 25 restored locomotives and rail cars! Visitors who are here after the last train ride of the day can see the engine run onto the turntable and into the Roundhouse, where it remains for the night on cool evenings.

EASTER BUNNY EXPRESS

Ride the train with the Easter Bunny. Admission for ages (3+). Easter egg hunt. Easter Bunny luncheon (extra fee – reservations required) (2 weekends around Easter)

RAIL DAYS

Re-live the golden years of railroading with a weekend full of family fun! Train rides, model trains, live music, children's activities and the Rail Days CASI Chili Cook-off. Fee. (last weekend in April)

DAY OUT WITH THOMAS™

Take a 25-minute train ride with Thomas the Tank Engine™, a real steam locomotive. Bob the Builder will perform live on stage. Meet Sir Topham Hatt™, see a magician show, play in bounce castles, get a temporary tattoo, and much more. Model train layouts, live railroad music and a Caboose Train are part of the fun. (fee, tickets required) (last weekend of September and first weekend in October)

SANTA TRAIN, JINGLE BELL EXPRESS, COOKIES & COCOA

Santa rides the 25-minute train, passing out oranges and candy canes, a Southern Railway tradition. Storytelling of classic Christmas tales and an ornament-making activity are also part of the fun. Jingle Bell: Children hear readings of Christmas stories while riding the museum's 25-minute on-site train during this event for school and other children's groups. Cookies & Cocoa with Santa: Take a 25-minute evening train ride to the Roundhouse and enjoy a treat with Santa, and hear Christmas stories read by one of Santa's helpers. Limited space available; advance reservations required. Special fees apply. (weekends in December)

Statesville

CHILDREN'S MUSEUM - IREDELL MUSEUMS

Statesville - 1613 East Broad street (Signal Hill Mall) 28687. Phone: (704) 872-7508. www.iredellmuseums.org/prog-children.htm. Hours: Monday-Saturday 10:00am-5:00pm. Admission: $2.00 per Adult; Children under 12 play for FREE.

Art supplies abound to allow children to experiment with different textures and styles of art. Then, kids love to pound on African drums, bells, or rainstick in the music exhibit. The stage area has a costume and puppet show performance space. Kids dress up or re-create a storybook scene with puppets. A child-sized kitchen and café puts kids to work preparing and serving "meals" or cleaning up afterwards. Your kids can also play with blocks or look at live nature exhibits including fish, turtles and snakes.

CAROLINA BALLOONFEST

Statesville - Statesville Regional Airport. www.carolinaballoonfest.com. One of the oldest and biggest balloon rallies on the East Coast. 50 or more balloons, kids fun zone, crafts, balloon rides. Admission. (late October weekend)

HARVEST DAY AT THE CABINS

Statesville - Heritage Farmstead Log Cabins, 1335 Museum Road, I-40 exit 150, near the 1899 Water Pump Station. (704) 873-4734. www.iredellmuseums.org. Step back in time as you walk through the cabin site, witness demonstrations from the blacksmith and learn how to make Apple Butter in a copper kettle. Listen to the sounds of the dulcimer, smell the wood fires and taste the food cooked on the open hearth. Talk to the costumed staff and volunteers to learn how the way life use to be in Iredell County two hundred years ago. (second Saturday in October)

CROSSROADS PUMPKIN FEST

Statesville -   (704) 873-2892. Pummel pumpkins at the smashorama, pig out on pumpkin pie, try pumpkin bowling, watch a pumpkin catapult contest and make a scarecrow. Activity fees. (first Saturday in November)

LAKE NORMAN STATE PARK

Statesville (Troutman) - 159 Inland Sea Lane (I-77 by taking exit 42 onto US 21 north. Travel north on US 21 to Troutman. In Troutman, turn left on Wagner St.) 28166. Phone: (704) 528-6350. www.ncparks.gov/Visit/parks/lano/main.php Hours: Daily 8:00am-dusk. Admission: FREE. Fee for camping and rentals.

It's the largest manmade lake in the state - thus its nickname, the "Inland Sea." Thirteen miles of the shoreline are in the state park, which provides boating access. On another hand, the park boasts its own 33-acre lake where fishing and boating are enjoyed. Alder Trail: Begin this easy .8-mile loop at the parking lot near the swim beach. The trail crosses the picnic area, circles the peninsula between Norwood and Hicks creeks, and then skirts the edge of the lake. Take a short side path to the dam and view the spillway and gates that control the lake's water level before returning to the trailhead. Itusi Trail: Designed, built and maintained by volunteers, this 4.2-mile mountain bicycle trail winds through mature hardwood forests and offers a unique mountain bicycling experience. And with hiking trails, picnic areas, interpretive programs and campgrounds, there's more to Lake Norman State Park than merely water.

Thomasville

WORLD'S LARGEST CHAIR

Thomasville - 6 West Main Street (downtown, off I-85 south) 27360. Phone: (800) 611-9907.   www.thomasvilletourism.com/attractions/bigchair.htm.   Hours: Daytime.

Thomasville, know as the "Chair City," appropriately named its most conspicuous landmark, a 30 foot replica of a Duncan Phyfe armchair, as its first official local historic landmark. The chair, located in the heart of downtown Thomasville, is not only symbolic of the furniture industry's presence in the area, but has also held the distinction of being called the world's largest chair, and has even attracted American Presidents.

Welcome

RCR (RICHARD CHILDRESS) MUSEUM

Welcome - 299 Austin Lane (NC 8 halfway between Winston-Salem and Lexington) 27374. Phone: (336) 731-3389 or (800) 476-3389. www.rcrracing.com Hours: Monday-Friday 9:00am-5:00pm, Saturday 9:00am-3:00pm. Admission: $12.00 adult, $8.00 senior (55+), $5.00 student (7-18).

The RCR Racing Museum is a facility that encompasses the original No. 3 race shop built at the RCR campus in 1986 and the original RCR Museum built in 1991. The site allows fans to see many of RCR's greatest race cars along with famous machines from Indy car races and NHRA. See the winning car that Dale Earnhardt drove to victory in the 1998 Daytona 500. Inside, there are 47 race vehicles (46 cars and one NASCAR Truck) and a tractor-trailer transporter rig. Of those 46 race cars, 22 are black No. 3 GM Goodwrench, Chevrolet Monte Carlos or Luminas driven by Dale Earnhardt. There are 16 video screens in the facility, showcasing key victories in RCR history. This is one of the most comprehensive displays of #3 Dale Earnhardt race cars (different paint schemes) in the country and it's a self-guided, video directed tour so take your time, fans.

Winston-Salem

CHILDREN'S MUSEUM OF WINSTON-SALEM

Winston-Salem - 390 South Liberty Street (I40 Business to exit 5 C or D. Follow to corner of Brookstown and Liberty) 27101. www.childrensmuseumofws.org . Phone: (336) 723-9111. Hours: Tuesday-Saturday 9:30am-5:00pm, Sunday 1:00-5:00pm. Open Mondays during Summer break and public school holidays. Admission: $7.00 general (age 1+). Discount days or nights online. Miscellaneous: Gift shop.

The museum is designed around the themes of storytelling and children's books, and is targeted to an audience of birth through fifth grade. Upon entering the fairy tale village, visitors are immediately drawn to the 32-foot beanstalk, which is suspended within two miles of cable. Children can climb into Jack's Beanstalk and scale the overlapping, carpeted leaves to the second floor. Once there, they are invited to scamper around the Animal Alphabet to identify all 26 letters in the giant playroom. Nearby, doughnuts tumble down the conveyer belt as children race back and forth in the Doughnut Factory working to fill their boxes and then empty them again. Children can also play with giant foam logs and differently shaped blocks made of wood, plastic and foam in the Build It! exhibit. Additional exhibits include the Supermarket and the Surprise Garden.

OLD SALEM

Winston-Salem - 900 Old Salem Road (southwest of the intersection of Business 40 and U.S. Hwy. 52, look for brown signs) 27101. Phone: (336) 721-7300 or (888) 348-5420. www.oldsalem.org. Hours: Old Salem Interpretive Buildings: Monday-Saturday 9:30am-4:30pm, Sunday 1:00 - 5:00pm (except Thanksgiving, December 24, Christmas Day and Easter Sunday). Old Salem Museums are closed on Mondays in January and February. Visitors Center open before/after buildings close. Admission: $21.00 adult, $10.00 child (6-16). Includes admission to the self-guided historic tour buildings plus three museums. About half the shops and the visitors center are FREE to roam around, browse and shop at. If you just want to go to the Toy & Children's Museums - it's $6.00 per person. Miscellaneous: Deli, Tavern and Soda Shop open for light lunch fare most of the village hours. The Winkler bakery is especially good. Grab a homemade reward for walking the town. Saturdays often include arts and crafts for kids. Summer Camps include a Love Feast.

Founded in 1766 to house professional Moravian craftsmen, Salem was a haven for entrepreneurs. This living historical museum is in an outdoor town setting in which costumed guides recreate common Salem household activities

and trades of the 18th and 19th century Colonial life. Begin with a short video presentation at the Visitors Center. Your tour will help you take a look at the ways in which these pioneers worked, taught, played, worshipped, performed - and how their lives changed as the community and the country grew. In the village, visit with a Tavern wait staff or crafters such as a Tinsmith. Watch him make spoons from scratch. Learn things about their customs. Did you know Moravian girls studied and went to college just like the boys? Why did ladies wear colored ribbons?

Jenny in Moravian Costume

Churches: Why did the races worship together, then apart? See the oldest African-American church. What was the Love Feast? But, don't ask too many questions because the best part is yet to come—The Old Salem Children's Museum and The Old Salem Toy Museum (actually closest to the Visitors Center but may be best to visit last when the younger kids are fidgety or bored with the history tour buildings).

The TOY MUSEUM is an amazing collection of old, colorful, dollhouses, room boxes, animals and marbles. Some items are really old - like 1,700 years old! The CHILDREN'S MUSEUM is next door. The Museum is a hands-on "fun space" designed especially for children ages 4-9. Along with a child's size Miksch House, a secret tunnel, and a marble roll, the Museum features a two-story modern climbing sculpture. For more fun, children can have a profile drawn, try on costumes from long ago, or build with "bricks." (includes occasional afternoon puppet shows each summer)

FOURTH OF JULY

Interpretations of the Fourth starting in 1783 through the 1860s, plus dinner foods and a medicine show. Admission.

HOLIDAY SEASON AT OLD SALEM

Take time to enjoy a traditional holiday celebration including a visit by St. Nicholas, candlelight evening tours (CandleTea), etc. Admission. (day after Thanksgiving thru day after New Years)

WINSTON CUP MUSEUM

Winston-Salem - 1355 N. Martin Luther King Jr. 27101. Phone: (336) 724-4557. www.winstoncupmuseum.com. Hours: Tuesday-Saturday 10:00am-5:00pm. Days and hours may vary during race weeks at Lowes Speedway, certain holidays and special events. Admission: $5.00 adult, $3.00 child (5-12).

The Winston Cup Museum highlights R.J. Reynolds Tobacco Company's 33-year sponsorship of the NASCAR Winston Cup Series and houses more than 30 authentic Winston Cup race cars. It features one-of-a-kind racing artifacts including trophies, uniforms, helmets, winner's checks, autographed pictures and signed original racing posters. Of course, a souvenir store is on the premises.

SCI WORKS

Winston-Salem - 400 West Hanes Mill Road (Highway 52 North, take exit 116 (Hanes Mill Road) and follow the signs) 27105. www.sciworks.org. Phone: (336) 767-6730.   Hours: Monday-Friday 10:00am-4:00pm, Saturday 11:00am-5:00pm. Monday-Saturday 10:00am-5:00pm (summers only). Admission: $10.00 adult, $7.00 youth (6-19) and senior, $5.00 child (2-5). Miscellaneous: Museum Shop w/ gift bags starting at $1.00. FoodWorks on premises. Original Krispy Kreme is at 259 S. Stratford Road (336-724-2484 or www.krispykreme.com)…not too far away. Educators: Ask for the Scavenger Hunt sheets or Science Fair info online.

Explore the wonders and mysteries of our world at this science museum that features 25,000 square feet of interactive, hands-on exhibits, as well as a

15-acre Environmental Park with trails lined with live animals and native plants, and a 120 seat planetarium. In one place you'll be able to wish upon a star in the planetarium and learn about the earth and the solar system or maybe watch chemicals fizz and react. Walk inside a 20 ft. tall and 10 ft. wide tree to see the concentric rings and root system... then slide back down to the bottom. Is there science to sound? - Soundworks will tell ya. At the Tot Spot, younger children can practice the catch and release method of fishing in a simulated trout stream while older visitors can see live specimens in the trout tank. In addition, there's a beaver dam and touch pool. The Science Lab includes hands-on microscopes, an air quality station, and a demonstration on sand dune erosion. See organs, cells and teeth up close. Also, remember the game "Operation"? They have one that's the size of your kitchen table.

> Krispy Kreme's **"Hot Doughnuts Now"** signs started in Winston-Salem. Home to the original glazed doughnut giant founded in 1937. Look for the "Hot" sign lit and see them roll hot off the conveyor.

HISTORIC BETHABARA PARK

Winston-Salem - 2147 Bethabara Road (Business I-40, off University Pkwy/Cherry Street) 27106. Phone: (336) 924-8191. www.bethabarapark.org.   Admission: $1.00-$2.00.

This 175-acre historic park is dedicated to presenting the history of the religious sect that settled this village in 1753. It was a frontier trade center from 1753 to 1772 in an 18th-century wilderness, full of bears, wolves, Indians and outlaws. The Moravians, a German speaking Protestant sect, migrated to North Carolina from Pennsylvania and constructed this village which features a reconstructed church, a French and Indian War fort, colonial and medical gardens, Moravian-costumed guides, and a visitors center with an introductory video. Outside, explore the trails to the mill site, stroll the boardwalk over the beaver pond and spot otters, mink, foxes, deer and woodchucks or picnic overlooking the village. The fort and boardwalk trails are what the kids gravitate to as this historic attraction is in more of a park setting and a more casual (and less expensive) approach to observing Salem history.

LITTLE THEATRE OF WINSTON-SALEM

Winston-Salem - 610 Coliseum Drive 27106. www.littletheatreonline.com. Phone: (336) 748-0857.

This nonprofit theatre group has presented professional level productions of musicals, dramas and comedies. The average season includes two musicals and four plays. In addition to preparing and presenting shows, the organization also offers educational programs including drama classes for children from kindergarten through high school.

BOWMAN GRAY RACING

Winston-Salem - 1250 S Martin Luther King Jr. Dr (I-40 to 52 north (exit 193-B), exit Stadium Drive (exit 108-C) then follow signs) 27107. www.bowmangrayracing.com. Phone: (336) 723-1819.

NASCAR racing was established in 1949 at this stadium that features a flat, quarter mile oval racetrack. From 1958 to 1971, this asphalt track hosted 28 events in NASCAR's premier series. The Dodge Weekly Series, a NASCAR-sanctioned event, remains the featured division Saturday nights from May to August. Admission ($6.00-$10.00 general, Kids $1.00).

MUSEUM OF ANTHROPOLOGY, WAKE FOREST UNIVERSITY

Winston-Salem - 1834 Wake Forest Road (US 52 at the University Pkwy South exit, behind the Kentner Stadium) 27109. Phone: (336) 758-5282. www.wfu.edu/MOA/. Hours: Tuesday-Saturday 10:00am-4:30pm. Admission: FREE. Miscellaneous: Cultures Up Close On Second Sundays 2:30pm-4:00pm. A family-oriented program for elementary school-aged children and accompanying adults to examine a different culture and art form each session.

The only museum in the Southeast that is dedicated to the study of world cultures, this museum explores the cultures and people of the Americas, Asia, Africa, and Oceania including household and ceremonial items, textiles, hunting and fishing gear, and objects of personal adornment. Materials collected by Moravian missionaries can be found here, as well as prehistoric artifacts from North Carolina's Yadkin River Valley (from archeological digs). "How Do They Know…? The Science of Archeology in the Yadkin River Valley" really brings out the treasure seeker in you. The kimonos and masks are also big hits with the kids. As the visitor explores each themed room, a printed gallery scavenger hunt sheet allows the kids to search and find. Learn how to make a Kimono (w/paper). Play a painted gourd or sleep on a wooden head rest. They offer lots of inexpensive culture toys in their gift shop. Small but wonderful.

CELTIC FESTIVAL & HIGHLAND GAMES

Winston-Salem - www.bethabarapark.org. Salute the Celtic contribution to colonial Bethabara with music, food, step dancing, border collie demonstrations, Highland athletics, the annual Parade of Tartans, children's activities and pipe and drum bands. Bethabara Park. (second Saturday)

MRS. HANES HANDMADE MORAVIAN COOKIES TOUR

Winston-Salem (Clemmons) - 4643 Friedberg Church Road (Hwy 150 west (Peters Creek Parkway), turn right on Central Road. Go to Friedberg Church Road, turn left.) 27012. Phone: (336) 764-1402 or (888) 764-1402. www.hanescookies.com. Miscellaneous: Nearby, Tanglewood Park, a 1,100-acre county park in Clemmons, features an arboretum and rose garden, plus a championship golf course, horseback riding, an outdoor play aquatic center, tennis and canoe/paddleboat rentals.

Their cookies are made from an old family recipe that has been handed down over seven generations. Each cookie is rolled and cut by hand, the same way it was made a century ago. Then flavor is literally rolled into the cookies...in six delicious flavors: Ginger, Sugar, Lemon, Chocolate, Butterscotch, and Black Walnut. Guess what, you get to be taste-testers! A sample of one of the 6 different flavors is given at each "station". They make around 10 million Moravian cookies, each cut out one by one using a cookie cutter! Each year they use approximately: 65,000 lbs. of flour, 40,000 lbs. of Molasses, 35,000 lbs. of Sugar, and 450 lbs. of Ginger. Only the family is involved in the dough making process (secret family recipe, ya know). How do they keep the cookies from breaking? Believe us, this will be one of the most amusing (and yummy) tours you will ever take. Parents: Kids even learn about weights, measurements and estimating...and, working hard has benefits. Finally, a special note - Jenny and Daniel and their cousins LOVE these cookies!

> If you don't have time to arrange a group tour, you can see cookie crisp bakers at work hand cutting and rolling cookies through a specially placed window in the lobby.

FESTIVAL OF LIGHTS

Winston-Salem (Clemmons) - Tanglewood Park. www.tanglewoodpark.org. (336) 778-6300. Southeast's biggest display. Viewers drive along an almost 4-mile route past more than 1,000,000 colorful lights in 180 themed displays (many animated). Hayrides and carriage rides are also available. Admission. (mid-November thru December nights)

KÖRNERS FOLLY

Winston-Salem (Kernersville) - 413 South Main Street (I-40 Business to Kernersville Main Street exit, south one mile) 27284. www.kornersfolly.org. Phone: (336) 996-7922. Admission: $8.00 adult, $4.00 youth (6-18). Miscellaneous: Körner's Folly opened the

newly renovated Aunt Dealy's House for public tours a few years ago. Built in 1885 by Jule Körner, the museum area contains a collection of Aunt Dealy's remaining possessions, including a chair, a lantern and a copy of her last will and testament. You'll see this at the end of your tour, out back. There's a gift shop there, too.

Touted the "strangest house in the world," this oddity was built by Jule Körner and rises to 100 feet in height, creating a structure that includes 22 rooms on three floors and seven levels with ceilings ranging from six to 25 feet, and no two doors or windows in a room that are alike. Körner's Folly was always open to the children's (Gilmer and Doré) playmates for games and activities. The

A Strange and Fun House !

house includes a theatre that was used by the Körner children, 20 unique fireplaces of differing designs, decorative murals, and elaborate tile and

A Children's Theatre is in the large attic of the House

woodwork. How do the trap doors, tunnels and fake windows actually air condition the house? Körner's Folly is a home chock-full of contrasts and comparisons (that's what makes it fun to tour, every room is its own surprise). Kid's favorites may be the many hidden nooks and crannies. This home is quirky but so full of whimsy! Children are very welcome.

Chapter 3
North East

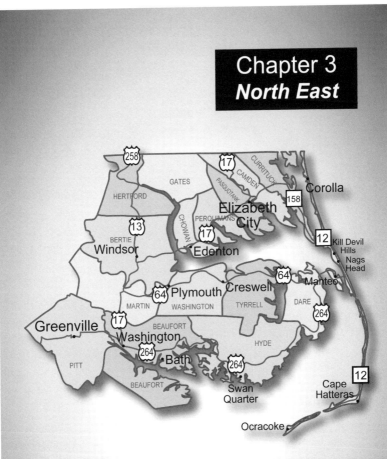

A Quick Tour of our Hand-Picked Favorites Around...

North East North Carolina

Welcome to the **Outer Banks**. The Outer Banks is a string of sandy barrier islands more than 130 miles long that bow out into the Atlantic Ocean and cup the shoreline. There's no escaping it. With beautiful sunshiny days and just a hint of seasonal change, you'll find there's much to do on the North Carolina coast all year round.

A sunrise walk on a North Carolina beach offers a wealth of seashells, treasures from the sea for those willing to get up early. You can find shells here year-round, but in early spring after a storm or during hurricane season are particularly good times for shelling. One hour before and one hour after low tide are prime shelling times, too. This coast is also the home for as many as 1,000 species of mollusks. Where's the best place to find shells in North Carolina? Shell collectors say **Cape Hatteras National Seashore** and **Ocracoke Island** are all excellent places to find these treasures.

Any time of the year is a great time for hiking, biking, watersports, or exploring the many state parks and natural areas of the Coast. Birding, fishing and canoeing activities abound and the unique region near **Swan Quarter** is the place to go to see thousands of tundra swans that make the area their winter home.

If you're looking for adventure, try hang gliding, body surfing or dune climbing near **Jockey's Ridge State Park**. The park encompasses the highest living sand dune on the Atlantic Coast and gives visitors a feeling of a windy desert. If that's too much adventure, you can relive the original flight at Kitty Hawk made by Wilbur and Orville at the **Wright Brothers National Memorial.** Retrace those 12 seconds that changed the world, and get a bird's eye view of the past. Spend the next day in the 16th Century at the **Roanoke Island Festival Park**. The park offers a living history of the first English colonists in America with special events scheduled throughout the year. Make sure you purchase tickets for the lavish production, the **Lost**

Colony, based on early colonists who vanished into thin air. It is one of the best outdoor dramas we've ever seen.

Near the southernmost tip of this region, the 208-foot **Cape Hatteras Lighthouse** is the tallest lighthouse in America. Its signature black/white tower stands over dangerous Diamond Shoals, warning travelers away from the area known as the "**Graveyard of the Atlantic**."

There are many wonderful ways to travel when visiting the spectacular sites of the North Carolina Coast. But, perhaps the most scenic, serene and peaceful route is that of the **Ocracoke Ferry**. Stretching along the eastern portion of the state, the ferry system transports more than 2 million visitors each year. Extending among the Outer Banks, it is a very necessary form of transportation that efficiently takes you from island to island. In fact, if your schedule allows, we suggest a trip to the coast to go ferry hopping (with snacks and games in tow)!

Sites and attractions are listed in order by City, Zip Code, and Name. Symbols indicated represent:

 Festivals   Restaurants   Lodging

Bath

BATH STATE HISTORIC SITE

Bath - 207 Carteret Street (US 264 east to south on NC 92 to downtown) 27808. Phone: (252) 923-3971. www.ah.dcr.state.nc.us/sections/hs/bath/bath.htm. Hours: Monday-Saturday 9:00am-5:00pm, Sunday 1:00-5:00pm (April-October). Tuesday-Saturday 10:00am-4:00pm, Sunday 1:00-4:00pm (November-March). Closed winter holidays. Admission: $1.00-$2.00. Includes tours of the Palmer-Marsh and Bonner Houses. Miscellaneous: Several geocaching sites are within 10 miles of historic Bath. Children's History Programs and Day Camps.

Guided tours originate at the visitor center. The video, "Bath: The First Town" is shown every fifteen minutes. Learn about the early nineteenth century, the Marsh and Bonner families and how folks like Jacob Van Der Veer added to the vitality of the town as merchants, shippers, and active citizens. Van Der Veer manufactured rope outside of town and was a partner with Joseph Bonner in an early steam sawmill. Bonner also operated a turpentine distillery. Bath was also the haunt of Edward Teach, better known as the pirate "Blackbeard." An expedition of the British Navy killed him in a naval battle near Ocracoke in 1718. Now, take the guided tour of some of the buildings filled with historical artifacts. Restoration efforts in Bath have saved the St. Thomas Church, the Palmer-Marsh House, Van Der Veer House (ca. 1790), and the Bonner House (ca. 1830).

CHRISTMAS OPEN HOUSE

Tour the 1751 Palmer-Marsh House, the 1830 Bonner House, the 1790 Van Der Veer House and the 1734 St. Thomas Episcopal Church, decorated in period holiday fashion. Enjoy music, apple cider and fresh-baked gingerbread. (second Saturday)

Columbia

POCOSIN LAKES NATIONAL WILDLIFE REFUGE & CENTER FOR THE SOUNDS

Columbia - 205 S. Ludington (on the south side of Highway 64 on the Scuppernong River) 27925. Phone: (252) 796-3004 or (800) 344-9453. http://pocosinlakes.fws.gov/. Admission: FREE

Pocosin is an Indian word meaning "swamp on a hill." These refuge lands were once the southern extremity of the Great Dismal Swamp. You'll find concentrations of ducks, geese tundra swans, raptors and black bears. The visitor center hosts exhibits and a film about the area. The Scuppernong River runs through the property and the Interpretive Trail is a 3/4 mile loop and boardwalk actually through the bottomland swamp. Interpretive signs explain the workings of the blackwater swamp ecosystem and encourage visitors to look, listen, and learn while they stroll along the path during daylight hours.

Corolla

CURRITUCK BEACH LIGHTHOUSE

Corolla - 1101 Corolla Village Road (Route 12 heading north towards Duck and Corolla) 27927. Phone: (252) 453-8152. www.currituckbeachlight.com. Hours: Daily 10:00am-5:00pm (Eastertime - Thanksgiving time). Open later in the summer. Admission: There is a nominal fee to climb the tower for everyone 8 years of age and older.

This lighthouse illuminates the northernmost island on the Outer Banks. At 158 feet, the unpainted red brick structure's light can be seen for 18 miles at sea. Built in 1875, it was the last brick lighthouse built on the Outer Banks.

Visitors can climb the 124 steps to the top observation deck. The lighthouse was constructed to fill the dark gap between Bodie Island and Cape Henry where many cargoes and lives had been lost in years past.

OUTER BANKS CENTER FOR WILDLIFE EDUCATION

Corolla - P O Box 502, 1160 Village Lane (located in Currituck Heritage Park on Highway 12 -near the historic Whalehead Club) 27927. Phone: (252) 453-0221. www.ncwildlife.org/fs_index_08_education.htm. Hours: Daily 9:00am-5:00pm. Closed state holidays in winter. Admission is FREE. Please call to sign up for programs.

Visitors to the center have opportunities to learn about the wildlife of North Carolina's northeastern coastal region. Exhibits include an 8,000-gallon aquarium stocked with native fish of Currituck Sound, a special decoy gallery with more than 250 antique waterfowl decoys, and a life-size diorama of a duck blind in a salt marsh. A 20-minute feature presentation, "Life by Water's Rhythms," screens daily in the auditorium. Because the center is located on the Currituck Sound, it offers visitors a chance to experience a barrier island first-hand. Kids can participate in the animal tracking, birdwatching, and marshwalk activities.

> NC Wildlife Resources Commission has an Outdoor Kids page online with easy nature projects, games & profile sheets on many popular NC wildlife.

They may also fish and kayak in the sound for FREE through the center. The wildlife guides provide all supplies for the activities, as well as act as instructors and nature guides. They also have herp hunt, duck calling and decoy making programs.

JULY 4TH FESTIVAL AND FIREWORKS

Corolla Currituck Heritage Park - food, fun and entertainment from 6 to 11. Parade earlier in nearby Duck. No alcohol; no on-street parking. $1 donation per person. (July 4th)

EASTER EGGSTRAVAGANZA

Corolla - Dare County Parks and Recreation. (252) 453-2838 or (252) 202-3796. Free egg hunt early after lunch. Games, food, rides, animals. FREE. (Sunday before Easter)

Creswell

PETTIGREW STATE PARK

Creswell - 2252 Lake Shore Road (seven miles south of Creswell off US 64, 20 miles west of Nags Head) 27928. www.ncparks.gov/Visit/parks/pett/main.php. Phone: (252) 797-4475. Hours: 8:00am-dusk. Admission: FREE

This park is home to Lake Phelps, a 16,600 acre natural lake and a virgin forest. Recreational facilities include a family campground, trails, boating, and fishing. A cloud of mystery shrouds the park's Lake Phelps. Scientists have debated the lake's beginning for centuries. Fed only by rainfall, the lake has an average depth of 4.5 feet and a beautiful, clear appearance – quite a contrast to many other lakes in this region. The lake is ideal for shallow draft sailboats, canoeing and windsurfing. Today, a carriage road makes up a portion of the Bee Tree Trail. Beginning at the park office, a one-mile section winds past the campground and Somerset Place. After wandering through a sweet gum forest, the trail leads to Bee Tree Overlook, a wooden platform offering a view of the lake and a place to observe wintering waterfowl.

VISITORS CENTER: In the exhibit hall, view displays of prehistoric Indian culture or head outdoors, near the lake, and dugout canoes. Among many of the fascinating artifacts uncovered, perhaps the most amazing is a series of 30 dugout canoes, which sank in the lake; the oldest is estimated to be 4,400 years old. It is believed that the Algonquian Indians placed the canoes in shallow water for seasonal hunting and they somehow sank over time. Two of the canoes, in fact the nation's longest and second oldest such relics, are displayed at the park's visitor center. Guests are invited to rent a modern canoe to explore the area just as the early Native American explorers did.

SOMERSET PLACE STATE HISTORIC SITE

Creswell - 2572 Lake Shore Road (U.S. 64 in Creswell follow the brown signs south through downtown, past Pettigrew State Park) 27928. Phone: (252) 797-4560. www.ah.dcr.state.nc.us/sections/hs/somerset/somerset.htm. Hours: Monday-Saturday 9:00am-5:00pm, Sunday 1:00-5:00pm (April - October). Monday-

Saturday 10:00am-4:00pm, Sunday 1:00-4:00pm (November-March). **Admission: FREE. Educators: A Hands-On Educational Program is offered.** Many well-edited writings about this time period and historic site are presented online (great to use for research papers). **Miscellaneous: Nature trails link Somerset Place with Pettigrew State Park. Picnic facilities and gift shop.**

Originally, this atypical plantation encompassed more than 100,000 densely wooded, predominantly swampy acres bordering Lake Phelps. During its 80-year tenure as an active plantation (1785-1865), hundreds of acres were converted into high yielding fields of rice, corn, oats, wheat, beans, peas, and flax; and sophisticated sawmills turned out thousands of feet of lumber. Somerset Place offers a view of the diverse lifestyles of the plantation's residents, from the perspective of owners and slaves, employed whites and free blacks. After the Civil War, nearly all of the newly emancipated black families left the plantation before 1870. We like the fact that through one general tour, visitors explore the lives of the plantation's owners, enslaved community, employed whites, and free blacks. The mansion and support buildings are preserved from that time. The visitor center has additional exhibits on the unique history of the site.

CHRISTMAS OPEN HOUSE

Enjoy historic decorations, homemade desserts, a free meal of black-eyed peas cooked over the open flame and cornbread cooked the old fashioned way in the fireplace hearth. (first Sunday in December)

Edenton

EDENTON NATIONAL FISH HATCHERY

Edenton - 1104 West Queen Street (US 17 S) 27932. www.fws.gov/edenton/. Phone: (252) 482-4118. Hours: Weekdays 7:00am-3:30pm. The hatchery is also open week-ends and holidays July thru mid-December (no staffing on weekends) Admission: FREE.

A facility operated by the U.S. Fish and Wildlife Service, the hatchery is one of over 80 federal hatcheries located throughout the country dedicated to the preservation of America's Fishing tradition. Edenton National Fish Hatchery is a warm water hatchery which means they raise fish that do best in water temperature above 65 degrees. The hatchery has a public aquarium, a raised boardwalk through a wetland area, and classroom facilities. All facilities are open to the public for self-guided tours. The Hatchery is featured on the Charles

Kuralt Trail. Edenton produces 2-4 million striped bass yearly for stocking the local rivers. The nearby Chowan River, Albemarle Sound and county creeks offer abundant fishing opportunities for large-mouth bass, crappie, striped bass, bluegill and white perch.

EDENTON TROLLEY TOURS

Edenton - 108 North Broad Street (departs from the Visitors Center) 27932. Phone: (252) 482-2637 or (800) 775-0111. www.edenton.com. Admission: $10.00 per adult, $2.00 per student. Miscellaneous: The Visitors Center provides a 14 minute audiovisual program and some exhibits to browse before or after your tour.

Have kids? We've found the best way to historically tour is by trolley (vs. walking tours). On this 45 minute tour, you'll see the 1758 Cupola House; the restored 1767 Courthouse and the St. Paul's Church, the second oldest in the state. All students of history are familiar with the Boston Tea Party. But how many have ever heard of the Edenton Tea Party? Hear about the beautiful teapot that commemorates the 1774 Edenton Tea Party, colonial America's first political action by women. Learn that, on a per capita basis, Edenton is one of the state's largest boat-building towns, as well as a farming and lumbering community.

Elizabeth City

MUSEUM OF THE ALBEMARLE

Elizabeth City - 501 South Water Street 27909. www.museumofthealbemarle.com. Phone: (252) 335-1453. Hours: Tuesday-Saturday 9:00am-5:00pm, Sunday 2:00-5:00pm. Closed major state holidays.

Located in Elizabeth City, NC, the Museum of the Albemarle is the northeastern regional branch of the North Carolina Museum of History. Serving thirteen counties in northeastern North Carolina, the Museum allows visitors to explore the history of the oldest section of North Carolina, many times considered the birthplace of English America. The Discovery Room features many "hands-on" history displays and interactives for families ("play" with 19th century fabrics and pretend school). The exhibit space titled "Our Story" is where all the real artifacts are. The Jackson House and the Proctor Smokehouse remain as anchors to the gallery.

CIVIL WAR LIVING HISTORY DAY

Visitors from across the Albemarle Area will commemorate the Battle of Elizabeth City, fought February 10, 1862 with a living history reenactments, demonstrations, displays, exhibit tours, lectures and more. (Saturday closest to Feb. 10)

Gatesville

MERCHANTS MILLPOND STATE PARK

Gatesville - 71 US Hwy 158E (From I-95, take US 158 east) 27938. Phone: (252) 357-1191. www.ncparks.gov/Visit/parks/memi/main.php. Hours: Daily 8:00am-dusk. Admission: FREE. Fee for camping and canoe rentals. Educators: The Merchants Millpond program introduces students to basic animal characteristics, focusing on the beaver. Majors concepts covered include adaptation, habitat, beaver-human similarities, animal signs and stewardship. Accompanying the program is a teacher's booklet and workshop, free of charge to educators.

An "enchanted forest," primitive species of fish relatively unchanged over thousands of years, towering bald cypress trees with massive trunks, luxuriant growths of Spanish moss—this is Merchants Millpond State Park. Discover a rare ecological community full of massive cypress and gum trees covered with Spanish moss, near the dark swamp waters. Paddle through the pond and creek where you might encounter beavers, owls, otters and fish. Cypress Point Trail, 1/3 mile in length, is wheelchair accessible. A total of nine miles of trails traverse the park however they are heavily infested with ticks during warm weather months. The park also offers an accessible campsite and picnic tables.

Greenville

SCIENCE AND NATURE CENTER, WALTER STASAVICH

Greenville - 1000 Mumford Road (River Park North) 27834. Phone: (252) 329-4562. www.reflector.com/featr/content/shared/living/interactives/riverpark/. Hours: Tuesday-Saturday 9:30am-5:00pm, Sunday 1:00-5:00pm. Educators: Take a virtual tour of the Walter L. Stasavich Science and Nature Center to see what is available for students to see and do. Included are interactives showing shells, native species of fish and turtles, and a quiz on animal tracks. The website also has Nature Activity Sheets for elementary age students.

The Center houses a 70 seat theater and a variety of exhibits including a turtle touch tank, waterfowl of the Atlantic Flyway, a 10,000 gallon freshwater aquarium, live snakes, and the North American Diorama. River Park North is a 324 acre park and has 3 miles of hiking trails where visitors can see deer, birds, fish, and even snakes. While at the park, stop in at the Adventures in Health hands-on exhibits on anatomy and physiology. Take a stress test or learn safety tips. Small admission fee is charged to Center.

PITT COUNTY FAIR

Greenville - Pitt County Fairgrounds/ Hwy 264 Extension. (252) 329-4200 or (800) 537-5564. Besides your regular county fair exhibits, competitions and food, the East Carolina Village of Yesteryear is open for touring. Depicting Eastern North Carolina from 1840 to 1940, the village maintains a country store, a traditional school house, a log church, farm machinery, and other artifacts from the period. (first week of October)

Hamilton

BATTLE OF FORT BRANCH REENACTMENT

Hamilton - Fort Branch. (252) 792-4902 or www.fortbranchcivilwarsite.com. Re-enactors perform drills, encampments, cannon firings and battles. Museum is open also. FREE. (first weekend in November)

Hatteras Island

CAPE HATTERAS LIGHTHOUSE

Hatteras Island - **Highway 12 (north end of city, look for brown signs) 27920. Phone: (252) 995-4474. www.nps.gov/caha/planyourvisit/. Hours: Lighthouse: Daily 9:00am-5:00pm (Good Friday-Columbus Day). Visitor Center/Museum: Daily 8:00am-5:00pm (except Christmas). Admission: Museum: FREE. Lighthouse: $7.00 adult, $3.50 senior (62+) and child (12 and under). Miscellaneous: Ranger-led historical and environmental tours are offered from mid-June through mid-August. Talks are held many times daily in the summer. Live View Cam: http://www.nps.gov/archive/caha/livecam.htm.**

> It is said that the engineer got the plans mixed up and the diamond-shaped figures, suitable for warning traffic away from Diamond Shoals, went to Cape Lookout and this lighthouse instead became ''The Big Barber Pole.''

The black-and-white, barber-shop-striped lighthouse recently reopened after renovations and being moved 2,900 feet inland for protection from the encroaching shoreline. Because of its recent monumental move, Cape Hatteras has received the most media attention of the North Carolina

lighthouses. The nation's tallest brick beacon (made from 1.25 million bricks), standing a proud 208 feet high, can be seen from 20 miles out to sea. Visitors are welcome to climb the 268 steps for a spectacular view of the national seashore. For more than 100 years, it has warned sailors of the treacherous Diamond Shoals, the shallow sandbars that extend into the ocean. So many ships and lives were lost here in the 1500s, that the area was named the "Graveyard of the Atlantic." Adjacent to the lighthouse site are framed buildings that originally served as quarters to the keepers of the light and now serve as a visitor center and maritime museum. It's a beauty and a fun climb!

What a view from the top!

HATTERAS KITE FESTIVAL

Hatteras Island - Hatteras Landing. (877) FLY-THIS or (252) 441-4124. www. kittyhawkkites.com. Casual competitions, games, and exhibitions of stunt and power kites. Climbing wall, face painting and kite making. (weekdays, late July)

DAY AT THE DOCKS - A CELEBRATION OF HATTERAS ISLAND WATERMEN

Hatteras Island - Hatteras Village. The commercial and charter fishing fleets will display their boats, skills, products and gear in a variety of competitions and demonstrations. There will be a number of maritime-inspired games for children and fresh, local seafood will be featured in a chowder cook-off and cooking demos. Traditional wooden boats, including a shad boat, NC's State Boat, a beach dory and a mullet skiff will be on site. Musical entertainment throughout the day. Blessing of the Fleet begins at 5:30 p.m. For more information visit www.dayatthedocks.org. (third Saturday in September)

FRISCO NATIVE AMERICAN MUSEUM & NATURAL HISTORY CENTER

Hatteras Island (Frisco) - (NC Hwy 12) 27936. www.nativeamericanmuseum.org. Phone: (252) 995-4440. Hours: Tuesday-Sunday 11:00am-5:00pm, Monday by appointment only. Admission: $5.00 per person, $3.00 senior, $15.00 per family

The Museum takes visitors back in time to follow the development and achievements of the island's earliest Native inhabitants. Artifacts from Hatteras Island's earliest inhabitants as well as from Native Americans across the US are displayed in galleries and art shows. Local finds include a dug-out canoe discovered on museum property as well as items recovered from the site of East Carolina University's archaeological dig at Buxton Village. Visitors can also enjoy the museum's nature trails, which wind through several acres of beautiful maritime forest, and feature labeled specimens and exhibits, open space with benches for resting, and roped walkways through wooded areas.

INTER-TRIBAL POWWOW, JOURNEY HOME

Traditional Powwow set in a beautiful maritime forest with activities for the entire family. Drumming, singing, dancing, native crafts, exhibits, displays, story telling, native food and more! Open to the public. Admission. (last weekend in April)

CHICAMACOMICO LIFESAVING STATION

Hatteras Island (Rodanthe) - milepost 39.5 (NC Hwy 12 near Rodanthe, south of Manteo) 27968. Phone: (252) 987-2401. www.chicamacomico.net. Hours: Monday-Friday Noon-5:00pm (mid-April thru November). Weekends only in season, weather permitting. Admission: $6.00 adult, $4.00 senior (65+) and students. $15.00 family rate.

Established in 1873 for crews to patrol the beaches looking for ships in distress along the coastal "Graveyard of the Atlantic", the stations were built at seven-mile intervals. Each station was patrolled by a crew of five to ten men on foot or horseback. Chicamacomico became the most famous of the stations, given its crews' many daring rescues. The buildings on the site today survive as one of the most complete US Lifesaving Service/Coast Guard Station complexes on the Atlantic. Exhibits display pieces of the hundreds of vessels shipwrecked off the coast of North Carolina during a 400-year time span.

GRAVEYARD OF THE ATLANTIC MUSEUM

Hatteras Island (Village) - (adjacent to the ferry docks, you can't miss its outstanding structure) 27943. Phone: (252) 986-2995/2996. www.graveyardoftheatlantic.com. Hours: Tuesday-Saturday 10:00am-4:00pm. Admission: FREE

The museum has a special preview exhibit area in the lobby gallery while construction continues throughout the rest of the museum. You will get a taste of eye-opening exhibits that chronicle 400 years of maritime history and artifacts. Learn how this coastline earned the nickname "Graveyard of the Atlantic". Witness the conservation of prized artifacts: German U-boat, the first enemy sub destroyed off the coast in WWII; a

> Support the museum by making a purchase in the gift shop. The sooner they raise funds, the sooner the exhibits open permanently.

ship's bell; a captain's desk from the Deering, the "Ghost Ship of Diamond Shoals"; the wheel from the John Duke; assorted beach finds and salvaged cargo; medals from the King of Norway; special exhibit of General Billy Mitchell on Hatteras Island; and the Huron shipwreck that started the Lifesaving Service reorganized to Coast Guard. Check out the building's unique architecture, too. What is it shaped like?

VISIBLE SHIPWRECKS along the Outer Banks: Schooner Francis Waters is on display at the Nags Head Town Hall (sank in October 1889); Schooner Laura Barnes (sank June 1921) on display at Coquina Beach in the Cape Hatteras National Shoreline; Trawler Lois Joyce (sank December 1981) is visible in the surf at Oregon Inlet; Federal Transport Oriental (sank May 1862) - her boiler stack is visible from the second beach access after the Oregon Inlet Bridge; an Unknown Barge is visible at low tide directly across from the Pea Island US Fish & Wildlife Station, just north of Rodanthe; Schooner Kohler (sank August 1933) is visible on the beach at Ramp 27, just north of Avon; and Schooner Altoona (sank 1878) is visible north of the pond at Cape Point, Buxton.

Hertford

NEWBOLD-WHITE HOUSE: A COLONIAL QUAKER HOMESTEAD

Hertford - 151 Newbold White Road (midway between Edenton and Elizabeth City, off of Highway 17 on Harvey Point Rd) 27944. www.newboldwhitehouse.com. Phone: (252) 426-7567. Admission: $3.00-$5.00 (age 6+). Miscellaneous: The Periauger Project to construct a replica of an eighteenth-century workboat docked at this site. It is 30 ft overall, with 7 ft beam and was originally designed to carry many barrels and/or sacks of corn, wheat & rice, bricks, rum, etc., or to be fitted out for military duty. Visitors can also watch a video on the Periauger.

From the shores of the Perquimans River, the site tells a story about Abraham and Judith Sanders, a Colonial Quaker family from the early 1700s. Sanders' riverside plantation was a diverse agricultural operation that included raising corn, cotton, wheat, flax, indigo, tobacco and rice. He also produced wood products such as barrels and shingles or shakes for roofs. The house is authentically restored and features period furnishings, enormous fireplaces, pine woodwork and a winding corner stair. The historic house is currently undergoing restoration and provides visitors with a unique and close-up look at the historic restoration process.

HEARTH & HARVEST FESTIVAL

A family event featuring period crafters and sutlers, children's games, tours, food and music from eighteenth century coastal North Carolina. Colonial encampment also on site with reenactments scheduled for Saturday and Sunday. History of the American Flag ceremony takes place at 1:30pm. Knife and tomahawk throwing competition and shooting competition held by reenactors. A free shuttle bus runs between downtown Hertford and the Hearth and Harvest at the Newbold-White House on Saturday. Admission. (weekend after Labor Day in September)

COLONIAL CHRISTMAS OPEN HOUSE

Gather around the Yule Log and enjoy musical performances by a children's choir, a harpist and a barbershop quartet. Cookies, hot mulled cider, cakes, and much more available. See the Newbold-White House decorated for Christmas in the eighteenth century style and then cap off the evening with the Lord Mayor in a fireside ceremony to bless the New Year. Admission is free although donations are welcomed. (second or third Friday in December)

Kill Devil Hills

WRIGHT BROTHERS NATIONAL MEMORIAL

Kill Devil Hills - (milepost 8 on the US 158 Bypass) 27948. Phone: (252) 441-7430. www.nps.gov/wrbr. Hours: Daily 9:00am-5:00pm. Until 6:00pm (summer). Closed Christmas. Admission: $4.00 adult (over 16), FREE child. Educators: First Flight online simulations - click Teachers icon.

The Outer Banks became known as "Home of the First Flight" following the monumental aviation event that took place over 100 years ago on December 17, 1903. Bicycle shop owners Orville and Wilbur Wright spent years developing the 40-foot glider that would become a history-making aircraft. As

their glider lifted off the ground at 10:35 that morning, the Wright Brothers achieved the first successful powered flight along the beaches of Kitty Hawk. Though the glider flew for only 12 seconds and 120 feet, it was an accomplishment that forever changed transportation. Numbered markers indicate the distance of each of the four flights made that historic day. The site also hosts a visitors center with exhibits that

Stand on the same spots where the Wrights their first flights !

include a full-scale replica of the Wright Brothers' original plane, the "Wright Flyer", and reproductions of the camp buildings used by the brothers - one as a hanger and the other as a workshop and living quarters. Be sure to sit

through a ranger talk given in the visitors center - it's very well done and easy to follow. The new Centennial Pavilion has exhibits that depict various aspects of aviation and space travel as well as the Outer Banks at the turn of the century, including walking through a camp tent or

THE BIRTHPLACE OF AVIATION
Here, on December 17, 1903, Wilbur and Orville Wright made the first successful power-driven flight in world history.

watching video of making a reproduction bi-plane. Outside, climb Big Kill Devil Hill for a breath taking view of the area from sound to sea. Atop the Hill, stands the 60ft. Pylon - the site the Wilbur and Orville used for their glider experiments.

WILBUR WRIGHT'S BIRTHDAY

This festive celebration will be a full day of family fun, play, picnic, and learning just as the Wright Brothers had at their own birthday celebrations more than 100 years ago. (mid-April Sunday)

Wright Brothers National Memorial (cont.)

WRIGHT KITE FESTIVAL

This kite festival celebrates 100+ years of flight with professional kite fliers from all over the world. Spectators can see a large kite including a 75ft. octopus and 40ft. Manta Ray's, fly in the air at the base of the Wright Brothers Monument. Stunt kite demos, games, kid's kite making, etc. will all be highlights of this event. For more information call 1-877-FLY-THIS or visit www.kittyhawk.com. (second weekend in July)

NATIONAL AVIATION DAY

In 1939, President Franklin D. Roosevelt established August 19th, Orville Wright's birthday, as National Aviation Day to honor the Wright Brothers and all flying pioneers and heroes. Special aviation related activities. (August 19)

OUTER BANKS STUNT KITE COMPETITION

This Eastern League event brings the best kite fliers on the circuit to The Wright Brothers National Memorial for stunt kite competition. Come see kite flying ballets, team competition, etc. Kid's games and lesson from professionals will be available as well. For more information visit www.kittyhawk.com or call (877) FLY-THIS. (third weekend in October)

WRIGHT BROTHERS' "FIRST FLIGHT" CEREMONY

Kill Devil Hills - Wright Brothers National Memorial. www.firstflight.org. Celebrate the anniversary of the first powered flight. (December 17th)

CLARION HOTEL ON THE OCEAN

Kill Devil Hills - 1601 S. Virginia Dare Trail. (252) 441-6333 or www.clarionhotel.com. The Clarion Hotel On the Ocean is located in the beautiful and historic Outer Banks. Watch the sun rise over the Atlantic Ocean and set over the Roanoke Sound. This full-service hotel has the family amenities we look for: free continental breakfast, spacious rooms, frig and microwave, warm outdoor pool with hot tub, and easy ocean access and showers plus small patio snack bar. The restaurant serves hot breakfast and surf and turf dinners, too. Kids eat free with adult purchase. Peak rates start around $90 a night.

Manteo

CAPE HATTERAS NATIONAL SEASHORE

Manteo - 1401 National Park Drive (NC Highway 12) 27954. Phone: (252) 473-2111. www.nps.gov/caha. Hours: Visitor Centers open Daily 9:00am-5:00pm. Open until 6:00pm (summer). Closed Christmas. Admission: FREE. Miscellaneous: Bikers are encouraged to visit the website: www.outerbanks.org. for information on routes and a link to the Wheels of Dare Bicycle Club. Educators: A Lifesaving Station Lesson Plan is online.

The Seashore stretches 70 miles north to south across three barrier islands - Bodie, Hatteras and Ocracoke. The islands are linked by a narrow, paved road and the Hatteras Inlet Ferry. Recreational opportunities include fishing,

surfing, sunning, swimming, beach combing, boating, canoeing, kayaking, sailing and surfing. Among the sand dunes, marshes and woodlands, many like to auto tour, bike, bird watch, camp and hike. Bicycle paths are prevalent in Sanderling, Duck, Southern Shores, Kitty Hawk, Kill Devil Hills, Nags Head and Roanoke Island. These are paved separate routes that wind along parallel to the highway or through wooded areas. The islands are a wintering area for migrating waterfowl. In Ocracoke Village, view wild ponies that have roamed the salt marshes for more than 200 years. Visitors can view the ponies from a wooden platform overlooking the fenced pasture and picnic tables are on site.

The Seashore offers three visitor centers, each one is located in a famous lighthouse station - BODIE ISLAND, CAPE HATTERAS and OCRACOKE LIGHTHOUSES.

FORT RALEIGH NATIONAL HISTORIC SITE

Manteo - (north end of Roanoke Island, 3 miles from Manteo) 27954. Phone: (252) 473-5772. www.nps.gov/fora. Hours: Daily 9:00am-5:00pm, except Christmas. Visitor center open until 6:00pm when the Lost Colony outdoor drama is presented. Admission: FREE. Educators: Roanoke Revisited curriculum supplements and Handbook online under "For Teachers" icon.

The park commemorates the first English attempts to colonize the New World from 1585-1587. The site is the acclaimed birthplace of Virginia Dare, the first child born of English parents in America before the colony vanished without a trace. The park is home to a visitors center, museum, Elizabethan Gardens (www.elizabethangardens.org), "The Lost Colony" outdoor drama, historic earthen fort works, gift shop and picnic area. The Nature Trail offers a 20-minute pocket wilderness experience of the island's natural setting. Wayside signs on the trail relate what English explorers observed of the natural resources and the commodities that could be made from them. The other trail, the Freedom Trail leads 1.25 miles from the Elizabethan Gardens to the western edge, offing a similar view that the native Algonquians enjoyed. Other trial signs discuss the Civil War Battle of Roanoke Island and the freedom found on the island by escaped slaves. Be sure to view the 17-minute film "Roanoke" at the center to learn the background of the Roanoke voyages and Sir Walter Raleigh's efforts to colonize the area.

> Roanoke Island is the birthplace of Virginia Dare, the first English-speaking child born in the New World.

GUIDED WATER TOURS - OUTER BANKS

Manteo -

If paddling one's own boat isn't appealing, there are 14 area operators who provide guided water tours of the area. They offer a range of site seeing cruises, from daytime harbor tours during which visitors can look for schools of dolphin and indigenous species of birds to moonlit sailings.

OUTER BANKS CRUISES. A SHRIMPING-CRABBING CRUISE. (252) 473-1475 or www.outerbankscruises.com. Pulls a small commercial-type shrimp net behind its boat so passengers can sort the catch and examine the fish, shrimp, crabs and other marine life that's harvested.

NAGS HEAD DOLPHIN WATCH. (252) 449-8999 or www.dolphinwatch.com. Operates a 40-foot covered pontoon boat that spends the summer in Roanoke Sound to introduce cruisers to some of the dolphins there. Reservations a must.

<u>**DOWNEAST ROVER**</u>. (252) 473-4866 or www.downeastrover.com. A 55-foot topsail schooner takes passengers on a two-hour sunset cruise from Roanoke Island.

LOST COLONY OUTDOOR DRAMA

Manteo - Waterside Theatre (Fort Raleigh National Historic Site) 27954. Phone: (800) 488-5012. www.thelostcolony.org. Hours: Nightly at 8:30pm, except Sundays (late May-late August). Admission: $20.00 producer circle seats, $16.00 adult, $15.00 senior, $8.00 child (under 12). FAMILY VALUE: Each child accompanied by a paying adult admitted free on Mondays and half-price on Fridays and Saturdays. TICKETS ARE NON-REFUNDABLE UNLESS CANCELLED DUE TO RAIN. Miscellaneous: Concessions and gift shop. Educators: On their online "For Educators" page, you will find resources and tools you can use in your classroom as part of a Lost Colony curriculum. Excellent worksheets!

In order to colonize the New World, Sir Walter Raleigh sent an expedition of three ships led by John White to the Outer Banks. The expedition, which included women and children for the first time, arrived at Roanoke Island in 1587. Colonists used the abandoned quarters of former British explorers as their settlement. John White left the 117 colonists on the Outer Banks to return to England for food, supplies, and more colonists. When he returned, three years later, the colony had disappeared and the settlement was deserted. White's family and other English colonists had vanished, leaving no trace except for two cryptic carvings. "Croatoan" was etched into one tree near the fort (an important clue). There were no signs of struggle but the settlement was never found. "The Lost Colony" is America's longest running outdoor symphonic drama (over 60 years). Best of all, it keeps the kids' interest! As the story unfolds, can you solve the mystery? God Save The Queen! (and, my aren't the costumes gorgeous - especially the Queen!)

VIRGINIA DARE FAIRE

Celebrate Virginia Dare's birthday. Attend a day of free activities with music, games and fun for the family. Reserve your seats early for the evening performance of The Lost Colony that cameos infant actors as baby Virginia. (August 18)

Lost Colony Outdoor Drama (cont.)

LOST COLONY BACKSTAGE TOURS & TEA WITH THE QUEEN

Experience behind-the-scenes at the Waterside Theatre. Tours include the theatre, costume shop, props and history of the drama. Tea with the Queen at Elizabethan Gardens features high tea followed by a behind-the-scenes tour of the theatre. Reservations & Admission required. (tours are nightly @6:30pm during season - $5.00 per person, tea once a month)

NORTH CAROLINA AQUARIUM ON ROANOKE ISLAND

Manteo - 374 Airport Road, off Business 64 (northern end of Roanoke Island, overlooking Croatan Sound) 27954. Phone: (252) 473-3494. www.ncaquariums.com. Hours: Daily 9:00am-5:00pm, except Thanksgiving, Christmas and New Year's Day. Admission: $8.00 adult, $7.00 senior & military, $6.00 child (6-17). Families: Many participate in programs and activities such as, "Breakfast with the Rays," and "Snack with the Sharks." (extra fee). Educators: Pre-and-Post visit activities available online.

The 68,000 square-foot building houses seven major exhibits and 18 tanks from 300 - 285,000 gallons. The biggest tank is 17 feet deep and roughly the

Daniel's little alligator friend...

size and shape of a baseball infield (with a replica warship sunk inside). It features 450 fish and a number of sharks; and a live webcam monitors the tank's activity for internet visitors. In "Storms", you'll hear commentary from actual hurricane victims. Kids can touch a stingray or marvel at river otters swimming freely in their pond. They can see alligators (the way the tank is designed, it's the closest you'll probably ever get to one!), sea turtles, moray eels, snakes and other marine life. The "Sea Turtle Maze" is an interactive exhibit for all ages. As you make your way through the maze, you are taught to think like a sea turtle. Wrong answers to certain questions will leave you at a dead end. When you leave the maze, you will know more about the thoughts of the sea turtle than you ever imagined. There are daily dive shows, animal feedings, a webcam birds-eye view of a real osprey's nest...live, and a variety of educational videos. Outside is a nature trail, shoreline boardwalk with observation decks and mounted telescopes, and an excavation area where visitors can dig for fossilized shark's teeth.

NORTH CAROLINA MARITIME MUSEUM

Manteo - (downtown, Roanoke Island) 27954. www.obxmaritime.org. Phone: (252) 728-7317. Hours: Generally, Daily Monday-Friday 9:00am-5:00pm, Saturday 10:00am-5:00pm, Sunday 1:00-5:00pm. Museum hours do vary seasonally. Closed holidays. Admission: FREE.

Among the museum's exhibits, visitors can view: artifacts recovered from the shipwreck of the Queen Anne's Revenge, Blackbeard's flagship; collections of shells (5,000+) from 100 countries; fossilized remains of marine life and prehistoric animals; venomous snakes of North Carolina; working watercraft, including a dugout canoe, flat-bottom and spritsail skiffs; commercial fishing displays about whales and whaling, oystering and fishing; and displays of waterfowl hunting and decoys. On the waterfront across from the museum is the George Washington Creef Boat House. Visitors to the boathouse are met by the smell of cedar and a group of enthusiastic volunteers and staff. Here, visitors can observe restoration of wooden boats and a Model Shop demonstrates the art of ship model-making. Many items and demos here may be "first-time" learning…especially the boats and model projects.

PEA ISLAND NATIONAL WILDLIFE REFUGE

Manteo - Hwy 12, Sound side (northernmost section of Hatteras Island, between Oregon Inlet and Rodanthe) 27954. http://peaisland.fws.gov/qa.html. Phone: (252) 473-1131. Hours: Refuge open year round during daylight hours. Visitor Center: Daily 9:00am-4:00pm (March-November), Thursday-Sunday only during winter months. Admission: FREE, small charge for guided canoe tours.

The refuge is comprised of beautiful, barrier island beach, sand dunes, upland, fresh and brackish water ponds, salt flats and salt marsh. More than 400 species of wintering waterfowl regularly visit the refuge, including snow geese, egrets, herons and a large variety of wading, shore and song birds. Several shorebird nesting areas and wading bird rookeries are located on the refuge, too. It's "Birder's Paradise". The refuge is also home to 25 species of mammals, 24 species of reptiles and five species of amphibians. Endangered species include: peregrine falcons, American bald eagles, loggerhead sea turtles and piping plover. The refuge itself features a visitor center, two wildlife trails, observation platforms and towers with spotting scopes, guided canoe tours and children's programs in the summer months.

Pea Island National Wildlife Refuge (cont.)

WINGS OVER WATER

The premier birding & nature festival on the Outer Banks, offering over 100 birding, paddling & natural history tours throughout eastern North Carolina. For more information visit wingsoverwater.org. (six days early November)

ROANOKE ISLAND FESTIVAL PARK

Manteo - One Festival Park (over the bridge from Manteo) 27954. Phone: (252) 475-1500. www.roanokeisland.com. Hours: Daily 10:00am-5:00pm (6:00pm April-October). Closed Christmastime and January thru mid-February for maintenance. Admission: $8.00 adult, $5.00 student (age 6-17). There is no charge to visit the picnic areas, boardwalks, fossil site, museum store, and parking is free. Admission stickers are honored for two consecutive days to allow visitors unhurried enjoyment of all the attractions. Miscellaneous: Illuminations summer performing arts series, Children's Performance Series, Picnic areas, fossil pit and boardwalks. Many summer daytime performances are free with museum admission tickets. Educators: Online workbook and activity sheets.

Posing for tourists

The Park presents the evolution of Roanoke Island and the Outer Banks from the late 16th century to the early 20th century. Begin your journey on the island by viewing "The Legend of Two Path" film that gives the Native American reaction to the arrival of the English settlers on Roanoke Island and the permanent changes it brought the Algonquians (45 minutes long). Kids can then go outside and climb aboard Elizabeth II, a

sailing ship representative of those sent by Sir Walter Raleigh to the New World in the 16th century. Interpreters dressed as Elizabethan sailors tell seafaring tales to bring the story to life. Visitors can also explore the Settlement Site, a recreated military camp manned by costumed soldiers who are constantly on the lookout for Spaniards and Algonquin Indians. Visitors learn by doing as they explore the camp, tent and equipment. For entertainment, try playing board games or 9-pin bowling. Finally, back inside, tour the

Roanoke Adventure Museum, where interactive exhibits explore 400 years of Outer Banks history. Don a cloak (you too, Mom and Dad) as you venture through history. Answer these questions: Did the English abandon the Colonists? What became of the Lost Colony? Did anyone try to find the lost colonists? The museum chronicles boat-building, shipwrecks, pirates, lighthouse keepers, the Lost Colony, the Freedom Colony, the Civil War, and Lifesaving Services up to the 1950s. Very colorful and interactive with lots of hands-on history fun! Want to continue this re-enacting play at home? Purchase The Adventure Bag as a token reminder of your visit. It includes: Pirate Eye Patch, Civil War Enlistment Form, Sand Dollar, Sailor's Knot Tying Bookmark, Postcard of The Elizabeth II, Lolly Stick Candy, Gold Treasure Coin, and a Pencil.

Waiting patiently for the English to return....

ROANOKE ISLAND 1862 - A CIVIL WAR LIVING HISTORY WEEKEND

This Civil War Living History Weekend commemorates the Anniversary of The Battle of Roanoke Island. The festival features re-enactors of Union and Confederate soldiers and Civil War-era sailors and civilians. Other events include period activities such as artillery demonstrations, drills, living history encampments, blacksmithing, woodworking, crafts, presentations, lectures, civil war surgeon, book signings, enlistment station, period music performances and children's activities. (first weekend in March)

FOURTH OF JULY CELEBRATION

Waterfront Pavilion, www.NCSASummerFest.org. NCSA's Woodwind Quintet, Jazz Ensemble and jazz singers perform an evening of patriotic music to precede and accompany fireworks by the Town of Manteo. Don't miss this July 4th tradition on the Outer Banks! FREE! (July 4th)

Roanoke Island Festival Park (cont.)

ELIZABETHAN CHRISTMAS

Don't let the holiday spirit fade! A few days after Christmas, come join in the fun as Roanoke Island Festival Park celebrates the third day of Christmas. Visitors to the Park get a taste of 16th century holiday traditions as they make decorations, learn special dances, sing songs, discover food and drink of the season, and indulge in merriment with members of the Guild of St. Andrew. Many events are held inside and the celebration goes on, rain or shine. In the Settlement Site visitors join with the interpreters as they "recreate" their celebration in the American wilderness, with simple decorations and a roast over the open fire. Admission. (a few days after Christmas in December)

ALLIGATOR RIVER NATIONAL WILDLIFE REFUGE

Manteo (East Lake) - (west of Manteo on US 64/264) 27954. Phone: (252) 473-1131. www.outer-banks.com/alligator-river. Hours: Daily during daylight hours. Admission: FREE. Nominal fee for guided canoe tours.

The refuge is home to at least 200 species of birds, including owls, ducks and warblers. Endangered and threatened species that can be found on the refuge include the American alligator and the red-cockaded woodpecker. One of the largest remaining concentrations of black bears along the mid-Atlantic coast also has found a home at the refuge. During the winter months you might even hear the howl of a red wolf. There are hiking trails, wildlife trails and canoe and kayak trails, as well as a fishing dock. Creef Cut Wildlife Trail and Fishing Area is fully handicapped accessible. A half-mile paved trail leads to a 50 foot boardwalk with an observation platform that overlooks Creef Moist Soil Unit and a 250 foot boardwalk over a freshwater marsh. Look for waterfowl during the winter months, black bear, woodpeckers and birds of prey. At the beginning of the trail, behind the interpretive kiosk, is a handicapped accessible fishing dock. Perhaps the best way to see the refuge, though, is by water.

Nags Head

JOCKEY'S RIDGE STATE PARK

Nags Head - (US 158 Bypass at milepost 12.5) 27959. Phone: (252) 441-7132. www.ncparks.gov/Visit/parks/jori/main.php Hours: Park open daylight hours. Exhibit Hall open 8:00am-5:00pm daily. Admission: FREE. Miscellaneous: Sand is typically 30 degrees hotter than air. Wear durable sandals or shoes.

The State Park gives visitors a chance to experience the world of the desert. Shifting sands, high winds, extreme temperatures and a lack of water make the park resemble barren environments such as the Sahara Desert. Visitors can climb the 90-foot dune or park staff can drive people needing assistance to the top. Besides the adventure of climbing a dune (aerobic)

> This park has the highest living sand dune on the Atlantic Coast.

and the view of panoramic vistas of the Ocean and Roanoke Sound, families can also hike one of the park's two self-guided nature trails, kite-fly, sand-board or picnic. Soft sand and easy runs down the dune are the best part. Most people also tour the exhibit hall. They discover what dunes are made of, how they are created and how they are shaped. Kids can play

several matching games in which they match tracks to the animals that created them and dune names to their locations across the country. Next, study the history of storms and their effect on the dunes. Ever seen petrified lightning? You will here! Wonder where the names "Kill Devil Hills" and "Nags Head" came from? Visit the exhibit hall to find out more about these and other legends, including Blackbeard's treasure.

FLY INTO SPRING KITE FESTIVAL

Come and kick-off spring with Kitty Hawk Kites first festival of the year! Professional kite fliers from all over the country are on hand to demo stunt kites, teach lessons and display their large show kites! Children's activities are also available at Jockey's Ridge, as well as across the street at Kitty Hawk Kites. This festival also celebrates National Kite Month. For more information, www.kittyhawk.com. (877) FLY-THIS. (first weekend in April)

Jockey's Ridge State Park (cont.)

HANG GLIDING SPECTACULAR

Come see the best sport hang gliders from around the world compete on the dunes of Jockey's Ridge State Park. During this competition there are also activities for the whole family taking place across the street from Jockey's Ridge State Park at Kitty Hawk Kites. Activities include: climbing wall, face painting, kite making, etc. For more information call 1-888-FLY-THIS or visit www.kittyhawk.com. (second or third weekend in May)

ROGALLO KITE FESTIVAL

Honoring Francis Rogallo, inventor of the flexible wing and resident of the Outer Banks. The festival takes place atop Jockey's Ridge State Park. Across the street at the Kitty Hawk Kites store there are kids activities including face painting, kite making, etc. For more information call 1-877-FLY-THIS or visit www.kittyhawk.com.

KITES WITH LIGHTS

Kids can get their picture taken with Santa each day at Kitty Hawk Kites. On Saturday, come see the kites with lights display on top of Jockey's Ridge State Park at sunset. Christmas carols, hot apple cider and cookies served. For more information call (877) FLY-THIS or visit www.kittyhawk.com. (Saturday after Thanksgiving)

KITTY HAWK KITES EASTER EGGSTRAVAGANZA

Nags Head - (877) FLY-THIS or (252) 441-4124. www.kittyhawkkites.com. Kite making games, chalk coloring contests, and surprise visits from Wil-Bear and friends. 2,000 toy-filled plastic eggs are waiting to be found. Easter Bunny visit. (Saturday before Easter)

OUTER BANKS PIRATE FESTIVAL

Nags Head - MP 12.5, Kitty Hawk Kites, Nags Head. Appearances at several local businesses by pirates. The main event is on Saturday with an entire day of pirate appearances, games and stories. For more information and schedule of events visit www.kittyhawk.com. (third week of September)

NE Area

Ocracoke

OCRACOKE ISLAND / LIGHTHOUSE

Ocracoke - www.ocracoke-nc.com.

Ocracoke is a small fishing village lined with small hotels, down-home restaurants and quiet residents. Several public beaches dot the area. One may also catch a glimpse of the wild ponies that call the island home. Ocracoke Island was known to be a hideout of the infamous pirate, Blackbeard, who lost his head on the island in the 1700s. Local legend says that he still roams the island in search of it. Built in 1823, the OCRACOKE LIGHTHOUSE is the oldest North Carolina lighthouse and the second oldest lighthouse in the United States. The 76 foot high structure is also the shortest among the North Carolina beacons. Visitors are invited to tour the grounds surrounding the lighthouse; however, the structure itself is not open to the public. Ocracoke Island can only be reached by ferry.

OCRACOKE / NORTH CAROLINA FERRIES

Ocracoke - 27960. Phone: (800) BY-FERRY. www.ncferry.org. Hours: See or call about schedule. Varies on season and weather. Make reservations. Admission: FREE for link to Hatteras. Nominal charge for Cedar Island to Ocracoke. Generally 15.00 per vehicle-one way. Reservations required for the ferries from Ocracoke. Miscellaneous: there are vending machines (soda, coffee and snacks) on the fee ferry. Restrooms on board. The long rides also have arcade games. Restroom facilities are available at all ferry terminals and on all ferry vessels. Pets are permitted on the ferries as long as they are either in the vehicle or on a leash.

North Carolina boasts approximately 10 one-way ferry passages. Once on the ferry, guests can either relax in the comfort of their own vehicle or walk around the deck of the ship. This provides an amazing chance to take photos as well as meet other passengers along the way. Gaggles of seagulls dance and dive along the wake of the traveling ship. Dolphins often follow playfully, hoping for a handout or even more attention from their adoring fans.

We suggest bringing along travel games to play.

Starting in the most northern part of the state, the first ferry is a transport from Knotts Island to Currituck. Locals use it as others would the subway. The ferries even transport school buses with students to and from school each day. The next step along the ferry journey is from Hatteras to Ocracoke Island. Although only a 45-minute journey, the route is reminiscent of sailors'

journeys long ago when they ventured into seas undiscovered. Leaving Ocracoke, the longest ferry ride along the NC Coast, guests may go atop the boat to be greeted with coffee, video games and vending machines. The two-hour-plus ride leaves you no choice but to relax and enjoy the sound of the waves. We set up chairs and played travel games on top of our large cooler - only interrupted by an occasional seagull looking for a snack.

PORTMOUTH ISLAND ATV TOURS

Ocracoke - Jolly Roger Marina & Restaurant (Hwy 12) 27960. Phone: (252) 928-4484. www.portsmouthislandatvs.com. Admission: $85.00 per person, max. 6/tour.

"Discover an Island Frozen in Time" with this tour company and visit some secret spots. Tours begin with a twenty minute boat ride from Silver Lake Harbor to Portsmouth Island where you will discover the historical settlement that was once a thriving port town with over 685 residents in 1860. On the beach you can discover excellent shorebird and dolphin watching, sea turtle tracks and other fascinating seashore creatures. Wear your bathing suits for a dip in the ocean and they'll supply the shell bags for the best shelling on the Outer Banks.

Plymouth

BATTLE OF PLYMOUTH LIVING HISTORY WEEKEND

Plymouth - Port-O-Plymouth Museum, 302 E. Water Street. (252) 793-1377 or www.livinghistoryweekend.com/civilwar.htm. This weekend highlights the Civil War Battle of Plymouth in 1864 and was not only the state's largest battle but also the last major Southern victory of the war. In the museum, view bullet shells and artifacts collected, as well as a 3/8 scale, 63-foot replica of the CSS Albemarle. Outside, they'll have artillery drills, boat rides and a battle reenactment on Sunday. Adult Admission, FREE for children. (last weekend in April)

South Mills

DISMAL SWAMP CANAL VISITOR CENTER & STATE NATURAL AREA

South Mills - 2356 Highway 17 North (3 miles south of the VA/NC border) 27976. Phone: (252) 771-8333. www.dismalswamp.com. Hours: Daily 9:00am-5:00pm (summer/fall). Rest of year, closed on Sundays and Mondays. Admission: FREE Miscellaneous: Gift Shop. Nature walks are available at the Great Dismal Swamp National Wildlife Refuge, approximately 40 miles from the Visitor Center. Locks, located at each end of the Canal in Deep Creek, VA, and South Mills, NC - open four times a day: 8:30am, 11:00 am, 1:30pm & 3:30pm.

The historic Swamp Canal Visitors Center is the only such center that can be accessed by either car or boat. It connects the Chesapeake Bay in Virginia and the Albemarle Sound in North Carolina. The Swamp supports a variety of mammals, including otter, bats, raccoon, mink, gray and red foxes, and gray squirrel. White-tailed deer are common, and black bear and bobcat also inhabit the area. Three species of poisonous snakes are found here, - cottonmouth, canebrake rattler, and the more common copperhead - along with 18 non-poisonous species. Yellow-bellied and spotted turtles are commonly seen, and an additional 56 species of turtles, lizards, salamanders, frogs, and toads have been observed on the Refuge. It may sound creepy to spend the day in a swamp, but oh how much wildlife your kids will get to see - firsthand.

Swan Quarter

MATTAMUSKEET WILDLIFE REFUGE

Swan Quarter - 38 Mattamuskeet Road/ US 94 & US 264 (on Hwy 94, approximately 1 mile North of the intersection of Hwys 264 & 94) 27885. Phone: (252) 926-4021. www.albemarle-nc.com/mattamuskeet/refuge/. Hours: Daylight hours only. Admission: FREE.

Established primarily as a resting and breeding area for migratory birds, the area consists of over 66,000 acres of water, salt marsh land and forested wetlands. Mattamuskeet and Swan Quarter NWR lie in the middle of the Atlantic Flyway and provide a valuable wintering area for the waterfowl using this migration route which extends from Canada southward. Thousands of Canada geese, snow geese, tundra swan and 22 species of ducks winter on the refuge annually. The Refuges also provides habitat for endangered species such as the bald eagle and peregrine

> Thousands of tundra swans make the area their winter home.

falcon. Deer, bobcats, otters, black bear, 240 species of birds and other wildlife species are common to the area. The refuge areas are open to the public for wildlife viewing, canoeing, hunting and fishing. The endangered bald eagle may be observed during the fall, winter and early spring.

Washington

GOOSE CREEK STATE PARK

Washington - 2190 Camp Leach Rd 27889. Phone: (252) 923-2191. Hours: Daily 8:00am to sunset. www.ncparks.gov/Visit/parks/gocr/main.php. Admission: FREE. Fee charged for camping.

Nature beckons you to the marsh and swamp along the borders on the Pamlico River and Goose Creek. Visitors can canoe the unhurried creeks, fish on the River shores or learn about these wetlands at the Environmental Education visitor Center. In the Discovery Room, aquariums are set up to simulate a hardwood swamp and brackish marsh. Mounts, replicas and animal signs, both on tabletops and in pullout drawers, allow close-up study and encourage hands-on learning. The Discovery Room also has a bird observation station with an excellent view of the bird feeder outside. Sit down and wait to see which birds stop by. In addition, a five-minute film is available to introduce visitors to the park and its creatures. Birders and hikers are welcome to explore the eight miles of well-marked hiking trails.

NORTH CAROLINA ESTUARIUM

Washington - 223 Water Street (on the Pamlico River, downtown) 27889. Phone: (252) 948-0000. www.partnershipforthesounds.org/NorthCarolinaEstuarium.aspx. Hours: Tuesday-Saturday 10:00am-4:00pm. Admission: $2.00-$3.00 (age 6+). Educators: Pre-visit materials are available including school Scavenger Hunts. The Estuarium will supply clip boards and pencils for use during the visit.

An estuary is formed where fresh water and salt water mix together. Situated on the waterfront, this estuarium tells the story of the state's sounds and coastal rivers, using the Pamlico/Tar River Esuary, the second largest in the nation behind Chesapeake Bay, as an example. Begin by watching the introductory film about the Pamlico region. Art and science exhibits feature living aquariums, historic artifacts, antique boats, hands-on displays, a film, plus a river tour. Program topics include Black Bears, Birds, Blue Crabs, Reptiles and Amphibians, or Wetlands. The buttons, gadgets, colors and sounds make the estuarium a fun and educational spot for children. Watch tubes drip water in different concentrations of salt to represent the amounts

For updates & travel games visit: **www.KidsLoveTravel.com**

of salt in the ocean, brackish water, estuaries vs. fresh water. Why is the wind so important in estuaries? Like chemistry? Try experiments and read gauges from samples of water collected just beyond the docks.

Windsor

CASHIE WETLANDS WALK & MINI ZOO

Windsor - 101 York St. 27983. Phone: (919) 794-5553. Hours: Monday-Friday 8:00am-8:00pm, Weekends 9:00am-9:00pm. Winter Hours: Daily 8:00am-5:00pm. www.albemarle-nc.com/windsor/attractn/wetwalk.htm. Admission: FREE. Canoes available at no charge.

The Zoo features over 30 different species of foreign and domestic animals including llamas, donkeys, goats, rheas, a bird house with all types of birds including turkeys, pea fowl, peacocks and Polish hens. Across the street from the Zoo is the Cashie Wetlands Walk. The Walk has an 1800 foot handicapped accessible walkway to the Cashie River and features a fishing pier at its end. The trees and shrubs in the Walk are labeled for identification. Various wild animals can be seen in their natural habitat, many of which are endangered species, such as the pileated woodpecker. The walk takes visitors to the edge of the Cashie River, which is 20 miles long and as deep as 80 feet. The observation deck allows views of several different species of endangered waterfowl and other swampland animals in their natural habitats.

HOPE PLANTATION

Windsor - 132 Hope House Road (four miles northwest of town on NC 308) 27983. Phone: (252) 794-3140. www.albemarle-nc.com/hope/. Hours: Monday-Saturday 10:00am-4:00pm, Sunday 2:00-5:00pm. Closed Thanksgiving Day and the entire Winter Break. Admission: $8.00 adult, $7.00 senior (65+), $3.00 students. Educators: Lesson units for Fourth and Eighth grade curriculums available upon request. Heritage Day and Living History Days.

Tour the authentically furnished c. 1803 Hope Plantation, home of Governor David Stone, the 1763 King-Bazemore House, and the Samuel Cox House. The Hope was the centerpiece of a completely self-sustaining plantation. At Hope they operated a water powered grist mill, a still, and as indicated by his inventory, a saw mill, a blacksmith shop, a cooper's shop and houses for spinning and weaving. His farm lands produced wheat, corn, oats, rye, flax, and cotton, for which he had a cotton machine. On his pastures he raised cattle, sheep and horses, in his woods he raised hogs, while his forests produced timber for the sawmill.

Walk the plantation grounds and the Hope Forest nature trails. The modern Roanoke-Chowan Heritage Center features regional exhibits and annual celebrations of Native American and African-American heritage. Admission charged.

A CHRISTMAS TRADITION....AT HISTORIC HOPE

The Mansion and the King Bazemore House are decorated for the season & open to everyone by donation. Holiday punch & cookies in the Heritage Center. There will be special musical treats, so be sure to stay on... (first Sunday in December)

ROANOKE RIVER NATIONAL WILDLIFE REFUGE

Windsor - 27983. Phone: (252) 794-5326. www.fws.gov/roanokeriver/index.html. Hours: Daily during daylight hours. Admission: FREE. Fee for camping.

The refuge is home to animals such as deer, otter, beaver, muskrat and black bear. There are more than 191 species of migrating birds that find seasonal homes here. The largest inland heron rookery in North Carolina is on refuge. The informal trail tracts are open to the public for hiking and birdwatching - although, some of the trails are only accessible by boat.

Chapter 4
South Central

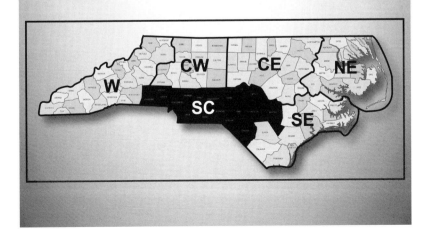

A Quick Tour of our Hand-Picked
Favorites Around...

South Central
North
Carolina

In Charlotte, you'll find rides that go in circles at **Carowinds,** or you can slow the pace with some indoor time at the **Levine Museum of the New South** in downtown Charlotte. What is the "New South?" Visitors enjoy an interactive, hands-on experience as they tour 6 different "environments" within the exhibit that begin right after the Civil War up to present day. Each space tells a different story but the kids must "unlock" the clues.

Need to refuel? Try lunch at a **Fuel Pizza,** located in old 50s gas stations, the theme and food are so fun! They have a kids menu and offer "play dough" while you wait for your food or Pizza Tour.

When you're finished there, race over to nearby **Lowe's Motor Speedway** for a complete NASCAR experience, including an exhilarating race track tour and visits to neighboring race team garages. Wait 'til you see what's inside those transport trailers!

What's your wing-span? Check it out at the **Carolina Raptor Center.** Meet one turkey vulture who likes to untie shoe laces. Another turkey vulture at the center, is a movie star. Did you know Bald Eagles nests can be as large as a small car?

Head a litte further east on SR 24/25 to Midland. The Old North State led the nation in gold production until 1848, when the great rush to California began. The gold business fizzled out here. But you can experience some of the excitement of days gone by at **Reed Gold Mine.** Learn how to pan for gold and explore a real gold mine!

Spend an afternoon in Fayetteville at the **Airborne & Special Operations Museum,** which honors the shared history of airborne and special operations soldiers at Fort Bragg. Parachutes dropping out of the sky, soldiers in bunkers, motion theatre and simulators make the drama of military action very real.

Sites and attractions are listed in order by City, Zip Code, and Name. Symbols indicated represent:

 Festivals   Restaurants   Lodging

Aberdeen

MALCOLM BLUE FARM

Aberdeen - 1177 Bethesda Rd. (Hwy 5 & E.L. Ives Drive) 28315. Phone: (910) 944-7558. www.malcolmbluefarm.com. Hours: Wednesday-Saturday 1:00-4:00pm. By appointment only November through February.

A tour of the 1825 farmhouse and museum provides insight into the lives of early pioneers in the Sandhills area known as "the Pine Barrens." The house is filled with authentic furnishings of everyday life during the early 1800's. Visitors get a first-hand feel for what life in the 1800's was about by touring the farmstead. The property contains the historic farmhouse and barns, an old gristmill, and a wooden water tower. Annual events are held here throughout the year.

HISTORICAL CRAFTS AND FARMSKILLS FESTIVAL

Approximately 1,800 school children visit the farm on Friday during School Children's Day to learn what daily life and work was like in the 19th century. Some of the crafts and skills demonstrated are pottery, basket making, woodworking, blacksmithing, spinning, weaving, soap and candle making and fringe tying. Farm animals fill the stable; pony and wagon rides are available for the young and young at heart. Folk and country musicians and dancers entertain during the three-day event. In the meadow, Civil War reenactment troops are encamped and steam engines are demonstrated. (last weekend of September)

EARLY AMERICAN CHRISTMAS

Open House with musicians, carolers, traditional food, 19th century children's games, quilters, cornhusk angels, garlands of popcorn and cranberries.

Albemarle

MORROW MOUNTAIN STATE PARK

Albemarle - 49104 Morrow Mountain Road (NC 24 east and veer right on NC 740. After about six miles, turn right on Morrow Mountain Road) 28001. Phone: (704) 982-4402. www.ncparks.gov/Visit/parks/momo/main.php Hours: Daily 8:00am to dusk. Exhibit Hall open 10:00am-5:00pm. Admission: FREE. Fee for boat rentals, cabins, camping and swimming.

These steep, rugged hills—unusual topography for the area—form a stark contrast with the rolling countryside of the piedmont plateau. The park offers an exhibit hall and a historical site. The hall includes exhibits about Native Americans, plant and animal communities, early explorers, and rocks and minerals. Visit the homestead of a 19th-century doctor, Dr. Francis Kron, the first physician in the area. His home, doctor's office and infirmary, and greenhouse were reconstructed and appear today much as they did in 1870. Recreation is plentiful in and around the waters of Lake Tillery and the Pee Dee River. Fishing, boating and swimming are popular pastimes. Nature lovers can pick from miles of trails to travel on foot or horseback. And for those who want to stay and take it all in, cabins and camping are available.

Carthage

BUGGY FESTIVAL

Carthage - (910) 947-2331. www.townofcarthage.com. For more than half a century, this town had the largest buggy factory in the nation during a time when carriages were essential to life in rural areas. The town celebrates with an all-buggy parade, food, live entertainment and fun. (second weekend in May)

Charlotte

CHARLOTTE SPORTS

CHARLOTTE BOBCATS - Charlotte Bobcats Arena. The Charlotte Bobcats are the latest in a league of up and coming young NBA teams. Their offense is fast paced, exciting, and they are willing to scrap for every point. The arena has colorful exhibits and displays plus a kid's interactive center. www.charlottebobcatsarena.com. Tickets start at $10.00.

CHARLOTTE CHECKERS - The AA ECHL Checkers play home games at St. Lawrence Homes Home Ice at Charlotte Bobcats Arena. The Checkers have affiliations with the New York Rangers of the National Hockey League and the Hartford Wolf Pack of the American Hockey League. Charlotte is known as the birthplace of pro hockey in the South. Many family-oriented events occur monthly. www.gocheckers.com.

CHARLOTTE KNIGHTS - The AAA affiliate of the Chicago White Soxs plays games in Knight Stadium, just over the border in South Carolina (off I-77). Meet their mascot, Homer the Dragon. Inexpensive general seats, a playground, post-game fireworks, and even a miniature golf course round out the fun for kids.

CAROLINA PANTHERS

Charlotte - 800 S. Mint Street (Bank of America Stadium) 28202. Phone: (704) 358-7800 tickets or (704) 358-7158 store. www.panthers.com.

NFL Heroes of the scrapping football team invite you to home football games every fall. Begin your game day experience on The Catwalk. Located outside the North Gate, all fans can enjoy free games, music, entertainment, and appearances by the TopCats, Sir Purr and former Panthers players. Activities begin 2 1/2 hours prior to kickoff and conclude at kickoff. The Carolina Panthers mascot, Sir Purr has been a beloved fixture of football in the Carolinas since the team's first season in 1995. Armed with nimble feet, a great smile and one big shaking belly, this cat is best known for his silly antics and creative skits that can be seen on game day.

CAROLINA PANTHERS STADIUM TOURS

Charlotte - Bank of America Stadium (meet at the Ticket Office, between East and South gates on Mint Street) 28202. www.panthers.com/stadium/ Phone: (704) 358-7538. Admission: $5.00 adult, $4.00 senior (55+), $3.00 child (5-15).

Tours of the Bank of America Stadium for the general public are offered each Wednesday, beginning at 10:00am. See the Panthers' Locker Room, Weight Room, Training Room, Luxury Suites, the Stadium Bowl, Practice Fields and even the Press Box. Behind-the-scenes stadium tours are the insider way to learn more about your favorite teams and their "workplace."

SC Area

DISCOVERY PLACE

Charlotte - 301 North Tryon Street (I-77 north exit 11, Brookshire Freeway. Right to Church St/Tryon St exit. Follow signs) 28202. Phone: (704) 372-6261. www. discoveryplace.org. Hours: Monday-Friday 9:00am-5:00pm, Saturday 9:00am-6:00pm, Sunday Noon-6:00pm. Closed Thanksgiving Day, Christmas Eve, Christmas Day and Easter Sunday. Admission: $8.00-$10.00 (age 2+). IMAX extra $7.00-$8.00. Combo tickets offer discounts.

One of the top hands-on science facilities in the nation, this unique center provides ever-changing and entertaining facilities such as an IMAX Dome Theatre, planetarium, Life Center, Einstein's Corner, Machine Shop (with giant levers), a wonderful aquarium w/ touch pools and a Rain Forest. In Science Theatre check out the show "Sparks Anyone?" or unravel the double helix with the film DNA: The Secret of Life. Reach out and touch a simulated tornado, check out the weather or view a gem collection while exploring video presentations and hands-on exhibits. Get a scoop of liquid nitrogen ice cream made in minutes right before your eyes. Explore the heart exhibit, As The Beat Goes On... , with its giant walk-through heart or check out the giant eyeball. And, for the preschoolers - their own KidsPlace space with water tables and a treehouse sized just for them. We promise stimulation abounds here!

LEVINE MUSEUM OF THE NEW SOUTH

Charlotte - 200 East 7th Street (I-277 North (exit 9B) to the College Street exit. Take College St. to 7th St. or I-77 exit 10B) 28202. www.museumofthenewsouth.org. Phone: (704) 333-1887. Hours: Monday-Saturday 10:00am-5:00pm, Sunday Noon-5:00pm. Closed Thanksgiving, Christmas and New Years. Admission: $6.00 adult, $5.00 senior (62+) and student (6-18), $17.00 family. Miscellaneous: Free 90 minute parking is available in the Seventh Street Station parking deck adjacent to the museum on weekdays. Parking is free on the weekends.

So what is the New South? The only regional history museum in the country that focuses on the New South period, this interactive museum takes at look at the history and culture of the South as it has evolved from the immediate post-Civil War era until the present day. Travel through the exhibit "Cotton Fields to Skyscrapers" to discover how the New South was reinvented from field to factory to finance. Visitors enjoy an interactive, hands-on experience as they tour 6 different "environments" within the exhibit: Step inside a one-room tenant farmer's house; Run a hand through a pile of seed cotton, then card, spin and weave cotton thread; Listen to the churning of the cotton mill; Play checkers on the front porch of a mill house; Sit in Good Samaritans Hospital Chapel, one of the first African-American hospitals in the South; Walk down main street and try on a hat in an early Belk department store; or, Sit at a lunch counter and hear personal accounts from local sit-in leaders. You can't really learn here unless you engage here - we liked the fact that the kids had to touch things in order to understand what they were.

Working at the cotton mill...

MINT MUSEUMS OF ART, CRAFT & DESIGN

Charlotte - 2730 Randolph Road/ 220 North Tryon Street (I- 77 Northbound:Take the Trade Street/Fifth Street exit 10. Turn right on Trade Street, head east toward downtown. Follow signs) 28202. www.themintmuseums.org. Phone: (704) 337-2000. Hours: Tuesday-Saturday 10:00am-5:00pm, Sunday 12:00-5:00pm. Closed Monday and major holidays (including New Year's Day, Easter Sunday, July 4th, Thanksgiving Day, Christmas Eve and Christmas Day) Admission: $6.00 adult, $5.00 senior (62+) and college student, $3.00 youth (6-17). Certain weekdays offer Free admission times. See website for details.

<u>**MINT MUSEUM OF ART**</u>: North Carolina's first art museum features many famous American and European paintings. The major focus of the collections exhibited by the museum traces American related art including the art of Native Americans and other cultures that influenced the shaping of American culture from pre-Colombian times through Colonial times to the present.

<u>**MINT MUSEUM OF CRAFT + DESIGN**</u>: This museum takes a look at the evolution of crafts and how the changing style of the artifacts produced by artisans reflects the various ages in which these objects were created. Unique objects on display include the traditional craft mediums of ceramic, fiber, glass, metal, and wood. Adult-child workshops introduce parents and young children to an exhibition, and finish with an art activity. After school and home school workshops introduce children to diverse art forms and world cultures, while weekend workshops and Family Days provide scavenger hunts and activities for the whole family's enjoyment. Summer art camps offer creative fun and inspiration for a variety of age levels and abilities.

CHARLOTTE TROLLEY

Charlotte - 2104 South Boulevard (South End) (I-77 S to West Blvd. Exit 9A. Left on West Blvd. Right on South Blvd. Depot at Atherton Mill, Historic South End 28203. Phone: (704) 375-0850. www.charlottetrolley.org. Hours: Fridays & Saturdays 10:00am – 9:00pm, Sundays & most weekdays 10:00am – 6:00pm. Carolina Panthers Game Days: 10:00 am until one hour after game ends. Admission: $1.00-$2.00. The Car Barn, Museum and Gift Shop are open during the same hours, and admission is free. Educators: Lesson plans (K-3) about transportation online.

Ring, Ring, Ring Goes the Trolley. A trip along the trolley route will take you past some of the most important and interesting sites of Charlotte's history, from the 19th Century right into the 21st. Drive by an original cotton mill or the factory that coined the phrase "air-conditioning". The trolley runs over the Westin Hotel's parking lot and through the Charlotte Convention Center via a 250-foot long tunnel that allows streetcars to rumble by without disrupting hotel guests. Volunteers serve as docents, riding the cars during peak tourist hours, explaining the role of the electric streetcar system and offering a guided tour of the personalities and landmarks associated with the trolley corridor. Get the lowdown on some of the funny, little-known stories about Charlotte's past.

CAROLINAS AVIATION MUSEUM

Charlotte - 4108 Minuteman Way (Charlotte/ Douglas International Airport, follow brown signs) 28208. Phone: (704) 359-8442. www.carolinasaviation.org. Hours: Tuesday-Friday 10:00am-4:00pm, Saturday 10:00am-5:00pm and Sunday 1:00-5:00pm. Admission: $8.00 adult, $5.00 senior & child (age 6+). Active duty military personnel with a valid military ID are admitted free of charge. Educators: View Takeoffs & Landings online.

Daring X-planes, jets defending our freedom, and choppers that brought our soldiers home. You'll see planes with names like Phantom or Shooting Star. Because this museum is located at a busy airport, your kids can watch modern planes arrive and depart.

CHARLOTTE NATURE MUSEUM

Charlotte - 1638 Sterling Road (I-77 exit 6A. Bear right on Woodlawn, heading east. Left on Park Rd. Right on Princeton. Left on Sterling. Adjacent to Freedom Park) 28209. Phone: (704) 372-6261. www.discoveryplace.org. Hours: Monday-Friday 9:00am-5:00pm, Saturday 10:00am-5:00pm, Sunday 1:00-5:00pm. Admission: $5.00 (age 2+).

The Charlotte Nature Museum is an urban science center that exhibits the animals and plants of the Piedmont including an ever-changing Butterfly Garden. The child-oriented museum features numerous hands-on exhibits that relate to natural history, as well as a live animal room, a puppet theatre, and a scenic Outdoor Exploring trail. The Outdoor Exploring Dome takes on the ambiance of a night in the forest around a campfire as Grandpa Tree tells about the nocturnal creatures. Insect Alley has games, videos and interactives and serves as a great primer for the Butterfly Garden. Make sure you meet the guard over the butterflies – Lovey Dovey. Or, meet Queen Charlotte, the groundhog. Live animals to see around every corner. Their Grandpa Tree room is the best show of its kind we've ever seen!

US NATIONAL WHITEWATER CENTER

Charlotte - 820 Hawfield Road (I-85 south to exit 29 (Sam Wilson Rd) 28214. Phone: (704) 391-3900. www.usnwc.org. Hours: Open daylight hours. Courses closed to public for competitions (spectators allowed). Trails not open during poor weather conditions. See website for current status. Admission: Trails are FREE. Flatwater Kayaking: 2 Hour Guided Trip- $35 per person (Ages 9+), $20 (Ages 5-8). Whitewater Kayak Sampler $55. Guided Climb-$23.00-1 hour guided climb belayed by staff. Ropes: Climb to Zip-$15.00, High Ropes-$33.00. Additional fees for gear or mountain bike rentals. Miscellaneous: Eddy Restaurant w/ panoramic view of rapids and wide selection of entrees and light fare.

Come see future Olympians from around the world compete - or, try some Class III/IV rapids yourself (ages 12 and up)! Cross the Catawba River and explore the world's largest manmade recirculating river with multiple channels. It's a sight to see - rapids in the middle of lowland Piedmont. Your tweens and teens will love the challenge of the rough rapids, while the younger set may opt for whitewater kayaking/flatwater courses for ages eight and up. They have one of the largest outdoor climbing facilities in the US and a unique ropes course and zip line, too. Not into the extreme sports? Try their seasonal bike or hike trails surrounding the facility.

> Eco Caching here gives explorers an opportunity to get into the woods. Use GPS-receivers with programmed treasure hunting destinations to log each find in your own "passport."

CHARLOTTE MUSEUM OF HISTORY

Charlotte - 3500 Shamrock Drive (I-85 N to exit 41. Turn Right onto Sugar Creek Rd. Bear Right onto Eastway Dr. Turn Left onto Shamrock). Follow Sugar Creek for approximately 3 miles. 28215. Phone: (704) 374-1565. www.charlottemuseum.org. Hours: Tuesday-Saturday 10:00am-5:00pm, Sunday 1:00-5:00pm. Closed major holidays. Admission: $6.00 adult, $5.00 senior and student, $3.00 child (6-12). Educators: The Hands-on-History Room in the museum provides interactive fun for children of all ages. The activities are based on current exhibits and colonial life. For written or craft activities, look at the online Activities page.

Located on the homestead site of Hezekiah Alexander, this museum displays artifacts and dioramas that relate to American and local history. The 18th century gallery takes you back to a time when this region was still rugged frontier. Long before the first European settlers came to the Piedmont, a group of Native American tribes inhabited the region. A visit to the 19th century gallery begins with the discovery of gold in the region, represented by a model gold mine and featuring a miner hard at work. The cotton industry grew substantially during this time and Mecklenburg became the third largest cotton-producing county in the State. The role of slave labor and local participation in the Civil War is here, too. The house on the grounds is the Revolutionary Era home of Hezekiah Alexander. Built in 1774, the house is decorated with historically correct period items. In addition to the House, the grounds offer elements of eighteenth century life in the kitchen, herb garden, and springhouse.

CHARLOTTE SYMPHONY ORCHESTRA

Charlotte - 201 South College Street, Suite 110 (concerts held in Belk Theater) 28244. Phone: (704) 972-2000 or (800) 972-2003. www.charlottesymphony.org

The largest and most active professional performing arts organization in the area, this symphony orchestra features over 100 professional musicians performing beautiful music from September through July. Lollipops concerts are especially great for families. Sometimes just music, but sometimes add in a movie or theatrical act. Shorter, funnier performances for youth with a lollypop treat at the end.

CAROWINDS & BOOMERANG BAY

Charlotte - 14523 Carowinds Blvd. (I-77 to SC exit 90, at the NC/SC border. Park is 15 minutes south of Uptown Charlotte & 15 north of Rock Hill, SC) 28273. Phone: (704) 588-2600 or (800) 888-4386. www.carowinds.com. Hours: Weekends (mid-March to mid-October). Daily (late May to Mid-August). Park generally opens at 10:00am, closes from 6:00-10:00pm. Boomerang Bay is open on public operating

days from Mid-May through Labor Day, hours vary. Admission: ~$46.00 (over 48")
and ~$30.00 (senior - 62+ and child - ages 3-6 or under 48"). Save $10.00-$20.00
per person at twilight or online discounts. The all-new Picnic Tic Package is a
convenient, yummy value – admission and picnic together is less than the price
of a regular adult admission at the Front Gate! Miscellaneous: Campground near
premises is a budget-friendly option for many families traveling to the area.

The premiere 105 acre water and theme park in the Carolinas, this park features
over 100 state-of-the-art rides, shows, and movie-themed experiences for all
ages, as well as a Zoom Zone children's area, and Boomerang Bay water
park. They now have the largest Nickelodeon area at any theme park in
the world. Nickelodeon Central is based on popular characters and shows.
NICKELODEON™ CENTRAL includes two rapids or waterfall rides and a
place to greet everyone's favorite lovable life-size Nickelodeon® characters
(like Dora). Challenge your friends to see who can capture the most ghosts
and Scooby Snacks™ in Scooby Doo's™ Haunted Mansion. Then, off to the
Rugrats™ RUNAWAY REPTAR™, a junior inverted roller coaster. Two newer
rides were our kids favorites: Phantom Flyers -all ages can steer their course
swooping up and down, weaving side to side, gliding thru the air; and the
Flying Dutchman's Revenge – all ages can navigate rotating mini-pirate ships
pivoting, twisting and turning a full 180 degrees while sloping up and down
along the terrain. Several rides are for the preschool set, other mini-coasters
for the preteens. Throughout the park, notice one thing: the name of the
ride pretty much tells the story. Example: Hurler (stomach leaves the body);
Cyclone (loopy); Richochet (jerky side-to-side motion). The waterpark area
was nice and compact but beware of pre-summer weekends when the water
feels cool for awhile. Bondi Beach is the park's new Wave Pool.

MCDOWELL NATURE CENTER & PRESERVE

Charlotte - 15222 York Road (I-77 Exit 90 onto Carowinds Boulevard. Go west
approximately 3 miles to Hwy 49 (York Road). Turn left on Hwy 49 and travel 4 miles)
28278. Phone: (704) 588-5224. www.parkandrec.com. Hours: Outdoor Exploring
Center: Monday-Saturday 9:00am-5:00pm, Sunday 1:00-5:00pm. Preserve: Daily
7:00am-sunset. Admission: FREE. A vehicle entrance fee of $3.00 (County
resident) and $5.00 (non-County resident) is charged to the Outdoor Exploring
preserve March 1 through October 31 on weekends and holidays. Miscellaneous:
Mountain bikes are permitted only on paved roads within the preserve.

Serving as the gateway to the 1,108 acre McDowell Outdoor Exploring Preserve,
this Outdoor Exploring center and preserve has numerous features including
live native animals, an outdoor amphitheater, an exhibit hall, educational

programs, a habitat garden with butterfly gardens, numerous picnic decks and tables, seven miles of hiking trails, fishing, canoeing (rentals), and a 58 site primitive and RV family campground. The Backyard Habitat Garden includes bird feeding stations, butterfly gardens, garden pond, and a demonstration compost area. The Four Seasons Trail, a 1-mile loop located near the nature center, is paved and handicap accessible. Mountain bikes are permitted only on paved roads within the preserve.

600 FESTIVAL

Charlotte - Uptown. www.600festival.com. (704) 455-6814. Race week is under way when thousands of fans pack the streets for the Parade, a colorful collection of NASCAR drivers, show cars, marching bands, clowns, floats and local celebrities. The streets of town showcase motorsports with non-stop entertainment on three stages, appearances by top NEXTEL Cup drivers, a large assembly of NASCAR show cars and simulators. (week before Memorial Day)

FUEL PIZZA

Charlotte - Need to refuel? Try lunch at Fuel Pizza. www.fuelpizza.com. Located in old 50s gas stations, the theme and food are so fun! They have a kids menu and offer play dough (real pizza dough), crayons and fun sheets. Try an Extreme Fuel, Whole Engine or Lasagna Pizza with a side of wings and garlic knots. They give Pizza Tours at some of their eight locations (mornings by appointment).

MARRIOTT COURTYARD CHARLOTTE - UNIVERSITY RESEARCH PARK

Charlotte - 333 West Harris Blvd. (I-85 exit 45A), (704) 549-4888. Rooms feature seasonal outdoor comfortable pool area, indoor jacuzzi, and moderate sized rooms. They are on the NASCAR side of town, close to the speedway and racing shops.

STAYBRIDGE SUITES SW CHARLOTTE

Charlotte - 7924 Forest Pine Dr. (704) 527-8889. www.ichotelsgroup.com. We'd recommend staying overnight at the Arrowood exit off I-77. Just a few miles from Carowinds park. All suites have kitchens (equipped) and free high speed internet. The property offers guests a convenience store, sport court, heated outdoor pool, BBQ pavilion, DVD rentals and a library. Oh, and the (hot/cold) items on the deluxe breakfast bar were good.

LOWE'S MOTOR SPEEDWAY TOURS (CHARLOTTE)

Charlotte (Concord) - 5555 Concord Parkway South (US 29 North) 28027. Phone: (704) 455-3200 or (800) 455-FANS (tickets). www.lowesmotorspeedway.com. Miscellaneous: Several go-kart speed racing tracks are nearby including NASCAR Speedpark (www.nascarspeedpark.com).

Located 12 miles northeast of Uptown Charlotte (the heart of stock car racing), Lowe's Motor Speedway is truly the "Mecca of Motorsports". The speedway annually hosts NASCAR Nextel Cup, Busch and Craftsman Truck Series races; gigantic AutoFairs, a 10-week Legends Car Summer Shootout Series, stock car driving schools and a variety of annual events at The Dirt Track.

FEEL THE THRILL TOUR: Your grand tour of LMS includes a close-up look at areas that are usually off-limits during a race. Go behind the scenes to the Nextel Cup Garage, travel down pit road where every second counts, and take a picture in the same Victory Circle that has hosted the greatest drivers in NASCAR history. Learn about the new Speedway lights built from an idea learned from the

The Thrill of Victory....

"Field of Dreams" movie (mirrored lighting in the corn fields). View Redneck Hill and Spotters Railing. The highlight of the tour is a fast (60-70 mph!) van ride around Charlotte's 1.5-mile oval where you will experience the full-tilt action of 24-degree banks! A thrilling tour for any race or speed enthusiasts!

600 RACING INC.

Charlotte (Harrisburg) - 5245 Hwy 49 28075. www.600racing.com. Phone: (704) 455-3896. Hours: Monday-Friday 9:00am-5:00pm, Saturday 9:00am-2:00pm (seasonal). Admission: Tours FREE.

This is the home of the Legends, Bandolero and Thunder Roadster cars. The Legends car - only sold as a "turnkey" car - is a 5/8 scale auto modeled after the great modifieds driven by NASCAR's earliest stars. The Bandolero, introduced in the late 1990s for drivers as young as eight, is a stepping stone to the Legends car. The Thunder Roadster, an open wheel, 96" wheelbase car, gives the driver the feel and comfort of a bigger race car. Tour the manufacturing facility and see the building of the cars. Be careful, you'll probably want to purchase one and start racing that day...

HENDRICK MOTORSPORTS

Charlotte (Harrisburg) - 4400 Papa Joe Hendrick Blvd. (I-85 exit 49 to Hwy 29 south. Right on Morehead, right on Stowe) 28075. Phone: (704) 455-3400 or (877) 467-4890. www.hendrickmotorsports.com. Hours: Monday-Friday 9:00am- 5:00pm. Periodically, the complex will close for holidays and vacations so we advise visitors to call ahead.

This sophisticated complex provides Hendrick Motorsports with facilities to design, test and make cars and engines for all of their race teams. Currently, site visitors are welcome to view Terry

The Thrill of Victory...

Labonte's Kellogg's/got milk?, Jeff Gordon's DuPont Motorsports Shop, Jimmie Johnson's Lowe's Racing Shop, and Junior's AMP #88. Visitors are also welcome to view the 15,000-square-foot Hendrick Museum and Speed Shop which showcases almost two decades of HMS racing. Special one-of-a-kind items include Rick Hendrick's very first car -- a 1931 Chevrolet. At age 14, he bought this 1931 Chevrolet in a "totally stock" condition, then rebuilt it for drag racing. Items also on display include the very first production ZR1 Chevrolet Corvette; the powerful, 1,000 horsepower "Spirit of Charlotte" GTP Corvette;

The Agony of Defeat....

one of the Chevrolet Lumina racecars used in the Days of Thunder feature film staring Tom Cruise; and many other collectibles. Even see a surviving crash vehicle and actual working shop floors. On a good day, you may be able to watch the pit crews practice in a back lot or observe the team loading up the truck for a race!

CENTER OF SCOTTISH HERITAGE AT RURAL HILL

Charlotte (Huntersville) - 4431 Neck Road (I-77 South to Exit #25) 28078. Phone: (704) 875-3113. www.ruralhillplantation.org. Hours: Monday-Saturday 9:00am-4:00pm. Closed: Week of Thanksgiving November 18-24, December 23-31. Admission: $4.00-$6.00 (age 6+). Please note SPECIAL EVENTS have different dates, times, and admission prices from regular daily hours and admission prices. Educators: Teacher's Guides online. Picnics and pets are allowed.

Rural Hill Plantation is a haven for area Scots. The homestead was built by Major John and Violet Davidson, who raised ten children here and became a prosperous plantation. A reproduction home can be toured, as well as the original smoke house, ash house, well, barn, chicken coop and granary. Two old schoolhouses are on the property also. Most educational tours last 2 hours so take note of that with antsy young ones. Want to enjoy more outside? Travel down the historic Mill Lane (dating back to the 1700's) or walk through the woods on our walking trails which extend 3-4 miles around the perimeter of present day Rural Hill.

LOCH NORMAN HIGHLAND GAMES

Rural Hill Plantation grounds are the place where World Class athletes come to compete in various competitions which include Heavy Athletics both professionally and amateurs, bag-piping, fiddle and harp, and Scottish Dance. Not only are there highly competitive events, but more than 90 Scottish and Scots-Irish Clans and organizations bring their banners to demonstrate their support and share family genealogy and heritage exhibits with visitors. Along with this family fun and educational atmosphere you can enjoy world renowned Celtic and Scottish bands while getting a taste of Scottish cuisine (Scotch Eggs and Meat Pies) along with other local delicacies like Carolina BBQ or Smoked Turkey Legs. Admission. (long weekend in mid-April)

Center Of Scottish Heritage At Rural Hill (cont.)

RURAL HILL REVOLUTIONARY WAR REENACTMENT

Visit with the soldiers and find out what life was like as a soldier in the army in 1781. There will be plenty of activities and exhibits for everyone to enjoy which will include: Colonial Games, Student Militia, Craftsmen and Artisans (Blacksmithing, basket making, candle making, cooking, weaving, carpentry), Colonial Merchandise Vendors, and Rural Hill-Museum and Exhibits are open. Vendors and Sutlers will be on site to provide food and beverages at an additional cost. Admission. (weekend in Mid-May)

AMAZING MAIZE MAZE

A historical or related theme to Rural Hill is carefully chosen for each maze. This is a great opportunity for families to work together in exploring and solving the clues to make it through the maze. Admission. (Thursday-Sunday in September/October)

SHEEP DOG TRIALS

Bring your family and friends and even your dogs out to Rural Hill to witness more than 75 Border Collies compete. The trials are a competition in performance not conformation. The competition is based on daily tasks that the dog is asked to do on the farm. Flying Disc dog activities, tractor show, unusual livestock expo and hayride tours will be provided. Admission. (first full long weekend in November)

1760 CAROLINA THANKSGIVING

In celebration of the Thanksgiving season Rural Hill hosts a 1760 style Thanksgiving living history event of the Colonial era which includes skilled craftsmen and artisan demonstrations and militia soldiers performing various drills and maneuvers. Other activities to see are 18th century children's games, musket firing demonstrations and open hearth Colonial style cooking - see the ladies prepare Thanksgiving dinner. One of the premiere demonstrations of the weekend is an actual log cabin raising. FREE. (near Thanksgiving weekend)

ENERGY EXPLORIUM - DUKE ENERGY

Charlotte (Huntersville) - 13339 Hagers Ferry Road (McGuire Nuclear Station) 28078. www.duke-energy.com/visitor-centers/energyexplorium.asp. Phone: (704) 875-5600.   Hours: Monday-Friday 9:00am-5:00pm, Weekends Noon-5:00pm. Admission: FREE.   Educators: Exhibit worksheets, video collection and educational backpacks are available for group visits.

The explorium is the facility where you can take a virtual tour of a real Nuclear Station. Here you can pretend to throw the switch, convert your own energy into enough electricity to power a TV, play computer games, or figure out how much energy you get for one dollar. Maybe watch a movie about Lake Norman or nuclear energy. Now, take some of that pent up energy outside to the mile-long nature trail along the shore of Lake Norman.

LATTA PLANTATION, HISTORIC

Charlotte (Huntersville) - 5225 Sample Road   28078. www.lattaplantation.org. Phone: (704) 875-2312.   Hours: Grounds open: Tuesday-Saturday 10:00am-4:30pm, Sunday 1:00-4:30pm. Admission: $6.00 adult, $5.00 senior (62+) and students.   Miscellaneous: Historic Latta Plantation is within Latta Plantation Park, on Mountain Island Lake. The park offers hiking and horseback riding trails, canoe rentals, and fishing. Teacher Resources online including vocabulary and pre- and post-test questions.

Historic Latta Plantation is a circa 1800 cotton plantation and living history farm. At the end of a country road, you see the Lattas' white two-story frame house. Enjoy wandering the grounds. See the barnyard animals (especially lambs and sheep). Visit the outbuildings, replica log house, and garden. Participate in a pre-arranged group tour led by a costumed docent and learn interesting, little-known facts about the Early Republic. Best to visit as a group or during special events. From Colonial to Revolutionary to Civil War periods - demonstrations of period cooking techniques, music, blacksmithing, basketmaking, weaving in the house and cabin, and outside war camp settings abound during event weekends.

A VICTORIAN VALENTINE

Celebrate Valentine's Day in 19th century style. Learn about Victorian valentine traditions, see antique valentines, take a valentine tour of the plantation home, learn English Country Dancing, smell treats cooking in the kitchen, make a craft, and more. Admission, age 5+. (Valentine's Day)

Latta Plantation, Historic (cont.)

EASTER EGG HUNT

Children ages 1 to 10 years old can hunt for thousands of Easter eggs across the beautiful plantation grounds. (Easter Saturday or Saturday before)

LATTA PLANTATION CHRISTMAS

The plantation home will be decorated for a 19th century Christmas and open for Christmas tours of the house throughout December. Candlelight Christmas: a candlelit evening filled with the sites, sounds, and smells of a Christmas from the past! Lantern led walks around the plantation will include the carriage barn, kitchen, plantation home, slave cabin, and more! Admission. (Tour times are: Tuesdays-Saturdays from 11:00am-4:00pm in December. Candlelight is first full weekend in December)

CAROLINA RAPTOR CENTER

Charlotte (Huntersville, Lake Norman) - 6000 Sample Road (I-77 N to exit 16B, Sunset Rd. Right on Beatties Ford Road, go 5 miles. Left on Sample Road and head straight into Latta Plantation Nature Preserve) 28031. Phone: (704) 875-6521. www.carolinaraptorcenter.org. Hours: Monday-Saturday 10:00am-5:00pm, Sunday Noon - 5:00pm. Closed New Year's Day, Easter Sunday, Thanksgiving, and Christmas Day. Admission: $7.00 adult, $6.00 senior, $5.00 student. Educators: Raptor Fact Sheets, games and vocabulary are online. Note: Carolina Raptor Center is an outdoor facility. Visitors are encouraged to prepare for inclement weather. Most of the outdoor center is shaded. Gift shop on premises.

> Raptors are a type of bird that preys on other animals. Hawks, eagles, falcons, and owls are examples of raptors you'll see.

Birds of prey, also known as raptors, often are the victims of harmful collisions with other species, including humans. Luckily, Carolina Raptor Center is there to nurse them back to health and often place them back in the wild. Stroll along the nature trail for a self-guided tour as you observe raptors in their aviaries. Along the way, watch a presentation of live raptors, chat with the Wild Wings Educators about your favorite bird of prey, or read personal stories about resident birds and how they came to live at Carolina Raptor Center. Meet one turkey vulture who likes to untie shoe laces. Another turkey vulture at the center is a movie star. The bird with the prickly personality appeared in The Chase, a film produced in Wilmy-wood, NC. In another aviary is a sweet albino hawk and an adorable small owl. Before a healed bird can be released, it must pass "Mouse School". It must be able to pass the "capture a rodent" test! A favorite area is the eagles' cages. Did you know Bald Eagles nests can be as large as a small car? Another fact: Barn owls can locate prey by sound alone - in the pitch dark. Before you leave, be sure to "Measure your Wing Span" against an eagle's span. Nice combo of nature trail and bird "zoo".

How big is a raptor's wingspan?
T H I S   B I G !!!

WALK THROUGH BETHLEHEM

Charlotte (Matthews) - Matthews United Methodist Church. 801 S. Trade Street. www.matthewsumc.org. "Walk Through Bethlehem" where 600 people participate and more then 5,000 people come and visit. The gym gets transformed in a market place in Bethlehem with booths that "sell" brass, baskets, wine, pottery, etc. (nothing is for sale) Outside are the carpenters, the butchers, candlemakers, etc. The Roman camp with the Roman soldiers make sure you write your name down at the census before entering Bethlehem. There are goats, sheep, a camel, donkeys, etc. After you make your way down the market, you pass the Inn and come in the courtyard where you find angels singing and Joseph and Mary with their newborn child. FREE (first Saturday of December)

POLK STATE HISTORIC SITE, JAMES A.

Charlotte (Pineville) - 308 S. Polk Street (I-77 south to I-485 east to Pineville exit US 521 south) 28134. www.ah.dcr.state.nc.us/sections/hs/polk/polk.htm. Phone: (704) 889-7145. Hours: Tuesday-Saturday 9:00am-5:00pm. Closed Sunday, Monday, and most major state holidays. Admission: FREE.

This site is located on land once owned by the parents of James K. Polk, the 11th U.S. president. Determined and stubborn, Polk entered the presidency with a clear-cut program. He set forth five goals, all of which he carried out successfully during his single term in office. The memorial commemorates significant events in the Polk administration: the Mexican War, settlement of the Oregon boundary dispute, and the annexation of California. Reconstructions of typical homestead buildings—a log house, separate kitchen, and barn—are authentically furnished. The Visitor Center features a 23-minute film on Polk's life and civic contributions.

Polk State Historic Site, James A. (cont.)

POLK BIRTHDAY CELEBRATION

This living history program brings back to life the Polk family of Mecklenburg County in November 1795, when James K. Polk was born into the family. Activities include a historic cooking demonstration, children's games and other hands on activities. (first Saturday in November)

CHRISTMAS PROGRAM

Come and participate in a day of Christmas festivities. Visitors see a living history vignette in the main house. Each building is decorated in the 19th century style! Come and learn about food and customs from Christmas in 1802! (second Saturday in December)

Cherryville

BEAM TRUCK MUSEUM

Cherryville - 111 N. Mountain Street (downtown, SR 150 & SR 274) 28021. Phone: (704) 435-3072. www.beamtruckmuseum.com. Hours: Friday 10:00am-5:00pm, Thursday & Saturday 10:00am-3:00pm. Admission: Small fee.

One of only three truck museums in the United States, this 7,500 square foot museum features a wonderful display of beautifully maintained vintage trucks. Located in an old-style service station with 14 trucks dating back to 1927, it is a tribute to Carolina Freight and its founder, C. Grier Beam. Visitors will be interested in learning that drivers were paid $12 to $15 per trip (during the Great Depression), which sometimes took more than a week and they had to pay their own expenses.

Concord

BOST GRIST MILL

Concord - 4701 Hwy 200 (off US 29 north) 28025. www.bostgristmill.com. Phone: (704) 782-1600.

Bost Grist Mill was established around 1810 (c.a.). The present building dates from the 1870's where the water wheel created 15 horsepower allowing the mill to produce 150 bushels a day. The Bost Grist Mill continues to use the same 48" French Buhr Millstone which was a prized possession in its day as (compared to local grinding stones).

SC Area

BATTLE AT BOST GRIST MILL

Surrounding the mill, re-enactors and visitors set up and walk around a Civil War camp. Real horses, tents and cannons are used to recreate an encampment scene. Vendors on site serving Breakfast, lunch, and various foods all day long. Admission. (weekend after Labor Day – **Note:** Held Every 2-4 Years - Contact for details)

ICE CREAM SUNDAY AT THE MILL

They are open for the public to visit and see the mill. Come enjoy a cone of Bryers Ice Cream on the front porch. Bring a pick picnic and sit under huge shade trees, relax and enjoy your Sunday with others. NO CHARGE ON SUNDAYS. (Sunday afternoons beginning late May through early October)

A TOUCH OF YESTERDAY

Come and take a guided tour of Bost Grist Mill and see the 1700 lb stone grind corn into cornmeal and grits. Learn the history of the mill and see articles dating back to the 1800 located around the grounds. They grind periodically throughout both days during the show. Door Prizes, Kiddy Tractor Pull, Gold Panning, Games, Lots of Tractors and equipment, live music, food, handmade crafts and much, much more. (first weekend in October)

BOST GRIST MILL CHRISTMAS OPEN HOUSE

The mill is decorated for Christmas with lights, greenery, and special added touches for the holidays. Light refreshments will be served. The mill is open for Christmas shopping. FREE. (first three weekends in December)

BACKING UP CLASSICS MOTOR CAR MUSEUM

Concord - 4545 Concord Parkway S (just one mile north of Lowe's Motor Speedway entrance) 28027. Phone: (704) 788-9500. www.backingupclassics.com. Hours: Open daily during gift shop business hours.

Camaros, Cadillacs and Corvettes (plus many more)...are displayed as you stroll down a memory lane of fine motorcars. A fascinating collection of antique, classic and race cars. Just 1 minute from racing mecca, they, too, have loads of NASCAR and auto-related gift items.

ROUSH RACING MUSEUM

Concord - 4600 Roush Place (I-85 exit 49, 10 minutes from Lowe's Speedway) 28027. Phone: (704) 720-4600. www.roushracing.com (Roush museums) Hours: Monday-Friday 10:00am-5:00pm. Special extended hours during May and October race weeks. Admission: FREE.

The team headquarters and team shops offer self-guided tour of historical photos, trophies and race vehicles from memorable events in racing history. Each of the shops has a viewing window. Sights and sounds can be seen and heard from inside the 60-seat theatre.

Ellerbe

RANKIN MUSEUM OF AMERICAN HERITAGE

Ellerbe - 131 West Church Street 28338. www.rankinmuseum.com. Phone: (910) 652-6378. Hours: Monday-Friday 10:00am-4:00pm, Saturday-Sunday 2:00-5:00pm.

Rare and unique artifacts and specimens constitute the museum's display of archaeology, paleontology, natural history and early Americana. The study and exhibits on Native American artifacts is superb for older elementary students studying early American history. Look for large fossils, giant shark teeth, beaded apparel and especially the masks and dishes from Southeast to Plains to Artic Indians. How was each culture different? The Natural History displays showcase full-size mounted animals such as polar bears, buffalo and mountain lions. All animals important to early natives. Each room chronologically links the stages of civilization and how they tie together - a welcome feature as parents try to sneak in a natural history lesson.

Fayetteville

FAYETTEVILLE MOTOR SPORTS PARK

Fayetteville - 283 Doc Bennett Road (I-95, take exit 46. Go South on Hwy. 87, turn right at the flashing lights on to Doc Bennett Rd) 28301. Phone: (910) 484-3677. www.fayettevillemotorsportspark.com.

Professional E.T. and Street E.T. drag racing that is sanctioned by the International Hot Rod Association is featured at this drag strip and sports park that also features stock car dirt-track racing April through September on Saturday evenings, as well as Streetcar Madness on Friday nights.

AIRBORNE AND SPECIAL OPERATIONS MUSEUM

Fayetteville - 100 Bragg Blvd (I-95 exit 52B to NC 24, left on Bragg) 28302. Phone: (910) 483-3003. www.asomf.org. Hours: Tuesday-Saturday 10:00am-5:00pm, Sunday Noon-5:00pm. Closed major winter holidays. Open many holiday Mondays. Admission: FREE. Fee for Vistascope or Simulator (age 8+) $4.00 each or both for $7.00.

Have you ever wondered what it was like for that first person to make the decision to jump from a moving airplane in order to serve his country? Well, now you may be able to learn the answer along with some other historically significant facts. The Airborne and Special Operations Museum is the only one of its kind and has newer, state-of-the-art exhibit spaces. The lobby exhibit features two fully deployed parachutes, a WWII era T-5 round chute and a modern MC-4 square chute. The mannequins look very real. Filmed in Vistascope, a high speed 8/35 mm process that presents a huge, stunningly clear image, the movie shown is designed to put the viewer into the exciting military action and to show military operations in a way never before experienced by the public. Similar to the movie, the Pitch, Roll, and Yaw, Vista-Dome Motion Simulator adds another dimension by physically moving a specially designed seating area up to 18 degrees in concert with the film. Suddenly a larger than life film of airborne and special operations becomes almost real. The 24-seat simulator provides visitors with an extreme taste of what the Army's finest are trained to do. Add to this, more extremely realistic dioramas of war action and camp scenes...and you've got the picture.

CAPE FEAR BOTANICAL GARDEN

Fayetteville - 536 North Eastern Blvd. (I-95, take Exit 52 (Hwy 24 West). Go approximately 5 miles. Turn right onto Hwy 301N (Eastern Blvd.) Go 1/8 mile. CFBG is on the right) 28302. Phone: (910) 486-0221. www.capefearbg.org. Hours: Monday-Saturday 10:00am-5:00pm, Sunday Noon-5:00pm. (closed Sundays from mid-December through February) Admission: $5.00 adult, $4.00 military, FREE child under 12. Miscellaneous: Nature Tales, Summer Day Camp. Treasure Hunt: each month, a new treasure hunt clue worksheet is introduced with different themes. Go out in search of numbered pine cones. Once completed, turn it in for 10% off a gift shop purchase.

Nestled on 85 acres that overlook Cross Creek and the Cape Fear River, this botanical garden includes numerous species of native plants, wild flowers, and majestic oaks. An authentic 1800s farmhouse and outbuildings are also on site, as well as nature trails, a Heritage Garden, a demonstration garden, and a large gazebo. In the Children's Garden: The Lilliput Labyrinth - based on the tale of Gulliver's Travels. The items Gulliver left behind are giant-sized, which sets the garden's theme of contrasting the immense with the miniature. Must see sculptures are a 15' swing, a 5' pair of eyeglasses, and a 17' chair. The Friendship Garden was established to recognize and appreciate ethnic diversity of the region through the exploration of our shared botanical heritage at a global level. Formed in the shape of a heart, the garden has seven beds, each representing plantings from each continent of the world.

HERITAGE FESTIVAL

Cape Fear Botanical Garden - Celebrate old-time farm life! Shell corn, scrub clothes, learn quilting and spinning, and have a healthy good time with refreshments and live bluegrass music! Hayrides, old-fashioned games, pony rides, and food. (first Sunday in October)

FASCINATE-U CHILDREN'S MUSEUM

Fayetteville - 116 Green Street (next to the Markethouse, downtown) 28302. Phone: (910) 433-1573. www.fascinate-u.com. Hours: Tuesday-Friday 9:00am-5:00pm, Saturday 10:00am-5:00pm, Sunday Noon-5:00pm. Open Wednesday evenings until 7:00pm. Admission: $3.00 child, $1.00 adult.

Fascinate-U began as the brainchild of two young mothers building educational opportunities for the area's children. Housed inside historic City Hall, this magnificent educational forum features a host of innovative role-playing and interactive exhibits that allow children to discover occupations such as banking, grocery, media, government, theater, medicine, and law. Come on in. You can touch and play with everything. In the mini-city everything is kid-sized. Children can go shopping at the Gro-Right Grocery & Deli, put on a judge's robe and pass their sentence-gavel in hand, respond to calls at the 911 Emergency Dispatch Center, and give the weather forecast at the WNUZ center. Let TAM show you how the body works.

FAYETTEVILLE MUSEUM OF ART

Fayetteville - 839 Stamper Road (I-95 take exit 56 (Highway 301). Right on Grove St, bear right on Bragg Blvd) 28302. www.fayettevillemuseumart.org. Phone: (910) 485-2121. Hours: Monday-Friday 10:00am-5:00pm, Weekends 1:00-5:00pm. Closed holidays. Admission: FREE. Educators: ArTrunks & Art Duffles boxes & bags with theme exploring artifacts. Read & Play Pouches are literacy tools for pre-K and K students. Each plastic carrying bag includes book(s) and a toy, puppet, stuffed animal, video or puzzle.

This museum offers a variety of unique and changing art exhibits, as well as concerts, educational programs, and workshops. The museum is on nearly six acres of park-like grounds and art sculptures. While most of the exhibits are modern, many may especially feature a different culture like Japan.

JAMBBAS RANCH

Fayetteville - 5386 Tabor Church Road (I95 exit 49, follow NC 53 east to flashing light, turn right and go two miles) 28302. www.jambbas.com. Phone: (910) 484-2798 or (910) 484-4808. Hours: Monday-Saturday 9:30am-5:00pm, Sunday 1:00-5:00pm. Admission: $6.00 adult, $4.00 child. Miscellaneous: Primitive camping at the Bass family ranch along the banks of the Cape Fear River.

A private zoological park and natural habitat offers tours of its extensive grounds which are home to numerous buffalos, llamas, deer, elk, cows, sheep, ducks, swans, and peacocks. The ranch raises Buffaloes, Deer, Elk and many other types of animals. It takes about 1.5 hours to walk through the ranch. You can pet and feed some of the smaller animals but only watch the larger ones. Scenic views and additional attractions include a Covered Bridge, Fort Rest, No Chance Gold Mine, Swinging Bridge, and the beautiful Cape Fear River.

CAPE FEAR REGIONAL THEATRE

Fayetteville - 1209 Hay Street 28305. Phone: (910) 323-4233. www.cfrt.org.

This award-winning theater has been performing elaborate musicals, classic dramas, off-Broadway productions, comedies, and children's shows/camps (Huck Finn) for over 40 years. Well known stars of the stage and screen are often seen performing here.

BEST CHRISTMAS PAGEANT EVER

Annual production of this modern holiday classic. This is the story of how the awful Herdman children learn the true meaning of Christmas and will delight children and adults alike. There will be both daytime school performances and weekend public performances. (runs two weeks mid-December)

COTTON BLUE FESTIVAL

Fayetteville (Laurinburg) - X-way Road. (910) 277-3582 or (910) 277-2585. Teams of mules hitched to a turnstile that powers a working pre-civil war cotton gin. The Cotton Blossom Railroad provides rides behind a real steam powered miniature locomotive. A shingle mill cuts wooden shingles, and fresh ground corn meal pours from an operating grist mill. Tour the historic John Blue House Museum. Live bands, food, hayrides, old-time games, petting farm, crafts, displays of early engines and tractors and demonstrations. Even an old style Sunday church service on the grounds on Sunday. Admission. (second weekend in October)

Fort Bragg

82ND AIRBORNE DIVISION WAR MEMORIAL MUSEUM

Fort Bragg - Ardennes Street 28307. Phone: (910) 432-3443 or (910) 432-5307. www.bragg.army.mil/18abn/museums.htm. Hours: Tuesday-Saturday 10:00am-4:30pm. Admission: FREE.

Dedicated to the glory and memory of all Airborne and Special Operations soldiers from 1940 to the present, and into the future, the museum houses photographic exhibits and artifacts but mostly real airplane displays outdoors. See the Curtis Commando - The first aircraft with jump doors on both sides of the fuselage. Used for Airborne operations from 1945 through the early 1950s. Skytrain - The C-47 was the workhorse of the Army Air Corps transport units. The C-47 carried 82d Airborne troops into battle at Sicily, Salerno, Normandy and Holland. The C-7 was used to provide logistic support (particularly in Vietnam) and support airborne training through the 1970s. It was even used by the U.S. Parachute Demonstration Team, The Golden Knights. See weapons displayed including: The Vulcan - a six barrel, 20mm-air defense weapon system which saw service with the 82nd from 1970-1994. This weapon fired on enemy aircraft during the Persian Gulf War. Also for viewing are Reconnaissance Tanks, Airborne Assault Vehicles, and many more.

PARACLETE XP SKYVENTURE

Fort Bragg (Raeford) - 190 Paraclete Drive (off US 401 W, 21 miles off I-95) 28376. Phone: (888) 4SKYFUN. www.paracletexp.com. Hours: Daily opens at 9:00am. Sunday-Thursday closes at 7:00pm. Friday-Saturday closes at 11:00pm. Admission: Basic (2 flights, flight training, gear and flight certificate) starts at $54.00. Specials include a flight t-shirt and DVD for $10-$20.00 more. Miscellaneous: Entire experience takes about one hour. Reservations are suggested.

Have you ever wished you could fly? Well you can! A new wind tunnel in North Carolina, called Paraclete XP, is the world's largest wind tunnel and opened in December 2007. While observers can watch from an observation level window, skydivers are taken to the training room to get suited up and learn the basic techniques of indoor vertical wind tunnel flight. Each person takes individual turns in the tunnel - with an instructor present to coach you. Remember to relax and enjoy this amazing experience. Kids are naturals and even parents learn easily, no matter how flexible you are. To commemorate this event, you'll receive a flight certificate and we highly recommend you order the flight DVD and t-shirt, too. What a rush!

WEYMOUTH WOODS SANDHILLS NATURE PRESERVE

Fort Bragg (Southern Pines) - 1024 North Ft. Bragg Road 28387. Phone: (910) 692-2167. www.ncparks.gov/Visit/parks/wewo/main.php. Hours: Daily 9:00am- dusk.

Home of the endangered red-cockaded woodpecker, a permanent resident of the Sandhills, this nature preserve features 898 acres of wildflowers, streams, and ponds, as well as over four miles of hiking trails, a beaver pond, and a museum with participation exhibits. A Sunday nature study program is offered each spring and summer. Inside the popular Interpretive Center: A 10-foot-high "wall of fire," a lighted photomural that introduces the role of prescribed burning in restoring the fabled longleaf pine forests of central North Carolina; An underground diorama where visitors can crawl beneath the forest to view wildlife that seek shelter there; and a large mural by illustrator Brooks Pearce that depicts flora and fauna in the park. Pushbuttons allow visitors to hear their calls; Another exhibit allows visitors to stir an old-time bucket of resin; and the nighttime diorama allows visitors to experience "Darkness in the Pines," "Ghosts of the Sandhills Swamps and Seeps" and "Things That Go Bump in the Night."

Gastonia

SCHIELE MUSEUM OF NATURAL HISTORY

Gastonia - 1500 East Garrison Blvd. (I-85 south to exit 20, New Hope. Follow signs to right on Garrison Blvd.) 28054. www.schielemuseum.org. Phone: (704) 866-6900. Hours: Monday-Saturday 9:00am-5:00pm, Sunday 1:00-5:00pm. Admission: $2.00-$4.00 (age 6+). Gastonia residents FREE. Educators: Print off online scavenger hunt ("Kids") before visit. Teachers can order Explorer Packs from the Schiele Museum Store that are packaged and ready for you to pick up at the end of your visit. Packs complement the programs and exhibits and help to provide continual learning long after your visit. Explorer Packs range in price. Miscellaneous: Planetarium (extra fee) shows. Half-mile Nature Trail (villages along the way). Gastonia is home to the WORLD'S LARGEST FLYING AMERICAN FLAG (visible for 30 miles from 4025 West Franklin blvd.)

Schiele Museum Of Natural History (cont.)

The largest collection of land mammal specimens in the Southeast is on display at this natural history museum. It includes six geographic areas of the state depicted at different seasons of the year: the Coastal Plain in the early summer, the Sandhills in early autumn, the Piedmont in mid-autumn, a cave in early winter, and the mountains in mid-winter. The Hall of Earth and Man encompasses the history of the Earth. Models, graphics, fossils, artifacts, and interpretive texts complement each exhibit and provide the visitor a glimpse of the Earth's past. Marine Touch Tanks, too. The 18th-century Backcountry Farm (located along the Nature Trail close to the main museum parking lot) contains a log cabin and kitchen, barn, blacksmith shop, woodworking shop, and several other outbuildings. The Catawba Indian Village contains a replicated prehistoric bark-covered house, a large council house, and two log cabins. We'd suggest coming for a group tour or Kids Club program. These are more engaging vs. exhibits behind glass.

GASTON COUNTY MUSEUM OF ART & HISTORY

Gastonia (Dallas) - 131 West Main Street 28034. www.gastoncountymuseum.org. Phone: (704) 922-7681. Hours: Tuesday-Friday 10:00am-5:00pm, Saturday Noon-4:00pm, every 1st Sunday 2:00-5:00pm. Admission: FREE. Miscellaneous: Terrific Toddler Tuesdays art or history stories, craft, song and tour.

Housed in an 1852 Greek Revival style old hotel, this museum features authentically furnished period rooms, a "hands-on" parlor, and changing art and history exhibits. The largest public collection of horse-drawn carriages and sleighs in North Carolina is also housed at this museum and a gift shop is on site. In the Carolinas Textile main exhibit, discover how cotton textile manufacturing transformed the Carolinas. Sights and sounds of the past combine with original objects, such as the world's longest running, original Edison generator (1884), the Loray Mill whistle, a ball gown and a baseball uniform. Most historical sites are old homes, not hotels, so this museum has more intrigue...wondering what famous Victorian folks stayed here and what they might have said if the walls could talk.

CROWDERS MOUNTAIN STATE PARK

Gastonia (Kings Mountain) - 522 Park Office Lane (southbound I-85, take exit 13 to Edgewood Road) 28086. Phone: (704) 853-5375. www.ncparks.gov/Visit/parks/crmo/main.php Hours: Daily 8:00am-dusk. Admission: FREE. Fee for camping

and canoe rental. **Educators: The Crowders Mountain program introduces students to basic geologic concepts, including the rock cycle, rock and mineral identification, weathering and erosion, and resource use. Accompanying the program is a teacher's booklet and workshop, free of charge to educators.**

Climb rugged peaks rising 800 feet above the surrounding countryside and watch raptors soar in the wind currents. The park includes two giant mountains: Crowders Mountain and Kings Pinnacle. The beauty and diversity of Crowders Mountain State Park is best appreciated on its miles of hiking trails. Hiking trails lined with wildflowers and mountain laurel lead along the ridges and to the summits of Crowders Mountain and Kings Pinnacle. Other trails are easier. Circle the lake on a gravel path or view aquatic plants and animals along a narrow creek. There is also a 9-acre lake, canoe rentals, hiking and nature trails and primitive camping.

Kannapolis

CANNON VILLAGE TEXTILE MUSEUM

Kannapolis - 200 West Avenue (Visitors Center) (From I-85 exit 60 and follow the signs) 28081. Phone: (704) 938-3200. www.cannonvillage.com. Hours: Monday-Saturday 9:00am-5:00pm. Miscellaneous: The Dale Earnhardt Statue and Tribute museum are in the Village, too. DEI up the road is the goal. Hands-on cotton exhibits are at the Levine Museum of the South and the Charlotte History Museum.

Once the world's largest producer of household textiles, the Cannon Mills name was synonymous with fine towels and linens. Feel the pride of the 25,000 workers who once occupied the nearby mill buildings as you view the manufacturing process video in the large theatre. The show will transport you inside the mill - right to the production floor. Now, experience the history of textiles through a self-guided, interactive tour featuring a hands-on demonstration of sheet fabric printing. See an antique handloom, 1,200 year-old textile samples and the world's largest towel.

Lillington

RAVEN ROCK STATE PARK

Lillington - 3009 Raven Rock Road (take US 421 east. Turn left onto Raven Rock Road, and follow it for three miles to the park) 27546. Phone: (910) 893-4888. Hours: Daily 8:00am-dusk. www.ncparks.gov/Visit/parks/raro/main.php. Admission: FREE. Fee for permit camping. Educators: The Raven Rock program introduces students to the geologic processes along the fall zone. Accompanying the program is a teacher's booklet and workshop, free of charge to educators.

Raven Rock State Park (cont.)

Raven Rock offers a variety of trails. Travel them on foot or on horseback (separate, undeveloped paths). A number of trails in the park traverse a variety of terrains. Raven Rock Loop Trail travels through a hardwood forest on its one-mile trip to the park's centerpiece, Raven Rock. Wooden stairs down the face of the river bluff lead to the base of Raven Rock where the river bank provides a place to examine the area beneath the overhang. A stone balcony along the way overlooks the river and the flood plains beyond. Other trails offer access to fishing holes and idyllic scenery. There are areas for picnicking and primitive backpack camping, too.

Lumberton

EXPLORATION STATION

Lumberton - 104 North Chestnut Street (I-95 exit 22 into town) 28358. Phone: (910) 738-1114. www.explorationkids.com. Hours: Tuesday-Friday 10:00am-5:00pm, Saturday 10:00am-4:00pm. Open until 8:00pm on Thursday. Admission: $1.00-$3.00 per person. Educators: Science, Spanish, Art and Music are offered on a weekly basis during the school year.

The Children's Museum contains eleven interactive spaces where kids can play educational make-believe. Dress up and play doctor in the hospital, milk a cow, teach a class in school, shop at the general store or watch ducks cascade down a waterfall. There's a separate play area for infants.

ROBESON PLANETARIUM & SCIENCE CENTER

Lumberton - 420 Caton Avenue (I-95 S to exit 17, Hwy 72 northwest past Board of Education Bldg.) 28358. Phone: (910) 671-6015. www.robesonsky.com Shows: Weekend public shows are generally held at 11:00am and 1:00pm. Admission: Varies depending on group. Small fee for monthly shows.

The science center is located in a one room schoolhouse and offers many hands-on exhibits and activities. The planetarium is located adjacent to the center and uses light, sound, and color to recreate the images of the universe. Some available programs of interest: Tonight's Sky (part of all programs); Space Station (NASA's exploration vision); Skytellers; and Apollo Magnus (pieces of the moon).

MUSEUM OF THE NATIVE AMERICAN RESOURCE CENTER

Lumberton (Pembroke) - Old Main Building, Univ. of NC at Pembroke (ten miles west of the intersection of U.S. 74 and I- 95) 28372. www.uncp.edu/nativemuseum/. Phone: (910) 521-2433. Hours: Monday-Friday 8:00am-5:00pm. Admission: FREE.

A very unique museum and resource center that contains 19th century artifacts, as well as arts and crafts from Lumbee Indian tribes plus displays contemporary Indian arts and drafts that represent Native Americans all over North America. Favorite family displays include an authentic log canoe and log cabin, Indian dress and music or video presentations. Many other items come from North Carolina Native Americans, with special emphasis on Robeson County Indian people. Particular focus is placed on the largest North Carolina tribe, the Lumbee. Today, the Lumbee number over 50,000, with the majority residing in Robeson and adjoining counties. According to local legends, the Indians of Robeson County are descendants of several tribal groups (three languages families - Eastern Siouan, Iroquoian and Algonkian) and John White's Lost Colony.

STRIKE AT THE WIND OUTDOOR DRAMA

Lumberton (Pembroke) - Adolph L. Dial Amphitheater, 638 Terry Sanford Rd. This 31-year-old drama depicts the life and mysterious disappearance of North Carolina Lumbee Indian outlaw Henry Berry Lowrie, whose exploits in the years after the Civil War earned him a reputation as the American Robin Hood. Admission. (910) 521-6287 (tickets); (910) 521-0835 (group rates); or www.strikeatthewind.com/. (8:30pm, Friday-Sunday, in July and August)

Midland

REED GOLD MINE STATE HISTORIC SITE

Midland - 9621 Reed Mine Road (U.S. 74 (Independence Boulevard) east to N.C. 24/27 (Albemarle Road). Follow N.C. 24/27 to Reed Mine Rd or US 601 to NC200) 28107. www.reedmine.com. Phone: (704) 721-GOLD (4653). Hours: Tuesday-Saturday 9:00am-5:00pm (spring/summer/fall). Tuesday-Saturday 10:00am-4:00pm (winter). Admission: No fee is charged for admission or tours of the mine. Gold panning is $2.00 per pan (April-October). Miscellaneous: Picnic area and easy walking trails wind past old digging holes left behind. The Lower Hill Trail features

Many industrious men made fortunes in North Carolina during the nation's first gold rush. But...it was a boy who started it all.

"Talking Rocks" that describe the mining activities. Educators: Their online Teachers Guide is very comprehensive covering History, Science, Math and Language Arts.

....workin' in a Gold Mine...

Reed Gold Mine is the site of the first documented gold find in the United States. From this discovery, gold mining spread gradually to nearby counties and eventually into other southern states. Mr. Reed's son found a large yellow rock out in the creek one day and the family initially used it as a doorstop. When a jeweler valued it as gold (a 17 lb. chunk), Reed and his fellow farmers began panning for gold during the off-season farming. Creek gold mining led to underground mining when it was learned in 1825 that the metal also existed in veins of white quartz rock. Portions of the underground tunnels at the Reed mine

have been restored for guided tours. The underground tour is so interesting! Pretty much everything you hear about in the movies, you'll see for real on the tour. A visitor center contains exhibits of gold and historical mining equipment. An orientation film highlights the first gold discovery and techniques of removal of gold from the earth. At the panning station, they will instruct you on the stages of removal of dirt and rock to get to the gold. Why are the ridges in the mining pan so important?

Mount Gilead

TOWN CREEK INDIAN MOUND STATE HISTORIC SITE

Mount Gilead - 509 Town Creek Mound road (Signs point the way south from N.C. 731 & north from N.C. 73) 27306. www.ah.dcr.state.nc.us/sections/hs/town/town.htm. Phone: (910) 439-6802. Hours: Tuesday-Saturday 9:00am-5:00pm, Sunday 1:00-5:00pm. Admission: FREE. Miscellaneous: Astronomy Night. Come view the stars at one of the last great dark sky sites in the Piedmont. Binoculars and telescopes encouraged. Site telescope will be available. Registration required.

Around A.D. 1200, a new cultural tradition arrived in the Pee Dee River Valley. That new culture, called "Pee Dee" by archaeologists, was part of a widespread tradition known as "South Appalachian Mississippian." Throughout Georgia, South Carolina, eastern Tennessee, western North Carolina, and the southern North Carolina Piedmont, the new culture gave rise to complex societies. These inhabitants built earthen mounds for their spiritual and political leaders, engaged in widespread trade, supported craft specialists, and celebrated a new kind of religion. The reconstructed ceremonial center includes the major temple on an earthen mound, minor temple, mortuary, game pole and stockade surrounding the ceremonial area. The burial hut contains an exhibit depicting a burial scene with an accompanying audio program. The modern visitors center shows a slide presentation and features exhibits of artifacts found in the area. A self-guided nature trail leads out to and past the reconstructed area.

TOWN CREEK HERITAGE FESTIVAL

Celebrating the Native American heritage of the region, features an authentic pow-wow with singing, dancing and drum. Admission. (last weekend in September)

Newton Grove

OLD MILL STREAM NATURE ADVENTURE

Newton Grove - 3225 Oak Grove Church Road (Old Mill Stream Nursery, southwest off SR 55 at Blackmans Mills) 28366. Phone: (910) 567-2305 or (800) 307-3793. www.oldmillstream.com/nature. Admission: $7.00 per student for hayride and tour. Educators: Download Activity Packets for four different lesson subjects.

Fun Filled Nature Adventures for groups. Nature Adventures provides educational field trips for school groups, birthday parties, scouts, and civic groups. Take a hayride through the countryside to explore a beaver dam, creatures, plants, and farm animals. Next, take a scenic walk on the beautiful nature trail. Pot a plant to take home and feed fish in the pond. Children participate in hands-on activities that correlate with the NC Standard Course of Study.

Wadesboro

PEE DEE NATIONAL WILDLIFE REFUGE

Wadesboro - 5770 US 52 North (seven miles north of Wadesboro, NC on U.S. Highway 52) 28170. Phone: (704) 694-4424. www.fws.gov/peedee/.

The refuge encompasses about 8,500 acres along the Pee Dee River. The diversity of habitats supports a broad range of wildlife species, including over 180 birds, 49 amphibians and reptiles, 28 mammals, and 20 fish species. This makes for excellent bird watching, fishing and trail hiking. The Gaddy Covered Bridge and the Griffin Low Grounds provide a winter home to a myriad of migrating waterfowl. Open daylight hours.

Waxhaw

MUSEUM OF THE WAXHAW

Waxhaw - 8215 Waxhaw Highway (NC 16 & NC 75) 28173. Phone: (704) 843-1832. www.perigee.net/~mwaxhaw/ Hours: Museum: Friday-Saturday 10:00am-5:00pm, Sunday 1:00-5:00pm. Admission: Museum: $2.00-$4.00 (age 6+). Miscellaneous: Nearby at the Museum of the Alphabet: The museum is divided into three major parts. History and Writing Development, Writing Systems, and Modern Alphabets. An average of 7,000 tourists per year go to the Museum of the Alphabet to learn about writing systems, unique languages, and many other things relating to alphabets and languages.

This museum collection contains historic artifacts that document the development of the region from the time of the Waxhaw Indians, for whom the region is named, until 1900. As part of the permanent exhibit, the museum shows a 12-minute introductory film that outlines the general history and important events of the region. Subjects include the first European explorers, early settlers, and the boyhood days of Andrew Jackson. Also the culture of the Scotch-Irish settlers who courageously forged a new civilization in the Carolina back county called "the Waxhaws" is remembered in this lasting memorial.

Chapter 5
South East

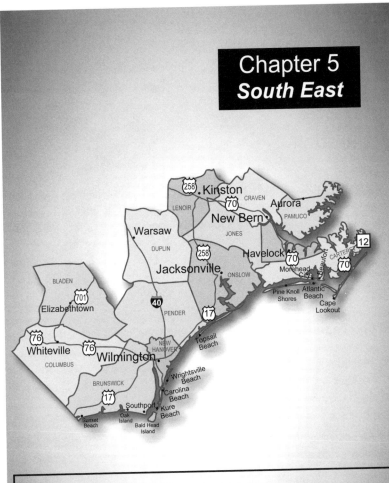

A Quick Tour of our Hand-Picked Favorites Around...

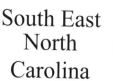

South East North Carolina

Along North Carolina's Crystal Coast, beaches, nature and history all wait to be explored. From the sands of Atlantic Beach and Emerald Isle to the history of Beaufort, this unspoiled stretch of the Southern Outer Banks coast is rich with beauty, heritage and activities in, on and around the water. The barrier islands take a curious southward curve, blessing the Crystal Coast with beaches that course east and west making it possible to admire the dazzlingly bright sun rise to greet the day and then slip into the shimmering translucent blue waters in the evening during a spectacular sunset.

The **Cape Lookout National Seashore** offers the perfect way to enjoy the ocean. It is not uncommon while dining at a waterfront café to see wild horses running freely on Carrot Island, just across the glassy waters of Taylor's Creek. The wreckage of legendary pirate Blackbeard's infamous ship, the Queen Anne's Revenge, rests in its watery grave just three miles off its sandy shores.

An eccentric history steeped in legendary tales of swashbuckling pirate adventures and ghostly encounters is the "feel" of the **Beaufort Historic Area**. Costumed guides narrate walking or double-decker bus tours of the town's narrow streets and historic buildings. You'll hear stories of pirates, sea captains, star-crossed lovers, and Confederate spies. Add more Pirates at the **NC Maritime Museum** and **Mystery Boat** tours. Which boat would you choose to use on a quest to find treasure?

A side trip inland leads to the quaint town of **New Bern** where we recommend the **Trolley Tour** first, followed by a stop at the **Birthplace of Pepsi** soda shop. Here you'll also find **Tryon Palace**, where colonial history comes alive (it's like a miniature Williamsburg).

Further south and back towards the Atlantic, Historic Wilmington & NC's Cape Fear Coast encompasses the city of Wilmington and the island communities of Carolina Beach, Kure Beach and Wrightsville Beach. Wilmington's picturesque riverfront emerges from the Cape Fear River. Across the river on Eagles Island rests the majestic **Battleship NORTH CAROLINA**, a restored World War II memorial. Lights, cameras and action await you at the **Screen Gems Studios** where you can tour the studio any time of year. Then take a walking tour or carriage ride through the downtown historic district of Wilmington. There are also other museums for children or railroad buffs, and North Carolina's oldest history museum.

Home to Carolina Beach and Kure Beach, Pleasure Island embodies coastal Americana. Its gazebo, Boardwalk, piers, marinas and amusement park add to its nostalgic appeal. Take in some natural history at **Carolina Beach State Park** where you can wind your way through nature trails in search of the rare indigenous Venus Flytrap. Step back in time at a Civil War battlefield and museum (**Fort Fisher/Fort Macon**), or while away hours at the **NC Aquarium**'s state-of-the-art ocean and Cape Fear River habitats.

North of Pleasure Island is Wrightsville Beach. Enjoy a leisurely bike ride or take a harbor cruise along the Intracoastal Waterway. From sea turtle-watches to exciting watersports, there's something for those seeking a slower pace.

SE Area

Sites and attractions are listed in order by City, Zip Code, and Name. Symbols indicated represent:

 Festivals    Restaurants   Lodging

Atlantic Beach

FORT MACON STATE PARK

Atlantic Beach - NC Hwy 58 (milepost #0) 28512. Phone: (252) 726-3775. Hours: Daily 9:00am-5:30pm except on Christmas Day. Fort area closes at dark. Admission: FREE. www.ncparks.gov/Visit/parks/foma/main.php. Educators: The Fort Macon program introduces students to the geologic process of barrier island movement and to the plants and animals that thrive in this shifting environment. Accompanying the program is a teacher's booklet and workshop, free of charge to educators.

Built between 1826 and 1834 to guard the entrance to Beaufort Harbor, this fort was used by Confederate and Union troops as a prison during the

Reconstruction Era, the Spanish-American War, and during World War II. The fort stands as one of the finest surviving examples of military architecture and fortification. Kids notice it looks like the pentagon with its odd, strong structured

walls. Explore the history of Fort Macon State Park in the museum room located in the fort casemates. Exhibits and displays acquaint you with the fort's history, and restored quarters offer a look into the lives of officers and soldiers. Admire the fort's powder magazines, counterfire rooms with cannon emplacements and wide moat that could be flooded to protect the fort during a siege. The fort features

BIG cannons were waiting for the enemy...

several original and replica cannons, a restored Hot Shot Furnace and Restored Bake Oven. Areas of the fort depict periods of soldier occupation using selected "talking rooms". Re-enactments or musket firings are often staged on the fort's parade grounds. If you climb to the top of the fort, you'll get a wonderful view of Navy installments off Radio Island. The large park has an inviting beach with picnicking facilities and summer bathhouse. It is a favorite spot for fishing, bird-watching and shelling, too.

NORTH CAROLINA AQUARIUM AT PINE KNOLL SHORES

Atlantic Beach - NC Hwy 58, 1 Roosevelt Drive (5 miles west of Atlantic Beach, milepost #7) 28512. Phone: (252) 247-4004. www.ncaquariums.com. Hours: Daily 9:00am-5:00pm. Closed only Thanksgiving, Christmas and New Years. FREE ADMISSION Martin Luther King Jr. Day & Veteran's Day. Admission: $8.00 adult, $7.00 senior (62+) & military, $6.00 child (6-17). Miscellaneous: The Aquarium also has a snack bar and a gift shop. Boat cruises, marsh explorations and other adventures (like "Get Hooked" fishing class), are available for a small additional fee.

This particular aquarium interprets waterways of North Carolina "From the Mountains to the Sea". The renovated aquarium is arranged in five themed areas: Mountain, Piedmont, Coastal Plain, Tidal Waters and Ocean. You can watch – and talk to – divers in the Living Shipwreck exhibit, meet an alligator or other animal face to face in daily programs in the theater and participate in a number of other fun activities. The aquarium's largest exhibit is the 306,000-gallon Living Shipwreck, featuring a three-quarter-size replica of the WWII German submarine, the U-352, which was sunk off of Cape Lookout. Around the sub are a variety of sea life, including a few large tiger sharks. Another popular new attraction is Queen Anne's Revenge, a 50,000-gallon depiction of the marine community and debris field of an 18th-century shipwreck discovered near Beaufort Inlet in 1996. The ship may very well be Blackbeard's flagship. Other cool finds are the Smoky Mountain waterfall, stingray touch pool and the amusing otter pools. Outdoors, the Aquarium has two nature trails, a marsh overlook, and a Fossil Hunt.

> **Turtle Trails is now online!** This project uses satellite transmitters attached to juvenile loggerhead sea turtles to follow their movements after rehab from the N.C. Aquariums. Travel the ocean and sounds with loggerheads as your guides!

Aurora

AURORA FOSSIL MUSEUM

Aurora - 400 Main Street 27806. www.pamlico.com/aurora/fossils. Phone: (252) 322-4238. Hours: Audio Visual Presentation: Monday - Friday 9:00am - 4:30pm, Saturday 10:00am - 4:30pm. Admission: FREE

Start your tour by watching the 18-minute video that traces the geological and paleontological history of the area in a setting that represents the formations as seen from the bottom of a mine. It's a great setting for kids to understand the evolution of geography and how the phosphate beds were formed that provide the fossilized bones, teeth and shells that are found today. There are rooms with exhibits of prehistoric man in eastern North Carolina, including the Algonkian Indians who met Sir Walter Raleigh's colonists in 1584. Another display has ceremonial pipes, shell beads, pottery, axes, and grinding stones from native villages. Newer displays compare modern shark teeth with fossilized shark teeth - and, everything you ever wanted to know about sharks. Kids, the perfect way to end your visit is to dig for your own fossils in the material provided from the nearby Phosphate mine. Find treasures of fossilized shark's teeth, coral and shells. The best part? You can take the findings home as a souvenir.

Bald Head Island

BALD HEAD ISLAND TOURS

Bald Head Island - Lighthouse Wynd 28461. www.oldbaldy.org. **Phone: (910) 457-5003. Old Baldy Lighthouse & Smith Island Museum: Tuesday-Saturday 10:00am-4:00pm, Sunday 11:00am-4:00pm (summer mostly). Admission: $3.00 per person includes museum, grounds and lighthouse. By reservation and type of tour. Miscellaneous: Bald Head Island Ferry - Ferry Schedule Daytrip: Cost is $15 per person round trip. Children 12-under $8.00. Reservations are encouraged. (Mainland Ferry Dock, Indigo Plantation Marina at 9th Street)**

Take a guided historic tour of Bald Head Island, which includes a stop at the Smith Island Museum, lighthouse and lunch or dinner. Old Baldy is the state's oldest standing lighthouse built in 1817. Looking for pirates? There's lots of history here.

Beaufort

BEAUFORT HISTORIC SITE TOURS

Beaufort - 130 Turner Street 28516. **Phone: (252) 728-5225 or (800) 575-7483.** http://beauforthistoricsite.org/tours.htm or www.historicbeaufort.com. **Hours: Welcome Center: Daily, except Sunday 9:30am-5:00pm (March-November), 10:00am-4:00pm (December-February). Admission: Welcome Center, FREE. Tours: $8.00 adult, $4.00 child (age 6+). Miscellaneous: the Old Beaufort Shop has many fun trinkets to browse and shop from - especially pirate stuff!**

Beaufort, an important Colonial seaport, preserves its colorful history with tours of town characterized by white picket fences, a seaside boardwalk, unique shops and restaurants. The town has been visited by patriots, privateers and pirates alike. Its residents have been fishermen, boat builders, merchants and skilled craftsmen. Tours of restored town buildings are hosted by costumed guides who also narrate tours of the town's historic district aboard an English double-decker bus. You'll hear stories of pirates, sea captains, star-crossed lovers, Confederate spies, and the ghosts of Old Beaufort by the Sea. Enjoy a walk through historic homes, the old jail, the courthouse, the apothecary shop, the art gallery and join in a tour of the Old Burying Ground. This is a great way to orient yourself to this seaside town. Ride on top, if you're taking the bus tour! Well done!

EASTER EGG HUNT

Children up to seven may participate throughout the historic downtown. (Saturday before Easter)

HARVEST TIME IN OCTOBER

Learn through living history re-enactments about coastal Colonial times. Held for nine days in late September and early October, students learn about life in Colonial times as they press apples, quilt, cook over an open fire, make herb pillows, churn butter, tie knots, and much more. (October)

COMMUNITY THANKSGIVING FEAST

Mid-day dinner is prepared by town restaurants and served for take-away or to enjoy at the Historic site. Fee for food purchased. Kindergarten students learn how early settlers lived and prepared for winter in a program especially designed for them. (Saturday before Thanksgiving)

MYSTERY BOAT TOURS

Beaufort - (Beaufort Waterfront or Big Rock Landing/Morehead City Waterfront) 28516. Phone: (252) 728-7827 or (866) 230-BOAT. www.mysteryboattours.com. Admission: Varies depending on cruise. Kids under 5 years old are generally $5.00. Miscellaneous: Diamond: Spacious climate-controlled lower deck and large, covered upper deck. Mystery: Canopy-covered.

Boy, this company offers a lot of choices...especially for families. We highly recommend the Sightseeing Harbor Tours or the Treasure Hunt if it's your first visit to Beaufort. Either way, make sure it's a Pirate tour. Here's some of the best for kids:

"TRUST ME", says the pirate...

TREASURE HUNT - search for buried treasures with a pirate on a deserted island. Children receive a treasure map and their own treasure chest to take home. Great for ages 4-12. Reservations required. $18.00 all ages.

GUARANTEED DOLPHIN WATCH - cruise inland waters in search of playful Atlantic Bottlenose Dolphin. They guarantee you'll see dolphin on your trip or your next one is free. $12.00-$15.00.

SHRIMP-A-ROO CRUISE - watch the sunset while feasting on all you can eat seafood. For the shrimp-lover families. $33.00/$19.00.

PIG PICKIN' FAMILY NIGHT SPECIAL - dinner cruise serving a buffet of NC pork BBQ, fried chicken and all the fixins. $27.00/$14.00.

SIGHTSEEING - see Fort Macon, historic homes, Blackbeard's House, fish factories, the wild ponies, dolphins and many birds. You might be attacked by a pirate ship and have a crafty pirate board and play tricks on the kids. Do you think he'll share his gold? Daily 1 1/2 hour narrated cruises daily at 2:00pm, 4:30pm and 7:00pm, April-October. $10.00-$15.00.

HALF-DAY ISLAND EXCURSION - visit Cape Lookout for shelling, swimming, surfing, fishing, hiking and birdwatching. Once on the island, take the beach "Mule Train" tour (see separate listing). $35.00/$25.00.

Really, the pirates were fun...
Does Daniel look scared?

NORTH CAROLINA MARITIME MUSEUM

Beaufort - 315 Front Street 28516. Phone: (252) 728-7317. Hours: Weekdays 9:00am-5:00pm, Saturday 10:00am-5:00pm, Sunday 1:00-5:00pm. Admission: FREE. www.ah.dcr.state.nc.us/sections/maritime/default.htm. Educators: The Junior Sailing Program (ages 8+) uses the fun of sailing and the competition of racing to teach sailing, seamanship, navigation skills and maritime traditions.

The Summer Science School has varied programs age appropriate for kids.

Exhibits take visitors from dugout canoes to sail rigs to traders and even pirates. Witness a giant collection of seashells, gently turn the ship's wheel of a real trading vessel from the

early 1900s, watch how whales eat, touch old boats, and feel old wood sterns and rudders. Touch computer screens teach you about commercial and sport fisheries and the "strange" seafoods you can eat in North Carolina. One of the most exciting exhibits at the Museum is artifacts of the shipwreck of Blackbeard's flagship, Queen Anne's Revenge, discovered in the late 1990s near Beaufort Inlet. This is one of the most significant marine archaeological discoveries of our time. But, is it truly Blackbeard's? Investigate for yourself as you view and read about the cannons and supplies found as evidence. In the Watercraft Center,

> The Museum conducts curator-led field trips to nearby barrier islands, marshes, tidal flats and coastal forests for kids of all ages.

visitors can observe the construction and restoration of full-sized wooden boats and ship models. On guided tours, museum staff can take you to the top where you can see horses on the Rachel Carson Estuarine Reserve and, frequently, dolphins in the harbor. This is a very interesting and easy to understand museum that is a good introduction to an old English marine town.

Carolina Beach

CAROLINA BEACH STATE PARK

Carolina Beach - 1010 State Park Road (Hwy 421 S) 28428. Phone: (910) 458-8206. www.ncparks.gov/Visit/parks/cabe/main.php. Hours: Daylight hours, 8:00am-8:00pm (extended during summer). Closed Christmas Day. Admission: FREE. Miscellaneous: Carolina Beach Skate Park is a huge skateboard park located inside Mike Chappell Park on Dow Road. Open daily.

> The popular Interactive Carnivorous Plants exhibit (Venus Flytraps) allows visitors to experience how these fascinating plants capture their prey. Now, venture outside... ...if you dare ;)

Venus flytraps, bladderworts, butterworts, pitcher plants and sundews are waiting to be discovered on the Flytrap Trail at this park. The easy, half-mile loop trail showcases these native plants in their natural habitats. These plants almost seem to defy nature by consuming animal protein. Carnivorous plants are forced to get their essential nutrients from insects and tiny animals. They're really not man-eating plants as shown in the movies! The park also has five other trails, campsites, a visitor center, marina and educational programs. The visitor hall offers maze and computer games. Visitors attempt to navigate a ball, which represents an insect in the park, around a maze without taking a wrong turn and being eaten by a carnivorous plant. Their universally accessible hiking trail allows persons with disabilities, the elderly, and children to enjoy.

CAROLINA COASTAL ADVENTURES

Carolina Beach - Bridge Barrier Road, near Snows Cut Bridge 28428. Phone: (910) 458-9111. www.carolinacoastaladventures.com.

Includes a small fleet of powerboats for fishing and sightseeing excursions. Surfboard, body board, boat and kayak rentals or licensed captains lead a variety of field trips and sightseeing and adventure programs.

ISLAND OF LIGHTS PARADE & FLOTILLA

Carolina Beach - Lake Park Blvd (Hwy 421). The Christmas parade furnishes exceptional night time electric displays, featuring floats, bands, queens, clowns, horses, Santa Claus and much more. The hour and a half parade brings festive fun and entertainment to all. Fishing boats and pleasure crafts electrically decorated with thousands of lights present a spectacular display on the Intracoastal Waterway. The parade of boats will cruise from Snows Cut to Carolina Beach Boat Basin and back. Bring your chairs, blankets and snacks to enjoy the fun time. www.islandoflights.org. (first weekend in December)

MICHAEL'S SEAFOOD RESTAURANT

Carolina Beach - 1206 N. Lake Park Blvd., www.michaelscfood.com. (910) 458-7761. Right after you cross the bridge over to Carolina Beach, look to your left for a wonderful seafood lunch or dinner. If you love seafood, try their Samplers or Fresh Catch Special with a bowl of Captain M's Seafood Chowder (award winning chowder in a rich cream base loaded with clams, crabmeat, scallops, veggies, potatoes, herbs and spices). If you're not in the seafood mood, try their salads or pizza. Entrees run: Light $10.00, Seafood Samplers average $20.00. Children's Menu: $3.00-$7.00 with variety of everything - even steak or shrimp.

Chadbourn

NORTH CAROLINA STRAWBERRY FESTIVAL

Chadbourn - US Highway 74/76 and Highway 410. www.ncstrawberryfestival.com. (910) 654-3518. Strawberry Jam concerts, strawberry spitting contest, parade, crafts, food competition and rides. Hot air balloon fiesta. (first long weekend in May)

Cherry Point

MCAS CHERRY POINT AIR SHOW

Cherry Point - MCAS. (800) WINGS-NC or www.cherrypointairshow.com. Military and civilian performances and a variety of ground events combine to make this a thrilling time for the aviation enthusiast. Largest air show in the state. (first weekend in May)

Currie

MOORE'S CREEK NATIONAL BATTLEFIELD

Currie - 40 Patriots Hall Drive (Hwy 210) 28435. www.nps.gov/mocr/. Phone: (910) 283-5591. Hours: Daily 9:00am-5:00pm. Closed November and December Holidays. Admission: FREE. Educators: Teachers Guide online includes vocabulary, reading, historical characters and quizzes.

A 1776 Patriot Victory! "King George and Broadswords!" shouted the loyalists as they charged across partially dismantled Moore's Creek bridge on February 27, 1776. Just beyond the bridge nearly a thousand North Carolina patriots waited quietly with cannons and muskets poised to fire. The loyalists weren't expecting this. As the loyalists advanced across the bridge, patriot shots rang out and dozens of loyalists fell, including their commanders. The loyalists surrendered, retreating in confusion. Wagons, weapons and British sterling worth more than $1 million by today's value were seized by the patriots in the days following the battle. The battle ended the royal Governor's hopes of regaining control of the colony for the British. It also raised morale for the Patriots and greatly influenced North Carolina to be the first colony to vote for independence. The park has two self-guided trails including the 1-mile History Trail (explains the battle and includes site where clash took place) and the 1/3 mile Tar Heel Trail (explains the naval stores industry during colonial times). Afternoon programs, talks, walks, and demos are held on summer weekends.

> The victory at the battle of Moores Creek Bridge resulted in N.C. being the first of the thirteen colonies to vote for independence.

SE Area

Moore's Creek National Battlefield (cont.)

ANNIVERSARY OF THE BATTLE OF MOORE'S CREEK BRIDGE

Enjoy a variety of activities including demonstrations of muskets, cannon, and broadswords, colonial music, surveying, cooking demonstrations, military drill, blacksmithing, and other activities. Two separate militia camps will portray the Loyalist and American troops who fought at Moore's Creek. Throughout the day scheduled weapons firings and musical performances are offered. A variety of children's programs are also offered, including militia drill, toy making, and surveying. Both days food is available in the park. Admission to all activities is free. (last weekend in February)

COLONIAL CRAFT & TRADE FAIRE

Moore's Creek comes alive with its annual trade faire. Historically trade faires brought together artisans, merchants, and traders to sell goods and share news. This weekend re-enactors demonstrate skills like gunsmithing, woodworking, blacksmithing, cooking, candle making, spinning and weaving, surveying, colonial medicine, and other activities. Some artisans have their goods for sale. Throughout each day there are special presentations of Militia drill, musket firing, and historic music. Food is available in the park this weekend. (first weekend in May)

INDEPENDENCE WEEKEND AT MOORE'S CREEK

Celebrate the nation's independence at the battle site that convinced North Carolina to be the first state to call for the final break with England. The American victory at Moore's Creek led North Carolina to instruct its delegates in the Continental Congress to vote for Independence. This weekend features a variety of activities, including militia camps, musket and cannon firing, colonial medicine, and other demonstrations. (July 4th weekend)

CANDLELIGHT TOURS OF MOORE'S CREEK

The park's annual candlelight tours will be held from 7:00-9:00pm. Tours will leave from the visitor center every 15 minutes, each group is limited to 30 people. Visitors learn about the events that led to the battle of Moore's Creek as they see the battlefield by candlelight. Tours are free but reservations are required.

(SE Area)

Elizabethtown

JONES LAKE STATE PARK

Elizabethtown - 113 Jones Lake Drive (NC 53 for approximately 40 miles, take a left onto NC 242 and travel north) 28337. Phone: (910) 588-4550. Hours: Daily 8:00am-dusk. www.ncparks.gov/Visit/parks/jone/main.php. Admission: FREE. Fee for camping, swimming and rentals. Educators: The Jones Lake program introduces students to the unique geology of Carolina bays. Accompanying the program is a teacher's booklet and workshop, free of charge to educators.

View one of the greatest geological mysteries of the eastern United States—the phenomenon of the Carolina bays. Adjacent to the Bladen Lakes State Forest and home of two natural lakes, Jones and Salters lakes, the 2,208-acre park is a nature lover's delight. Bay Trail is a five-mile loop around Jones Lake, offering an excellent chance to experience the habitats of a Carolina bay. Wander through dense vegetation and over boggy soil to view lovely lakeside flora. Large pond cypress trees, draped with Spanish moss, line the shore and grow in the shallow water. A variety of facilities make this state park a favorite for hiking, picnicking, swimming (cool, tea-colored lake and sandy beach), fishing and camping.

Harkers Island

CAPE LOOKOUT NATIONAL SEASHORE

Harkers Island - 131 Charles Street 28531. www.nps.gov/calo. Phone: (252) 728-2250. Hours: Harkers Island Visitor Center 8:00am-4:30pm. Park is accessible 24 hours. Admission: FREE admission and primitive camping (permit required). Educators: If you are a third through sixth grade teacher looking for a new way to give your students an exciting classroom experience, the Cape Lookout National Seashore Traveling Trunks Program may be what you are looking for. Transportation: Getting to Cape Lookout National Seashore can be an adventure! Several styles and sizes of boats are used as ferries with 16 passenger flat bottom skiffs predominating. Passengers are generally delivered directly onto the sound-side beach. The larger ferries, some carrying up to 80 passengers, make use of the docks. All are open to the elements. On windy or rainy days be prepared to get wet. See website for list of ferry services.

A combination of three beautifully natural islands, this area remains relatively unchanged since the pirate Blackbeard found safe harbor here 200 years ago. Accessible only by toll ferry or private boat, the seashore is the perfect destination for surf fishing, sunbathing, kayaking, beach camping and shelling.

Native wildlife species are the only permanent residents of the park. Except for the ferry landing areas, the islands are undeveloped and wild. Families can

A 4-wheel drive vehicle makes searching for that good shelling, surf-fishing or camping spot a little easier. If you don't have your own check with the ferry services for details on the beach shuttles.

observe endangered loggerhead sea turtle, rare waterfowl and a variety of lizards, insects, crabs and clams. Vacationers looking for less action are happy with beautiful beaches, shelling, and heritage attraction sites. Beaches of the Seashore are recognized by the Clean Beaches Council as one of the nation's "Clean and Safe" beaches. The beach does have picnic shelters and restrooms. What it doesn't have is drinking water, anything to buy or trash receptacles. Take all you need to eat or drink, sunscreen and bags to bring back shells, treasure and any trash that you generate. It's best to wear bathing suits under shorts and shirts when on "safari" here.

The original diamond-painted **CAPE LOOKOUT LIGHTHOUSE** and Keepers' Quarters still stand and the Quarters are available for touring April-November (Lighthouse conducts open houses only a few times/year with guides). Portsmouth Village, located on the northern end of North Core Banks, is the surviving remnant of the thriving pre-Civil War port that reached its zenith in the decade prior to 1860. Now it is practically a ghost town.

Another treasure of the Seashore is the wild **SHACKLEFORD HORSES** (www.shacklefordhorses.org, 252-728-6437). Besides small creatures, these horses are the only island residents, and they have been part of the island for more than 400 years. Brought to the Carolina Coast by colonial explorers, the wild "ponies" of Shackleford Banks descended from Iberian stock carried by Spanish supply ships to the island of Hispaniola. The horses are believed to have swum ashore from shipwrecks, and to have been left by an abandoned Spanish colony. Today, the federally protected herd is managed by a tradition of the annual roundup and pony penning. The herd's lifestyle thrives with limited human contact, socialization, and intervention. The park conducts guided horse watching trips, and passenger-only ferry services operate daily to take passengers for horse-watching and beach combing trips.

CORE SOUND WATERFOWL MUSEUM

Harkers Island - 1785 Island Road (east end of Island, neighboring the Cape Lookout Visitor Center) 28531. Phone: (252) 728-1500. www.coresound.com. Hours: Monday-Saturday 10:00am-5:00pm, Sunday 2:00-5:00pm. Admission: FREE, donations accepted.

Explore the waterfowling heritage of Core Sound through exhibits, traditional decoy carving and annual events. The museum is set on 16 acres of wooded maritime forest with a freshwater pond for native waterfowl and other wildlife. Interpretive hiking trails are open to enjoy. Carving demonstrations are offered at the museum each week.

Jacksonville

LYNNWOOD PARK ZOO

Jacksonville - 1071 Wells Rd. (off Hwy 258) 28540. http://lynwoodzoo.tripod.com/. Phone: (910) 938-5848. Hours: Friday-Monday 10:00am-5:00pm (general public). Admission: $6.00 adult, $5.00 child (2-12).

Home to more than 256 types of animals - land mammals, exotic birds, water fowl, hoofed stock and reptiles. During a tour of the zoo, which takes about an hour, visitors follow hard-packed dirt trails that stay shady and cool thanks to a natural canopy of trees and vegetation. The blackbuck antelope is a native of Africa; so is the serval. The capybara, the world's largest rodent, is from South America (looks like a giant guinea pig). There's also "Cousin Mo," an emu that hails from Australia; there's "Patton" (as in the general), an ocelot, a cat on the endangered species list; and good ol' "Buzz" a 6-year-old iguana.

Kenansville

CANDLELIGHT CHRISTMAS TOUR OF LIBERTY HALL

Kenansville - Liberty Hall, 409 S. Main Street. (910) 296-2175. Annual tour of Liberty Hall Plantation by candlelight. Guided tour of Kenan home decorated in 19th century style. Confederate encampment on the grounds. Reservations needed. Admission. (second weekend in December)

Kinston

NEUSEWAY NATURE AND SCIENCE CENTER

Kinston - 401 W. Caswell Street (On Highway 11/55 beside King Street Bridge. Off of Highway 70/258 Bypass) 28501. Phone: (252) 939-3367. www.neusewaypark.com/ Hours: Tuesday-Saturday 9:30am-5:00pm, Sunday 1:00-5:00pm. Admission: FREE.

Located on 55 acres along the Neuse River, this beautiful nature-based park is full of things to do - inside and outside. Inside the Nature Center, view over 40 different types of native and exotic animals, three large aquariums, fishponds stocked with catfish and a saltwater touch tank. Outside, enjoy the 18-foot climbing rock, nature trails, camping, fishing, and canoeing. The unique site also features a lower level cave with live exhibits focusing on the Neuse River.

The Health and Science Museum is adjacent to the Nature Center, resting on the Neuse River. The second floor is home of the planetarium which includes a 32 foot dome and projector that presents star patterns, constellations and video shows. This floor includes an observation deck with a telescope. On the first floor, interact with any of the hands-on exhibits, a butterfly garden, a hummingbird habitat, a mini-replica of the local hospital, computers and a giant "Operation" game.

CSS NEUSE

Kinston - 2612 West Vernon Avenue (US 70 Business) 28502. Phone: (252) 522-2091. www.ah.dcr.state.nc.us/sections/hs/neuse/neuse.htm. Hours: Monday-Saturday 9:00am-5:00pm. Admission: FREE

The Neuse was one of 22 ironclads commissioned by the Confederate navy. The boat had a wide, flat bottom resembling a river barge and was plated with iron armor. The vast pine forests of eastern North Carolina provided the needed lumber, and local carpenters served as shipwrights. Transportation problems and manufacturing difficulties delayed the completion of the ship. Once used, the new ironclad ran aground en route to an attack site. It was the Confederate navy's ill-fated attempt to regain control. Shortly afterwards, the Neuse was burned by its crew, resulting in a large explosion in the port bow, which sank the ship. The Neuse remained in the river for nearly one hundred years. In the mid-1960s, the hull was raised and transported to the property where it now rests. You're looking at real remnants of a real boat built for the Civil War!

Also at the site is the Governor Richard Caswell Memorial, which honors one of Kinston's most important early citizens. A native of Maryland, Caswell founded the town of Kinston, and served as North Carolina's first elected governor.

Kure Beach

FORT FISHER STATE HISTORIC SITE & CIVIL WAR MUSEUM

Kure Beach - 1610 Fort Fisher Blvd. 28449. Phone: (910) 458-5538. www.ah.dcr. state.nc.us/sections/hs/fisher/fisher.htm. Hours: Monday-Saturday 9:00am-5:00pm, Sunday 1:00-5:00pm (April-October). Tuesday-Saturday 10:00am-4:00pm, Sunday 1:00-4:00pm (November-March). Admission: FREE, donations welcomed. Educators: wonderful topical papers are available online that kids can use to research reports before/after they visit.

Before its fall in January, 1865, Fort Fisher protected blockade runners en route to Wilmington. It was the largest earthen fort in the South and had the largest land-sea battle of the Civil War. Inside, a large lighted map follows the lines of battle by water and on

> The NC Underwater Archaeology Center operates a small museum with exhibits on dive sites and maritime history dating from prehistoric to the Civil War and the present (adjacent).

the beach. The emphasis here is on blockade runners and is a great way to understand their purpose and successfully help to block trade between Europe and the South. Fort Fisher was a sand and wood design to defend against the blockade runners ...unsuccessfully. The lifeline of the Confederacy fell into Union hands. Outside, wayside exhibits mark the tour trail, including a reproduction of a big Rifled heavy Seacoast cannon. Artillery demos are staged quarterly and are a great time to visit.

ANNIVERSARY OF THE CAPTURE OF FORT FISHER

A large living history program featuring special tours and demonstrations interpreting the battle. Later in the evening the dramatic surrender of the last major stronghold of the Confederacy is re-created. A fireworks display follows the program. Small Donation. (third Saturday in January)

NORTH CAROLINA AQUARIUM AT FORT FISHER

Kure Beach - 900 Loggerhead Road (20 miles south of Wilmington, just beyond Kure Beach) 28449. Phone: (910) 458-8258. www.ncaquariums.com. Hours: Daily 9:00am-5:00pm, except Thanksgiving, Christmas and New Year's Day. Admission: $8.00 adult, $7.00 senior & military, $6.00 child (6-17). Miscellaneous: Teacher resources online. The SharkBites/TCBY snack bar, located on the food deck outside the Gift Shop.

The theme for the huge aquarium is "Waters of the Cape Fear". Visitors journey from freshwater rivers and swamps to saltwater marshes into reefs

Diver shows entertain questions like: Do fish bite? Do fish eat your hair?

and the open ocean. The centerpiece, "Cape Fear Shoals", is a 235,000-gallon tank with sharks, barracudas, and loggerhead sea turtles. "Loggerhead Legacy" features a loggerhead sea turtle in its first year of life (baby turtles, they grow fast!). Get physical with sharks - see the inside and look at their guts. "Seahorses" showcases seahorses and their pipefish cousins. "Freshwater Wetlands of the Cape Fear" is housed in a large conservatory full of box turtles (watch some sleep and some play), gar, catfish, alligators and water snakes. If you dare, stare down a poison dart frog or venomous snake and then touch a live stingray! Outdoors, in the Gardens, is a new exhibit about water quality. Look for Venus flytraps naturally found in this area (look closely, though, they're low to the ground and hard to find). Listen for Conservatory songbirds. As with all NC Aquariums, this is so colorful and engaging, yet easy to manage at a fair price.

PLEASURE ISLAND SAFARI

Kure Beach - (15 miles south of Wilmington) 28449. www.pleasureislandsafari.com. Phone: (910) 538-7474.

Guided eco-tours for small groups (up to 10 people) led by marine biologist/ environmentalist in a large dune jeep. Participants will explore the natural wonders and maritime habitats of barrier islands. Topics range from unspoiled salt marshes, dune covered beaches, to maritime forests, plants, wildlife, or ecology. Tour lengths range from 1/2 day to full day. Outfitters cater to individuals, families and small groups with nature tours and instruction.

ISLAND OF LIGHTS NEW YEARS EVE COUNTDOWN

Kure Beach - The Island of Lights countdown features the lowering of a giant lighted beach ball. A street dance featuring live music precedes a spectacular fireworks display to welcome in the New Year. Refreshments are available at this entertainment event for all ages. Free. For more information call 910.458.9023 or visit www.islandoflights.org. (New Years Eve)

Morehead City

CRYSTAL COAST JAMBOREE

Morehead City - 1311 Arendell Street (Hwy 70) (less than one mile east of the Atlantic Beach Bridge) 28557. www.crystalcoastjamboree.com. Phone: (252) 726-1501 or (866) 580-SHOW.

A large cast of talented vocalists and musicians entertain you with country, gospel, bluegrass, comedy, dance and tribute shows. You get a little bit of everything in every show. Similar to shows you might find in Nashville or Pigeon Forge.

HISTORY PLACE, THE

Morehead City - 1008 Arendell Street 28557. www.thehistoryplace.org. Phone: (252) 247-7533. Hours: Tuesday-Saturday 10:00am-4:00pm. Admission: FREE Miscellaneous: The Tea Clipper, a tea room and café, is located inside the site where visitors can enjoy a light lunch.

The History Place showcases the cultural history of this seaside region from the Native Americans to resort developers. Families can literally walk through the exhibits and visit an Old General Store, an early school room, Victorian parlor, and doctor's office. Indian artifacts, vintage clothing, period furniture, medical equipment, farming, fishing and even the carriage that well-known confederate spy, Emeline Piggot, was riding in when she was arrested in 1865 are on display.

CAROLINA CHOCOLATE FESTIVAL

Morehead City - Crystal Coast Civic Center. www.carolinachocolatefestival.com. (252) 247-3883. Features chocolate specialties for sampling, dunking, buying and competing. Pudding eating contests for the kids are held on Saturday, which by the way, involves hands-free eating. Also scheduled - a chocolate ice cream eating (hands-free) contest on Sunday for the grown ups. The winner will receive his/her weight in ice cream (200 lb. limit). Admission. (first weekend in February)

CRYSTAL COAST CHRISTMAS FLOTILLA

Morehead City - Morehead City and Beaufort waterfronts. (252) 726-8148. Yachts and workboats are decorated for Christmas and have a waterfront parade starting around 5:30pm. (first Saturday in December)

JULY 4TH CELEBRATION

Morehead City & Crystal Coast - Morehead City & Crystal Coast. (252) 726-8148 or (800) 786-6962. Fireworks displays at venues in every town. www.sunnync.com. Harbor cruises.

NC SEAFOOD FESTIVAL

Morehead City (waterfront) - Seafood, music, entertainment and the cultural heritage and traditions that surround commercial fishing begin Friday night on Morehead City's downtown waterfront. Weekend events include a road race, family fishing contests, surfing and more. www.ncseafoodfestival.org. (first weekend in October)

New Bern

BIRTHPLACE OF PEPSI

New Bern - 256 Middle Street (corner of Middle & Pollock streets) 28560. Phone: (252) 636-5898. www.pepsistore.com. Hours: Monday-Saturday 10:00am-6:00pm. The History of Pepsi Showings: 11:00am, 1:00pm, 3:00pm & 5:00pm. Admission: FREE.

The summer of 1898 was hot and humid in North Carolina. A young pharmacist, Caleb Bradham, knew he needed to make interesting cool beverages to keep

Area SE (sidebar)

the customers coming to his soda fountain. So, he began experimenting with combinations of spices, juices and syrups. He concocted a mixture of kola nut extract, vanilla and rare oils to make a soft drink so popular, his customers began calling it "Brad's Drink". As the sale of his new drink started to grow, Caleb formed a company to market it, and so Pepsi-Cola Company, located in the back room of Caleb's pharmacy, opened its doors in 1902. Sit a spell at the old-fashioned soda fountain and enjoy a refreshing Pepsi-Cola - surrounded by Pepsi memorabilia history and video clips. You can even buy anything "Pepsi" at the gift shop on site.

A good place to sit a spell...

NEW BERN TROLLEY TOURS

New Bern - 333 Middle Street (departs at corner of Pollock and George Sts, Tryon Palace) 28560. Phone: (252) 637-7316. www.newberntours.com. Admission: $15.00 adult, $7.00 child (12 & under). Purchase on trolley or at office.

See a famous communion set gifted by King George at Christ Church

Explore downtown New Bern and learn about three centuries of history during this 90 minute trolley tour. Learn fascinating details of a former royal capital of North Carolina. Hear stories about duels fought and Barber Jack. Stop in the cemetery where the inventor of Pepsi is buried. When you re-embark the trolley, you'll be treated to a Pepsi. What did archeologists find in the New Bern Academy lot? (marbles from school kids). We ALWAYS recommend trolley tours of historic cities. You'll find the kids like the amusement of the trolley so much - they forget they're learning some history along the way!

See where Pepsi was invented in 1898

TRYON PALACE HISTORIC SITE

New Bern - 610 Pollock Street 28560. www.tryonpalace.org. Phone: (252) 514-4900 or (800) 767-1560. Hours: Monday-Saturday 9:00am-5:00pm, Sunday 1:00-5:00pm. Closed New Years, Thanksgiving, Christmastime. Admission: $15.00 adult, $8.00 student (grades 1-12). Educators: Teacher's Guides, crafts and puzzles online (Fun & Games icon). Home School Days. Miscellaneous: An audio-visual presentation is available to understand the time and place. The sites to visit are within a one-block radius. Tryon Palace Theater - Come experience the dramatic side of history. You may see an 18th century puppet show, a 19th century play, or another engaging historical vignette. Tickets required.

Welcome. Do come in. The history of colonial America awaits you - tales of ladies and gentlemen, servants, slaves, craftsmen and apprentices. Within these walls, British rule flourished, revolution came, independence took root, and a new state capital was formed. Visitors see the rooms as they might have been arranged during the royal governor's rule. Costumed hostesses lead informative tours through the Palace and East Wing, which houses the kitchen and servant's quarters, and where craftsmen demonstrate fireplace cooking, spinning, weaving, etc. In the East Wing are the stables. If you're fortunate, you might find Governor Tryon at home, or Mrs. Tryon playing the harpsichord. On the South lawn overlooking the Trent River, some gentlemen may be playing bowls - and invite you to join them. Surry and other slave and free black characters share the stories of the large African-American population that helped to build New Bern. This is kind of North Carolina's "Williamsburg."

FOURTH OF JULY, THE

Hear the Declaration read from the Palace steps by costumed characters portraying famous North Carolinians from the Revolutionary era; listen to the Tryon Palace Fife & Drum Corps; and participate in thematic and patriotic craft activities. Fireworks that evening at Union Point Park. FREE garden/outdoor activities. Buildings require tickets. (July 4th)

TRYON PALACE HOLIDAY CELEBRATION

See over 200 years of American Christmas traditions. Admission. (December, month long)

FIREMAN'S MUSEUM

New Bern - 408 Hancock Street (building next door to the modern station) 28562. Phone: (252) 636-4087. www.newbernmuseums.com. Hours: Monday-Saturday 10:00am-4:00pm. Winter hours may vary. Admission: $5.00 adult, $2.50 child (age 6+).

Learn about the development of the 19th century fire departments at this museum that features a collection of early fire fighting equipment, as well as Civil War relics, and steam pumpers. Hear the story of Fire Horse Fred and learn why the Dalmatian is the "Fire Dog". A rivalry between two companies left residents gathering at a blaze in anticipation of seeing which company would arrive first - competition in fire fighting?

NEW BERN CIVIC THEATRE

New Bern - 414 Pollock Street (performances at Saax Bradbury Playhouse) 28563. Phone: (252) 634-9057. www.newberncivictheatre.org.

The theater presents dramas, comedies, musicals and even performances in sign language. Classics like "The Sound of Music" and Stagehands family musicals (ASL children perform) and Children's Theatre summer workshops.

COASTAL CHRISTMAS FLOTILLA

New Bern -   Union Point Park. See the rivers of New Bern light up with boats in holiday glory. Boats compete for prizes. Free. (first Saturday in December)

EASTER EGG HUNT

New Bern (Cove City) - A Day at the Farm. (252) 514-9494 or www.adayatthefarm.com. Enjoy a hunt, hayride and farm tour. Admission. (first two Saturdays before Easter)

A DAY'S MAZE

New Bern (Cove City) - 183 Woodrow McCoy Road (Hwy 41 north, then northeast on Woodrow McCoy). www.adayatthefarm.com. (252) 514-9494. Enjoy a seasonal corn maze, swinging playground and ice cream parlor. The hayrides follow a scenic route along Grape Creek. Riders may see the fox and her cubs entering a nearby den and view various crops growing in the fields. Admission. (September-October, by appointment)

FALL ON THE FARM

New Bern (Cove City) - Kirkman Farm, 5255 Hwy 55 West (between New Bern and Kinston). (252) 638-1847. Get into the fall feeling with a hay ride on a decorated fall trail and purchase pumpkins. The farm is a real working farm. They grow such crops as corn, soybeans, wheat, rye, oats, hay and pumpkins. Spend time helping to feed and pet some of the many barnyard buddies. Admission. (by appointment, daily except Sundays, September – November)

CHRISTMAS ON THE FARM

New Bern (Cove City) - Kirkman Farm, 5255 Hwy 55 west (between New Bern and Kinston). (252) 638-1847. Hear those sleigh bells ring and take a hay ride on the farm to see all the decorations and lights as you travel through "Moo Town". Don't forget the "Reindeer Pony" rides for the children. Admission. (Daily, by appointment, except Sundays, in December)

Oak Island

SE Area

OAK ISLAND NATURE CENTER

Oak Island - 20th Street SE & 19th Place E (end of 52nd St, park across from Yacht Drive) 28465. www.southport-oakisland.com/attractions/index.htm. Phone: (910) 457-6964 or (800) 457-6964. Hours: Seasonal, depending on programs and weather. Trails are open most days during daylight hours. Admission: FREE. Miscellaneous: Oak Island Lighthouse - Located on the U.S. Coast Guard Station Oak Island in Caswell Beach. Completed in 1958, it stands 169 ft. The main light is a four light rotating fixture, reaching 24 nautical miles offshore and flashing every 10 seconds.

Overlooking the marsh and Intracoastal Waterway, the Oak Island Nature Center offers a wide range of educational activities for children and adults alike. The Talking Trees Walking Trail: stroll the interactive trail as trees like the Dogwood, Red Cedar, Southern Magnolia and Black Gum "talk to you". The Mineral, Rock & Animal Exhibits: Included in the animal exhibits are a ferret, prairie dog, hedgehog, guinea pig, rabbit, gecko, and moon crab. The Center also has a large touch tank with marine creatures native to the Oak Island community. The walkway spans the Davis Creek and connects to an extensive bike and walking path.

Ocean Isle Beach

NORTH CAROLINA OYSTER FESTIVAL

Ocean Isle Beach - (800) 426-6644. A champion oyster shucker is selected to compete in the national oyster-shucking competition with hopes of going to the international competition in Ireland. There is also an amateur division competition. Featuring mountains of oysters plus live music, entertainment for kids, and an oyster stew cook-off. www.brunswickcountychamber.org/OF-nc-oyster-festival.cfm. Small admission for adults. (October weekend)

Pine Knoll Shores

AMERISUITES ATLANTIC BEACH

Pine Knoll Shores - Highway 58 at Milepost 5. 118 Salter Path Road. (252) 247-5118 or www.amerisuites.com. The hotel offers clean, comfortable suites with pull-out couch/bed, microwave and refrigerator. Each morning a hot/cold complimentary breakfast with fresh fruit and hot food buffet is offered. Walk across the street to the public access boardwalk to the ocean/beach. Travelers will enjoy magnificent beaches for swimming, surfing, parasailing,  jet-skiing, or shell collecting. Afterwards, come back to the hotel and rinse off, then take a dip in the warm outdoor pool. Several mini-golf and raceway parks are on the strip and some grocery, restaurants, and shopping are within a block or two.

Southport

NORTH CAROLINA MARITIME MUSEUM AT SOUTHPORT

Southport - 116 North Howe Street 28461. Phone: (910) 457-0003. www.ah.dcr. state.nc.us/sections/maritime/branches/southport_default.htm. Hours: Tuesday-Saturday 9:00am-5:00pm. Admission: $1.00-$2.00 (age 16+).

The museum houses a collection of memorabilia pertaining to the vast nautical history of Southport, the Lower Cape Fear, and southeastern North Carolina.

SE Area

Self-guided tours through 12 designated stations, or ask a knowledgeable guide to lead the way. Read Gentleman Pirate Stede Bonnet's touching pleas for clemency, before he was hanged. Test your knowledge for trivia, from the jeopardy board. The "River Pilots, Rescues and Aids to Navigation" section offers a variety of nautical instruments, including a 48" Coast Guard nun buoy. Bounce and rock on the 5' model of a turn-of-the-century "Joggle Board". On to the shipwreck "City of Houston" display of rescued treasures from the depths of the Atlantic Ocean, near the Frying Pan Shoals. Learn about hurricanes and listen to the weather forecast on marine radio; when storms are present in the Atlantic, the site tracks them on a hurricane chart.

NORTH CAROLINA FOURTH OF JULY FESTIVAL

Southport - Southport & Oak Island. (910) 457-5578. Parade, fireman's games, food and fireworks over the water. There is a naturalization ceremony in which people of varying nationalities become citizens of the USA.

Sunset Beach

INGRAM PLANETARIUM

Sunset Beach - 7625 Highmarket (Village at Sunset Beach, Sunset Blvd. N) 28468. Phone: (910) 575-0033 or (910) 579-1016. www.ingramplanetarium.org. Hours: Tuesday-Saturday 2:00-8:00pm (summer). Friday, Saturday only 12:30-5:00pm (rest of year). Admission: $8.00 adult, $6.00 senior (60+) and student, $3.00 preschooler (includes Science Hall exhibits). Save some money with combo tickets to Museum of Coastal Carolina.

This newer, state-of-the-art planetarium offers shows (with multi-media presentations), a math and navigational display area and a gift shop. View the universe around us as you travel through space and time on Spaceship Earth. See the sky the way our ancestors did as they turn back the clock to view the constellations as they were originally recorded. Leap forward into time to witness planetary alignments as they will be seen by our childrens' grandchildren.

MUSEUM OF COASTAL CAROLINA

Sunset Beach (Ocean Isle Beach) - 21 East Second Street (Go across the bridge and turn left at the waterslide onto Second Street) 28469. Phone: (910) 579-1016. www.museumofcc.org. Hours: Friday-Saturday 10:00am-4:00pm, Sunday 1:00-4:00pm (spring). Monday-Saturday 10:00am-5:00pm, Sunday 1:00-5:00pm,

Monday & Thursday evenings until 8:00pm (summer). **Admission: $8.00 adult, $6.00 senior (60+) and student, $4.00 child (3-5).** Buy a combination pass for Ingram Planetarium and Museum of Coastal Carolina and save. **Educators: Guided Nature Walks, Museum Scavenger Hunt sheets, Questions & Vocabulary curriculum online (Group Visits).**

What do seashells and polar bears have in common? The answers are in exhibits including extensive collections of seashells, saltwater fish, birds, wetland animals, sea animals, snakes, animal skins, Native American artifacts, and Civil War memorabilia. The Museum of Coastal Carolina features the natural science, environment, and cultural history of the Coastal Carolina region. Excellent dioramas include The Swamp, The Reef, and Waterfowl. Streams to the Sea explains how stormwater runoff pollutes streams and rivers from higher ground as it flows to the Carolina Coast. Another part of the exhibit is an outdoor rain barrel that catches rainwater from the museum roof to water the plants around the entrance - pretty cool recycling. The Legacy of the Loggerhead is a model of a sand dune with a mother loggerhead turtle laying a nest and also hatchlings emerging from a nest. Visitors may walk through the dune to view the nests from the interior or watch a video about the life cycle of loggerhead turtles. Ringo, the Brunswick oak tree has a new look and there is an aviary for live finches. There's an always updating Touch Tank with live sea animals, too.

Swansboro

HAMMOCK'S BEACH STATE PARK

Swansboro - 1572 Hammocks Beach Road (only reached by boat or ferry) 28584. Phone: (910) 326-4881. Hours: Ferries run 9:30am-6:00pm (summer). Admission: FREE, but a fee is charged for ferry service and camping or swimming. **Educators: The Hammocks Beach program introduces students to the life history of sea turtles, focusing on the loggerhead sea turtle. The program's content includes information about animal adaptation, the sea turtle's lifecycle, endangered species, natural and human threats to wildlife, resource management and stewardship. Accompanying the program is a teacher's booklet and workshop, an electronic copy of the teacher's booklet is available, free of charge, to educators.**

This State Park is a barrier island with 3.5 miles of pristine beach. Backpack and primitive camping are allowed, as is swimming, wildlife viewing and shelling. No bikes allowed. Sand dunes on the island rise to 60 feet above sea level. Largely undeveloped, the park presently offers a bathhouse with restrooms, showers and a refreshment stand and picnic tables.

Topsail Beach

SEA TURTLE RESCUE & REHABILITATION CENTER, KAREN BEASLEY

Topsail Beach - 822 Carolina Avenue (across from the water tower in southern Topsail Beach. 28445. Phone: (910) 328-3377 or (800) 626-2780. www.seaturtlehospital.org. Admission: A suggested donation is requested for tours or even a visit. Call for details.

> **IT'S ALIVE !!**
> Check out the TURTLE CAM. Go to: www.topsail-island.info and watch sea turtles go through their day.

Topsail Island has 26 miles of coastline. Each mile is surveyed every morning to identify sea turtle tracks and nests from May through August. The Loggerhead Sea Turtle comes ashore to nest 3 to 5 times during a nesting year (usually at night). She deposits an average of 120 eggs per nest. The eggs will incubate in the sand for about 60 days. The hatchlings emerge and immediately try to make their way to sea. Only 1 in 1000 hatchlings survive their first year of life. 20-30 years later, the female turtles return to their natal beaches to nest. Volunteers stake off and protect the nests of endangered loggerhead sea turtles. The hospital also cares for sick and injured sea turtles.

Whiteville

LAKE WACCAMAW STATE PARK

Whiteville - 1866 State Park Drive (US 74/76) 28450. Phone: (910) 646-4748. Hours: Vary by season. www.ncparks.gov/Visit/parks/lawa/main.php. Admission: FREE Educators: The Lake Waccamaw program introduces students to the unique ecosystem of this particular Carolina bay, focusing on water chemistry and the lake's diversity of aquatic life. Accompanying the program is a teacher's booklet and workshop, free of charge to educators.

One of the most unique bodies of water in the world also contains some of the most unique plants. This park houses the native Venus flytrap, as well as pitcher plants and sundews. The best place to view the carnivorous plants is along the park's Sand Ridge Nature Trail.

NORTH CAROLINA MUSEUM OF FORESTRY

Whiteville - 415 S. Madison Street (corner of Madison and Columbus Streets in downtown Whiteville, beside City Hall) 28472. Phone: (910) 914-4185. Hours: Monday-Friday 9:00am-5:00pm, Saturday 1:00-4:00pm, Sunday 2:00-5:00pm. www.naturalsciences.org/visinfo/forestry.html. Admission: FREE. Educators: Online Treasure Hunt and Exhibit Guides (Education /Activity Guides), Fun Stuff has coloring pages.

The North Carolina Museum of Forestry is the only facility of its kind to exclusively interpret the forest and woodland of North Carolina. Interpretive and interactive exhibits and the preservation of natural and man-made materials demonstrate the ongoing relationships of forests and people. Examples include: a collection of North Carolina wood specimens collected in the 1920s, forest-related tools, and giant prehistoric ground sloth bones collected in Columbus County.

Wilmington

BATTLESHIP NORTH CAROLINA

Wilmington - Battleship Drive, Eagle Island (junction of highways 17/74/76/421 across from historic district) 28401. www.battleshipnc.com. Phone: (910) 251-5797. Hours: Daily 8:00am-8:00pm (mid-May to mid-September). Daily 8:00am-5:00pm, rest of year. Admission: $12.00 adult, $10.00 senior (65+)/military, $6.00 child (6-11). Miscellaneous: Want to go to battle? Check out the Kids' section online for games, puzzles, coloring and crafts related to the Battleship and Navy life.

Commissioned in 1941, "The Showboat" earned 15 battle stars and participated in every major naval offensive in the Pacific during World War II. This self-guided tour allows your family to walk the decks where you visit crew's quarters, a restored bridge and WWII exhibits of crew members' personal experiences. A visit to the North Carolina is like a visit

Just hold that big gun barrel for a little longer Daniel...

to a small city. A crew of over 2,300 worked on board in the hospital, bakery, butcher shop, print shop, general store, dark room, movie theatre or armed forces. The crews slept in metal bunks stacked five high. Look at the recipes in the galley. Pumpkin pie called for 6 cases of pumpkin, 100 pounds of sugar, etc. Can you believe the guns could fire shells the weight of a compact car almost 23 miles against a target? Kids like the fact that you can actually turn and manipulate all of the small-to-medium sized guns on deck. Look for "Charlie" the alligator in the swamp around the boat. Maybe grab a drink from a "Scuttlebutt" drinking fountain or "gossip center".

BATTLESHIP ALIVE

Watch and interact with World War II living history interpreters as they bring the ship to life by enacting daily duties and drills. Included with regular admission. (last weekend of April/ first weekend in May/last Saturday in September)

MEMORIAL DAY OBSERVANCE

Remember those who gave their lives in service and honor veterans at our traditional Memorial Day Observance featuring a military guest speaker, an all-service Color Guard, a 21-gun salute by a Marine Corps Honor Guard, military band, Taps, and a memorial wreath cast onto the waters. FREE. (Memorial Day)

HOLIDAY LIGHTING OF THE BATTLESHIP NORTH CAROLINA

A naval tradition continues as the Battleship is dressed in lights from the bow to the masts and stern. Best view from downtown Wilmington. (nightly dusk to dawn early December thru early January)

CAPE FEAR MUSEUM

Wilmington - 814 Market Street 28401. www.capefearmuseum.com. Phone: (910) 341-4350. Hours: Monday-Saturday 9:00am-5:00pm, Sunday 1:00-5:00pm (summer). Closed Mondays, rest of year. Admission: $6.00 adult, $5.00 senior/student/ military, $3.00 child (3-17). The first Sunday of every month is free for New Hanover County residents. Learning Center: The Museum's Learning Center is a place of discovery. Hands-on, facilitated activities encourage families to explore a different featured theme each month. The Learning Center is open Saturdays 10:00am-4:00pm. Activities are free with Museum admission and appropriate for children ages 5 to 12. Parental participation is required.

For updates & travel games visit: **www.KidsLoveTravel.com**

See the Cape Fear waterfront as it was during the Civil War, complete with a diorama of the Second Battle of Fort Fisher (with sound and light shows). Explore regional ecology in the Michael Jordan Discovery (hands-on) Gallery. Meet a giant sloth or gaze at Michael's jersey. Make your own sand dune or peek inside trash cans. How can you make light on the beach at night without electricity? (phytoplankton plants emit cold light). A large Venus flytrap model provides children with an interactive view of how the flytrap works. Is it really man-eating? Cape Fear Museum visitors can

The ferocious "pretend" man-eating Venus Flytrap!

explore watercraft people have used to get around the Cape Fear in the outdoor Maritime Pavilion. Check out the Simmons Sea Skiff in their lobby, too.

CHILDREN'S MUSEUM OF WILMINGTON

Wilmington - 116 Orange Street, downtown (corner of 2nd and Orange Streets) 28401. Phone: (910) 254-3534. www.playwilmington.org. Hours: Monday-Saturday 10:00am-5:00pm. Sunday 1:00-5:00pm. Open most holidays. Admission: $8.00 per person - 12 months and under FREE. Miscellaneous: The Toddler Exhibit is a space designed specifically for the youngest visitors—ages two and younger—and their caregivers.

Nurturing Imagination to explore and learn is their motto. Be a check-out clerk or stock the shelves to learn about the food groups, math and sorting. Pretend cook and serve a meal at the International Diner. Swab the decks maties as you pretend to be a crafty pirate aboard the ship. Next, discover the properties of sand by pouring and sifting. Culture boxes store a variety of activities, games and books from around the world in the Traveler's Stories exhibit. The circus area is actually run by the animals, with a lion as the ringmaster, and includes a performance ring, back stage dress-up area, clown car and a circus train carrying circus props and musical instruments as well as a tent wagon with many different types of blocks and building materials. Put together costumes and perform on stage at the Star Maker Sound Stage. Finally, play with gobs of blocks…maybe build a platform. In the Outdoor Courtyard, kids can jump like a frog, fly like a bird, climb like a monkey, creep like a spider, or wiggle like a worm as they crawl and climb in the body fitness, Animal Adventures. It's always changing and full-time art and science educators are on staff to supervise hands-on art and science projects.

Children's Museum Of Wilmington (cont.)

KIDFEST DOWNTOWN!

Kids can ring in the New Year with multi-cultural countdowns, glow-in-the-dark experiments, noise makers, silly hats and more. Admission. (5:00-9:00pm on New Years Eve)

HOLLYWOOD LOCATION WALK OF OLD WILMINGTON

Wilmington - (Tours Begin Riverfront At Market & Water Streets At The "Ghost Walk" Sign) 28401. Phone: (910) 794-7177. www.HollywoodNC.com. Admission: $12.00 for adults, $10.00 for seniors, students or military. Children ages 6 and under are FREE.

It's "Lights, Camera, Action!" as local actors lead visitors on a name dropping, movie & TV extravaganza through one of America's largest living film sets; Wilmington, North Carolina! Discover why, with over 400 film credits, Wilmington is known as "Hollywood East." See where some of Wilmywood's biggest movies were shot, including; Teenage Mutant Ninja Turtles, Divine Secrets Of The Ya-Ya Sisterhood, or Weekend At Bernie's. Also, see real locations & actual sets where your favorite TV Shows, movies & mini-series were shot, including Dawson's Creek, One Tree Hill, and Matlock. Then, see where the stars like to hang-out while working, vacationing or living there. This 90 minute fun-filled walking tour will have you laughing and crying, and you better do it on cue if you ever want to work in this town again!

> **DID YOU KNOW?**
>
> Wilmington generates more film income than any other American city except New York & Los Angeles !

WILMINGTON RAILROAD MUSEUM

Wilmington - 505 Nutt Street (corner of Red Cross and Water Streets in historic Atlantic Coast Line Center) 28401. Phone: (910) 763-2634. www.wrrm.org. Hours: Monday-Saturday 10:00am-5:00pm, Sunday 1:00-5:00pm (April-September). Only open to 4:00pm and closed Sundays, rest of year. Admission: $6.00 adult, $5.00 senior/military, $3.00 child (2-12).

Climb aboard a steam locomotive and bright red caboose. On the FUN side are a Thomas the Tank Train play area and operating HO and O scale trains.

Educationally, they trace the development of railroads in the Wilmington area as well as the careers of famous people who were involved with railroads, such as Thomas Edison and George Pullman. Learn about Wilmington's role as the center of railroad history along the coast. There are model exhibits of the Atlantic Coastline's Carolina routes from the 1940s and 50s.

WILMINGTON SPORTS

WILMINGTON HAMMERHEADS

www.wilmingtonhammerheads.com. Enjoy exciting USL-2 soccer action by this pro team each year from March through August.

WILMINGTON SEA DAWGS

www.goseadawgs.com. The Sea Dawgs are proud to be the newest professional sports organization in Wilmington, NC. The Sea Dawgs completed their inaugural professional season by winning the division making it all the way to the league "Final Four." For ticket information call (910) 256-2565. Schwartz Center .

CAPE FEAR RIVERBOATS

Wilmington - (docked at the foot of Market and Water Streets at Riverfront Park) 28402. Phone: (910) 343-1611. www.cfrboats.com.

Cruise into Wilmington's historic past aboard the Cape Fear River tour boats. Vintage WWII Navy launch boats offer cruises and taxi service to the Battleship NC and around the riverfront. The Henrietta III is available for sightseeing, dinner and fall nature cruises.

CAPE FEAR SERPENTARIUM

Wilmington - 20 Orange Street (historic downtown where Orange St. meets the Cape Fear River) 28402. Phone: (910) 762-1669. www.capefearserpentarium.com. Hours: Monday-Friday 11:00am-5:00pm, Saturday and Sunday until 6:00pm. Admission: $8.00 general (age 2+). Educators: Lesson plans and games online. See a new display of fantastic African tribal artifacts. See a real voodoo witch doctor's ceremonial costume, tribal swords and spears.

The site features 80 species of snakes (most of them venomous) from around the world, a Nile crocodile and an 8-foot water monitor lizard. The new 50-foot crocodile enclosure holds 2,000 gallons of water to house a very large crocodile. In addition to vipers, king cobras, Australian taipans, and long pythons, the facility features the world's largest collection of 30 bushmasters, the rarest venomous snakes on earth. All slither and slide here.

THALIAN ASSOCIATION CHILDREN'S THEATRE

Wilmington - 120 S. Second Street (Hannah Block 2nd Street Stage, Community Arts Center) 28402. Phone: (910) 251-1788. www.thalian.org.

The Thalian Association Children's Theatre (TACT) stages four productions a year. Dozens of local children get into the act for the Thalian Association Children's Theatre productions like Beauty and the Beast or Christmas-themed juvenile productions.

WILMINGTON TROLLEY COMPANY

Wilmington - (tours depart from Dock & Water Streets) 28402. Phone: (910) 763-4483. www.wilmingtontrolley.com. Admission: $11.00 adult, $5.00 child.

> The Cape Fear Historic Byway (www.ncdot.org) travels some of this route noted for its unique, exceptional historical, cultural or scenic characteristics.

The 45 minute narrated tour weaves through the bumpy brick laid streets as the guide gives life to the homes, people and events that give the town its character. The eight-mile sightseeing tour includes passing by mansions, haunted homes, TV & Movie locations, museums, birthplaces of famous locals, Civil War shipyards and some African-American historical sites. Note: Holiday Trolley Tours begin after Thanksgiving through Christmas.

AIRLIE GARDENS

Wilmington - 300 Airlie Road   28403. www.airliegardens.org. Phone: (910) 798-7564. Hours: Daily 9:00am-5:00pm. Closed winter Sundays. Open later in the spring bloom season. Admission: $3.00-$5.00 (age 6+).

The Butterfly House is here! Many colorful native species of butterflies take flight inside an open-air greenhouse that is open to visitors. Educational plaques focus on the butterfly life cycle and how to create your own backyard butterfly garden. The site is a combination of formal gardens, wildlife, historic structures, walking trails, sculptures, views of Bradley Creek, 10-acres of freshwater lakes, and the grandeur of the 462-year-old Airlie Oak. The Gardens are known for a collection of over 100,000 azaleas and countless camellia cultivars, which bloom throughout the winter and early spring. Displays around the Airlie Oak, Pergola Garden, and other areas bloom with continuous color year-round, as the displays are changed seasonally. While visiting, you will be able to set your own pace in the self-guided walking tour.

ENCHANTED AIRLIE: A HOLIDAY LIGHT EXTRAVAGANZA

One of the largest lighting displays along the NC Coast. 40 holiday events all month long (late November - early January)

JUNGLE RAPIDS FAMILY FUN PARK

Wilmington - 5320 Oleander Drive (I-40 becomes 132 College Road. Left on Oleander Drive (US76), one mile on right) 28403. www.junglerapids.com. Phone: (910) 791-0666. Hours: Opens at 10:00am daily. Water attractions open, seasonally, at 11:00am. Admission: Average $6.50 per person per game/activity. Range of $17.00-$24.00 for waterpark. Miscellaneous: Concessions, floats and gift shop on premises.

This large amusement park is home to a million gallon wave pool, speed slides, tube slides and body slides, a lazy river, and a large kids' splash pool. Some of the new theme tube rides are: Sidewinder (half-pipe) and Super Bowl ("toilet bowl") rides. Inside there's a large climbing wall, laser tag, playground, arcade, and café. Also outside are the go-kart track and jungle mini-golf.

TREGEMBO ANIMAL PARK

Wilmington - 5811 Carolina Beach Road 28403. www.tregemboanimalpark.com. Phone: (910) 791-0472. Hours: Open daily 9:00am-5:00pm (March - November). Admission:$8.00 adult, $6.00 child (2-12). Miscellaneous: large gift shop and petting zoo area.

Formerly known as the Tote-Em-In Zoo, Tregembo Animal Park carries on a family tradition that goes back over fifty years. Situated on five acres that create a forest-like atmosphere, this zoo features walkways that allow closeup observation of over 100 birds, mammals, and reptiles. The Tregembos have expanded and updated the zoo to create habitats for their animals from around the world. There are some of the familiar zoo favorites like Clyde, their 24-year-old camel, a lion named Simba and Ben the bear, along with some exotic new additions including a giraffe, a zebra and a group of ring-tailed lemurs that reside on their very own Lemur Island. Kids will have a great time feeding the ducks and goats, offering peanuts to the monkeys and watching their amusing primate antics.

SE Area

SCREEN GEMS STUDIOS / EUE TOURS

Wilmington - 1223 North Twenty-Third Street (off US 17/74, outskirts of downtown) 28405. Phone: (910) 343-3433. www.screengemsstudios.com. Admission: $12.00 adult, $10.00 students w/ ID/ military, $8.00 senior, $5.00 child (5-12).

This is the largest movie-making studio facility east of Hollywood (a.k.a. "Hollywood East") - and your family can tour it! Filmmakers like the mild

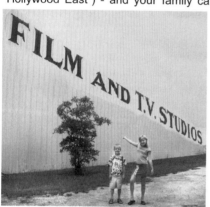

Lights...Camera...Action ! So many fun, unique things to see here...

climate, beautiful beaches, diverse architecture, varied landscapes and history along the Cape Fear River. The guided tour includes a visit to the sound stages, prop warehouses, and sets from current television series taped here. Most of the props you see are real. Spend some time in the kitchen, even the frig has real empty food cartons (companies have to authorize brand name use – it's called product placement). How do they use showers and kitchen sinks without the water hooked up? See a stairway to nowhere. Tour a locker room in a pretend high school or the many bedrooms on set. The tour changes as productions change so each one is a little different. Visit the actual set of the current WB hit show. The studio is always adding new props and items from the movies to Stage 1, which consists of items such as a jail cell (from "Matlock"), a coffin, electric chair, and lighthouse (from "Muppets From Space"), a "MINE" stamping machine (from "Elmo in Grouchland"), and set pieces from the "Dawson's Creek" series. A taste of "behind-the-scenes" Hollywood.

POPLAR GROVE PLANTATION

Wilmington - 10200 US 17 North (10 miles north of Wilmington) 28411. Phone: (910) 686-9518. www.poplargrove.com. Hours: Monday-Saturday 9:00am-5:00pm, Sunday Noon-5:00pm. Closed Easter Sunday and Thanksgiving Day. Closed the week of Christmas, reopens first Monday in February. Admission: $8.00 adult, $7.00 senior/ military, $5.00 child (6-15). Miscellaneous: Picnic area, restaurant and playground.

"A peanut here, a peanut there, pretty soon it adds up to some serious peanuts." Featuring outbuildings and crafts typical of an 1800s working community, this peanut plantation features a house, farmer's cabin, blacksmith's shop, and a peanut/agricultural exhibit building. Some of the discoveries made from the peanut were peanut butter, paint, salves, bleach, tan remover, wood filler, washing powder, metal polish, paper ink, plastics, shaving cream, rubbing oil, linoleum, shampoo, axle grease and others. Because of George Washington Carver, more farmers in North Carolina started planting peanuts instead of cotton. Today, peanuts are North Carolina's fifth largest cash crop. In the craft shops you can learn about basket making and weaving. They also have geese, goats, sheep, chickens and turkeys, and horses.

CHRISTMAS OPEN HOUSE

Sip some yuletide punch and nibble on a Christmas cookie in the warmth of a "Victorian Christmas" Manor House. You'll be back in antebellum times; stroll the decorated plantation, see the blacksmith or weaver creating their treasures, or visit the farm animals. FREE. (first Sunday in December)

NORTH CAROLINA AZALEA FESTIVAL

Wilmington - The Festival is a celebration of Wilmington's exceptional artwork, gardens, rich history and culture during its five days of entertainment that includes: a parade, street fair, circus, concerts, pageantry, and all that is Southern. Call (910) 794-4650 for more information. Various Locations. www.ncazaleafestival.org (five days in April)

JULY 4TH CELEBRATION

Wilmington - Riverfront, downtown. (910) 251-5797. Fireworks launched from the Battleship NC. Battleship Blast. Harbor cruises for fee. Best view from downtown. FREE.

WOODEN BOAT FESTIVAL

Wilmington - Presented by the CFCC Boat Building program, the festival serves as an annual celebration of the tradition and craft of wooden boat building. CFCC's wooden boat festival attracts thousands of visitors every year. This year, the event will feature over 50 wooden boats, including kayaks, skiffs, and boats from the Simmons Sea Skiff Club. Students in CFCC's Boat Building program will exhibit their own work and conduct demonstrations of traditional boat building techniques like bending wood using steam. Build Your Own Boat! If you have ever wanted to build your own boat, now is your chance! Cape Fear Comm. College Campus; Riverfront, Water Street. FREE for spectators. www.cfcc.edu/news/stories/boatfest/boatfest.htm (last Saturday in July)

RIVERFEST

Wilmington - Downtown Wilmington, Riverside - Water Street. Riverfest celebrates life and culture on the Cape Fear River with a variety of family-friendly events and activities, including a street fair, outdoor entertainment, ship tours, the Invasion of the Pirates Flotilla, and fireworks. www.wilmingtonriverfest.com. For more information call (910) 452-6862. (first long weekend in October)

COLONIAL CHRISTMAS

Wilmington -   Burgwin-Wright House Museum. www.burgwinwrighthouse.com. 224 Market Street. The house is decorated in the 1700's Christmas tradition during this two day event. Visitors are entertained by musicians playing 18th century music, food in colonial times is held in the colonial kitchen, hot wassail is served. A colonial surgeon is also available to demonstrate life during the colonial period, colonial dancers in authentic costumes dance and see weaving and spinning in the craft room above the kitchen. The old dungeon can be viewed in the cellar area. Admission. (second or third weekend before Christmas in December)

WORLD'S LARGEST LIVING CHRISTMAS TREE

Wilmington - Hilton Park, US Hwy 117 & Castle Hayne Rd. www.wilmingtonrecreation.com. The tree is lit the first weekend in December followed by holiday entertainment and Santa visits throughout the month. (month long in December)

Wrightsville Beach

WRIGHTSVILLE BEACH MUSEUM OF HISTORY

Wrightsville Beach - 303 West Salisbury Street 28480. www.wbmuseum.com. Phone: (910) 256-2569. Hours: Tuesday-Friday 10:00am-4:00pm, Saturday Noon-5:00pm, Sunday 1:00-5:00pm. Admission: $3.00 adult (age 13+).

The Museum is designed to reflect how life was lived in a typical home on the Beach, and throughout the community. One room is dedicated to the display of various exhibits pertaining to the area's history. At any one time you can catch exhibits on the history of the barrier islands, Wrightsville Beach and the Civil War, Hurricane Hazel, trolleys, surfing and Lumina Pavilion. The museum's centerpiece--a twelve foot model of Wrightsville Beach circa 1910. Couples dance at Lumina to the music of Benny Goodman. A young lady emerges from

For updates & travel games visit: **www.KidsLoveTravel.com**

the bathhouse sporting her new bathing suit. The trolley stops, dropping off its first passenger of the day to Wrightsville Beach.

WRIGHTSVILLE BEACH SCENIC CRUISES & WATER TAXI

Wrightsville Beach - (across from Blockade Runner resort) 28480. Phone: (910) 200-4002. www.capefearnaturalist.com. Admission: $20.00-25.00 adult, $5.00 -$10.00 child.

Narrated cruises around Harbor Island and nature excursions include funny stories about people who have anchored here. Also, hear stories about hurricanes and the story about a house with natural air-conditioning. See spots where movies have been filmed and famous stars

live. Treasure Island is here (where Blackbeard hid his treasures). Someone has since found the Spanish gold but others still look for more. Go under a drawbridge and then learn the amusing story of the "Palm Tree Island" parking meter.

<u>NATURE EXCURSION WITH MARINE BIOLOGIST</u>: This eco-minded tour explores Masonboro Island, NC. Masonboro Island is state owned wildlife sanctuary area. Here visitors, guided by a trained naturalist, can experience first hand the pristine ocean beaches, dunes and saltmarsh eco-system. Shelling trips leave at 10:00am. 1.5 hours. Adult $35.00.

CAPE FEAR KITE FESTIVAL

Wrightsville Beach - Shell Island Resort. Come watch as they paint the Cape Fear Sky! Flyers from all over join in for the Annual Cape Fear Kite Festival, held on Wrightsville Beach, in front of Shell Island Oceanfront Suites. See the sky filled with color from countless kites of unbelievable sizes and styles! Free. www.capefearkitefestival.com. (first weekend in November)

NORTH CAROLINA HOLIDAY FLOTILLA

Wrightsville Beach - Banks Channel. (800) 222-4757. A floating parade of brightly lit and wildly decorated boats of all shapes and sizes combine with a fireworks display at the beginning. A holiday fair, children's art show, rides, food and performing artists add to the festivities. (Saturday after Thanksgiving in November)

BLOCKADE RUNNER BEACH RESORT

Wrightsville Beach - 275 Waynick Blvd. www.blockade-runner.com. (910) 256-2251 or (800) 541-1161 or Located right on Wrightsville Beach Island, the resort fronts the Atlantic Ocean with a sandy beach and an Intracoastal Waterway on the other side. The largest guest rooms on the coast of North Carolina also have refrigerator wet bars in every room. The "SeaEscape" beach snack bar is surrounded by beach volleyball, sunbathing, surfing and swimming. A heated indoor channel leads to a heated outdoor pool, jacuzzi and sauna. They seasonally offer "Sand Campers" day and night activity programs. Average $150 per night w/ some rates starting at $99.00! Complimentary full American hot breakfast weekdays.

The sandy beach was great !

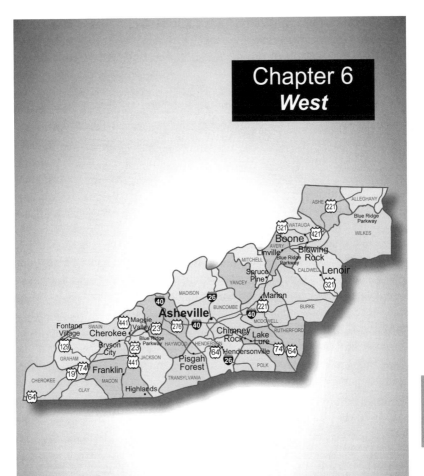

Chapter 6
West

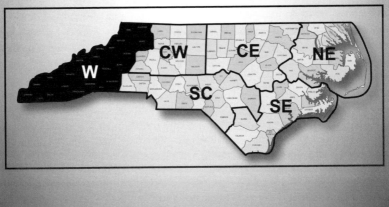

A Quick Tour of our Hand-Picked Favorites Around...

Western North Carolina

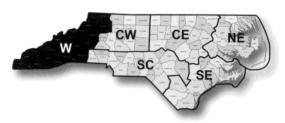

The Appalachian mountain chain runs through the western part of the state, forming the peaks and valleys of the region. The Great Smoky Mountains in southwestern North Carolina are one of the country's top natural destinations, and visitors can enjoy 250 miles of the world-famous Blue Ridge Parkway winding through North Carolina's mountains. Ride both a train and a ferris wheel at one park – **Tweetsie Railroad**. Traveling the Parkway in the rainy spring or fall months, you might feel you're on a cloud at **Grandfather Mountain** with its famous Mile High Swinging Bridge. Next, prepare to be elevated at **Chimney Rock**! Made famous in the movie *The Last of the Mohicans*, traverse a cool tunnel and then take the fast elevator up a 26-story shaft blasted through solid granite!

With the highest mountain peaks east of the Mississippi and some of the lowest average temperatures, outdoorsy families are provided with outstanding snow sports; a cool oasis for hiking, biking trails through enchanted Forests in the spring and summer; and an amazing season of fall foliage. Whitewater paddlers, anglers, hikers, mountain bikers and gem miners alike will find something fun to do here in this lush wilderness. In the summer, try a site at mountains base called **Lake Lure**. Taking a boat tour around the mountain lake, rafting or just splashing at the beach waterpark are all easy recreation activities at this resort town away from it all.

Ready for adventure? Indians once roamed these hills – and still do. Visit the **Cherokee Heritage Center** and the **Museum of the Cherokee Indian** and see the outdoor drama, **Unto These Hills** to learn more about the proud heritage of these Native Americans. While in the forest, visit The **Cradle of Forestry in America**. Pretend you're wildlife crawling the forest floor or don a swimsuit and swoosh down a natural 60-foot water slide called **Sliding Rock**.

And the great indoors is just as exhilarating as the outdoors. Spend an afternoon exploring America's largest home, at the **Biltmore Estate**. Be sure to ask for the scavenger hunt sheet to complete while you tour. Only the little detectives in your family may be able to "eye spy" everything on the list and win a prize! Nearby Pack Place Education, Arts & Science Center houses five of Asheville's premier attractions, including the **Colburn Earth Science Museum** and the **Health Adventure Museum**. Both keep young minds engaged and little hands busy. Test your heart and then touch some rocks.

Have an aspiring author or poet in your family? Writers and actors have always found the North Carolina mountains inspiring. Author **Thomas Wolfe** made his home in Asheville, while Historic Hendersonville and Flat Rock were home to poet **Carl Sandburg** (biography of Lincoln fame). Both homes will engage your kids literary senses – or maybe yours!

Sites and attractions are listed in order by City, Zip Code, and Name. Symbols indicated represent:

 Festivals   Restaurants   Lodging

Asheville

SMITH-MCDOWELL HOUSE MUSEUM

Asheville - 283 Victoria Road (campus of Tech College - off Hwy. 25 south of downtown, follow the signs to A-B Tech College.) 28801. Phone: (828) 253-9231. www.wnchistory.org   Hours: Tuesday-Saturday 10:00am-4:00pm, Sunday 1:00-4:00pm. Closed Mondays and major holidays. Admission: $3.00-$5.00 (age 5+). Add $2.00 for Christmas season tours.

A wealthy businessman by the name of James McConnell Smith built the mansion in 1840. He was the first child-settler born west of the North Carolina mountains. This National Register property was once the home of mayors, a Confederate Major, and friends of the Vanderbilts at nearby Biltmore Estate. While touring, notice much of the woodwork is original. Other interesting sights within the house include a journey through time including an 1840s kitchen, 1850s bedroom, 1880s parlor and 1890s dining room. Period furnishings are appropriate for each of the rooms. In addition, the museum offers a variety of educational programs and exhibits throughout the year.

Smith-McDowell House Museum (cont.)

VICTORIAN EASTER CELEBRATION

The town's oldest mansion is decorated with Easter baskets, old-fashioned bunnies and chicks, hand-painted eggs and colorful spring flowers. Daily except Mondays. (end of March thru mid-April)

CHRISTMAS AT THE SMITH-MCDOWELL HOUSE MUSEUM

Come visit the Smith-McDowell House Museum and see how popular culture effected trends and styles from the 1840s through 1890s. Each room in this restored circa 1840 mansion and local history museum is authentically decorated with fresh trees, garlands, ornaments, and toys of the Victorian Age. Admission. (mid-November thru New Years week)

THOMAS WOLFE MEMORIAL

Asheville - 52 North Market Street (I- 240, take the Merrimon Avenue Exit (5A) 28801. Phone: (828) 253-8304. www.ah.dcr.state.nc.us/sections/hs/wolfe/wolfe.htm. Hours: Tuesday-Saturday 9:00am-5:00pm, Sunday 1:00-5:00pm (April-October); Tuesday-Saturday 10:00am-4:00pm, Sunday 1:00-4:00pm (November-March). Admission: $0.50-$1.00 per student/adult. Educators: Wealth of biographical editorials online (for kids' research papers).

Portrayed as Dixieland in Wolfe's most famous novel, *Look Homeward, Angel*, the boarding house is the author's boyhood home (named Altamont in the book). A classic of American literature, *Look Homeward, Angel* has never gone out of print since its publication in 1929, keeping interest in Wolfe alive and attracting visitors to the setting for this great novel. A shrewd and hard-nosed businesswoman, family members remembered Wolfe's mother, Julia, as a "driver of hard bargains". Wolfe's writings were closely based on "characters" from his home town. Locals either despised or loved him for this "too close to home" approach. Kids learn the process of writing from a struggling, yet famous, author. The home is newly renovated and the Visitor Center has a short, comprehensive video shown, plus numerous displays.

W Area

ASHEVILLE HISTORIC TROLLEY TOURS

Asheville - 151 Haywood Street (Asheville Visitor Ctr., center of downtown or Grove Park Inn) 28802. www.ashevilletrolleytours.com. Phone: (828) 669-8046 or (888) 667-3600. Admission: $19.00 adult, $18.00 senior/AARP, $12.00 student (5-17).

See the best of Asheville aboard a vintage trolley and enjoy the narration covering all major points of interest in Asheville including: the Grove Park Inn, Biltmore Village, the downtown shopping and restaurants district, the Thomas Wolfe Memorial, the Asheville Museum and Art Gallery district, the Asheville Chamber and Visitors Center and much more. Learn how "Biltmore" got its name. Pass a house that celebrates Christmas every day. Your guide will combine humorous stories and historical information into a fun-filled experience. Disembark the trolley at any of the many convenient stops, then re-board and continue the tour.

COLBURN EARTH SCIENCE MUSEUM

Asheville - 2 South Pack Square (Pack Place Education, Arts & Science Center on historic Pack Square in downtown) 28802. www.colburnmuseum.org. Phone: (828) 254-7162. Hours: Tuesday-Saturday 10:00am-5:00pm, Sunday 1:00-5:00pm. Admission: $4.00 adult, $3.00 student/senior/child (age 4+). Miscellaneous: Monthly Homeschool, Preschool & After School classes offered.

Before you start, ask for an exploration guide and fill in the blanks to win a prize "gem" at the end. Now, start in The Hall of Minerals featuring specimens such as an amethyst crystal cluster; a green fluorite from a North Carolina mine; and a ruby in zoisite from Tanzania. The Gem Room includes a 220 carat blue topaz from Brazil and a 2,405.5 carat boulder opal from Australia. The North Carolina Gallery favorites include itacolumite (the bending rock) from Stokes County, North Carolina and an emerald crystal from the Old Plantation Mine in Cleveland County. Walk through an authentic replica of

Scratching soft minerals into powder...

a gem mine next. Also included is a gem location map, which identifies counties for gem collecting. The hands-on gallery explores the forces that shape the Earth such as the rock cycle, volcanoes, earthquakes, and plate tectonics. Highlights include a touch screen computer program on plate tectonics and large scale models of a volcano and the Earth. Visitors of all ages can investigate Weather, Climate and You - finding clues to the science behind weather reports. What happens when wind hits a mountain or floods rock the Piedmont. Even watch yourself on TV giving the weather report for the day. Fossils, Florescent Minerals and Crystals round out the collection. Throughout the museum, hands-on study areas include: Picking up a light rock (pumice) vs. a heavy rock (scoria), or even make your own powder from scraping a soft stone. And you thought rocks were dull!

> *The nearby Mast General Store is an enticement for kid-friendly shopping. At this store, you can still find baskets of candy and traditional mountain toys.*

HEALTH ADVENTURE

Asheville - 2 South Pack Square (Hwy 25 to Pack Place at Pack Square, downtown near Biltmore) 28802. Phone: (828) 254-6373.   www.thehealthadventure.org. Hours: Tuesday-Saturday 10:00am-5:00pm, Sunday 1:00-5:00pm. Closed Thanksgiving and Christmas days. Admission: $7.00 adult, $5.00 student, senior & child (2-15). Miscellaneous: Preschool Fabulous Fridays, Science Camps. Creative Playspace: This colorful area is specially designed for children under the age of six. A climbing structure, costumes, puppets, and a wealth of toys await.

> *Momentum: Science and Health Adventure Park is the name of this new indoor/outdoor museum space opening just one mile from downtown.*

Ever heard a glass lady talk? TAM (a transparent life-size doll) lights up, turns, and tells visitors (in Spanish and English) about how her body is constructed and functions (anatomy and physiology). TAM's counterpart, TechnoMan is a bionic figure with joints and anatomy replaced by high tech parts. In NUTRISPACE, practice brushing a giant set of teeth, measure the content of your food (quiz yourself), then try shopping at the grocery store. Many areas here also have "peeks" into life & nutrition. SCIENCESPACE is where you'll find an energy-generating bicycle

Flossing a GIANT's Teeth...

(try ringing the bell), a black light room, a Lok-It wall with "Be An Engineer" challenges involving momentum and gravity, and the "levitating mirror". You can also see the Super Sensory Science Stage Show, a popular demonstration program, or try one of many puzzles located on each floor. One traveling exhibit is displayed for several months at a time and some of the subjects they cover are very "Modern Science". We promise you'll leave here more sensitive to your senses and much more aware of good and bad foods you eat every day. Well done!

Here's the fat, salt, and sugar contents of my breakfast sausage biscuit - YUK!

BILTMORE HOUSE

Asheville - 1 Approach Road (Take I-40 West to Exit 50-B on US 25. Take US 25 exit of Blue Ridge Parkway) 28803. www.biltmore.com. Phone: (828) 225-1333 or

(800) 624-1575. Hours: Daily 9:00am–5:00pm (open 9:30am–4:30pm January – March). Some outdoor areas open later. Closed Thanksgiving & Christmas Days. Online Discounted pricing: $39.00 -$45.00 adult, Half Price for youth (ages 10-16). Children 9 and younger are admitted free year-round with a paying adult. Children ages 10-16 are also free most of winter and summer months. Pricing may differ for Christmas at Biltmore (November-early January).

Biltmore House has 250 rooms, or should we say, 235 more than our house...WOW!

Extra $8.00 for audio tours. Extra $15.00 for Behind the Scenes or Rooftop tours (recommended for frequent visitors). Educators: Top notch Student Resource Guides, Workbooks and Teacher Lesson Plans online. Miscellaneous: Grab lunch in the Stable Café, once used to house the horses and carriages on the Estate. New Kids' Land Rover Adventure Course: Youngsters are behind the wheel of electric mini Land Rovers driving around natural obstacles and gentle terrain. There's another challenging course with real Land Rovers for adult drivers.

Biltmore House (cont.)

Imagine the awe on your child's face at the first sight of this real-life castle! This was the home of "Richie Rich" in the movie of the same name (watch it before you go to get into the mood). In the 250-room Biltmore House, kids can imagine what it might have been like to live in a home with its own bowling alley and swimming pool. After you're greeted by the butler "Welcome Home", you'll take yourself on a self-guided visit through four floors of Biltmore House filled with art and antiques (look, don't touch), including the giant Banquet Hall (why are the acoustics so good?), the infamous Library (look for the secret stairway), the kitchens (with walk-in refrigerators), and servants' quarters. Stroll through century-old gardens designed by America's first landscape architect. Meet friendly farm

animals in the Farmyard at the River Bend Farm. Plan to spend half the day indoors, half outdoors on a hike or trail ride. Get the free Commodore's Treasure Hunt guide for your kids and explore upstairs, downstairs, and all around (they get a sticker prize if they complete the hunt). Another great way to increase the kids' interest in visiting this amazing house is to read *The Mystery of Biltmore House*, by Carole Marsh, available at KidsLoveTravel.com.

> Tailor your Biltmore House visit to your child's attention span and energy level. Take a breather and visit the Ice Cream Parlor or Bake Shop for a quick snack or water break. Run wild! Burn off pent-up energy with a race to the top of the Vista in front of Biltmore House.

EASTER AT BILTMORE HOUSE

Spring arrives at Biltmore Estate with Easter egg hunts held on the front lawn of Biltmore. Children ages 2-9 can participate in several hunts throughout the day with prizes, magic shows and visits/breakfast with Biltmore's 19th Century Easter Rabbit. Admission to home required. (Saturday of Easter weekend)

CHRISTMAS AT BILTMORE ESTATE

See dozens of trees dressed with glittering lights and elaborate ornaments, including a 34-foot Fraser fir that graces the Banquet Hall. Your senses will be thrilled with the spicy scent of evergreen and yuletide tunes from the Banquet Hall organ. Candlelight Christmas Evenings capture the magic of the holidays with candlelight and firelight, tinsel and glass ornaments, and choirs and musicians that fill the house with good cheer. Admission. (first weekend in November thru day after New Years)

BLUE RIDGE PARKWAY DESTINATION CENTER

Asheville - (milepost 384) 28805. www.blueridgeheritage.com. or www.nps.gov/blri/ Miscellaneous: The Go Blue Ridge Card will also be available here. The Go Card is also sold online and features more than 25 participating attractions. It's the perfect way to save time, save money and eliminate hassles on your Blue Ridge vacation! www.goblueridgecard.com.

The Blue Ridge Parkway is ranked "America's most scenic drive" by leading travel writers. The Parkway follows the mountain crests from Shenandoah National Park in Virginia to the Great Smokey Mountains National Park in North Carolina and Tennessee. This new 12,000-square-foot, environmentally friendly facility has native plants growing from a sod roof and glass panels in front to collect heat to warm the building. Inside, Blue Ridge National Heritage Area volunteers and staff will assist visitors with trip plans. An expansive, interactive map covers an entire wall of the structure. As visitors move a monitor across the length of the map, videos and photographs pop up with relevant travel information. Exhibits at the center focus on recreation, natural and cultural diversity and the economic strength of the region; a focus on the chestnut tree and its impact on Southern Appalachia is also there. To get the best "feel" for traveling the Parkway, watch the 25-minute movie. In addition, ten kiosks provide tickets to participating regional attractions, outdoor activities and tours.

With the highest mountain peak in the Eastern United States, the oldest river in North America, some of the oldest mountains in the world, the deepest gorge east of the Grand Canyon, the highest waterfall east of the Rockies and the two most visited National Park lands in the country, the natural heritage of the North Carolina Mountains is surpassed by none. Now that you're equipped with maps in hand, go out and explore! Note: most of our listings indicate what milepost on the Parkway to exit.

W Area

FOLK ART CENTER

Asheville - PO Box 9545 (I-40 exit 55 or milepost 382 on the Blue Ridge Parkway) 28805. www.southernhighlandguild.org. Phone: (828) 298-7928. Hours: Daily 9:00am - 5:00 or 6:00pm. Closed Thanksgiving, Christmas & New Year's Days Admission: FREE.

Didn't get enough crafters? Head west a little ways on US70 (940 Tunnel Rd, www.stuartnye.com) to the Stuart Nye Hand Wrought Jewelry studio. Here, they hammer and shape flower designs out of metal.

A Center representing the crafts culture of the Southern Appalachians. Works of Art guild members are displayed and sold and artisans frequently demonstrate their craft (March-December). We watched a quilter and a basket weaver (ever seen garlic and onion baskets?). Also a bookstore and Information center are on the premises.

SOUTHERN APPALACHIAN RADIO MUSEUM

Asheville - Asheville-Buncombe Technical Community College, Elm Bldg., Room 315 (I-40 exit 50, US 25 north. West on Victoria) 28805. Phone: (828) 299-1276. www.saradiomuseum.org. Hours: Friday afternoons from 1:00-3:00pm. Closed holidays, most of winter, and school vacations. Admission: $3.00 to $5.00 suggested donation, adult. FREE child (under 13).

See radios from the past such as Atwater-Kent and Philco. Talk over an amateur radio station (with a licensed operator) to stations far away. Learn how radio frequency waves move through the air. They want all visitors to feel at home; this is a museum where you can touch the radios and do things.

WESTERN NORTH CAROLINA NATURE CENTER

Asheville - 75 Gashes Creek Road (I- 40, take exit 53B. From I- 240, take exit 8) 28805. Phone: (828) 298-5600. www.wildwnc.org. Hours: Daily 10:00am-5:00pm. Closed Thanksgiving, Christmas, New Years and MLK day. Admission: $5.00 adult, $4.00 senior (65+), $3.00 child (3-15). $2.00 more for all adult non-residents. Miscellaneous: Trillium Outdoor Exploring Trail has boardwalk & dirt paths (takes ~30 minutes to hike). Petting area with goats and sheep.

Indoors, the Nature Center welcomes you with a hands on greeting. Children and adults are encouraged to get a feel for the outdoors by touching, feeling, and examining articles of mountain area natural history. Touch actual bear fur (the closest you'll ever get) or see turtles burying themselves in the sand. By utilizing the microscope and magnifying glass stations, you can zoom in on everything from a rattlesnake fang to a butterfly wing. Get up close and personal with a native reptile by handling harmless snakes or Box Turtles. Experience the world of night in the Nocturnal Hall. Screech owls make their calls into the night. You may <u>hear</u> these creatures at night, but how often do you <u>see</u> them? Meet the Skunk, Opossum, Deer Mice, Bats, Flying Squirrels,

> Pretend to be an otter as you slide down the very slippery otter slide. (CAUTION: Fast!)

and frogs. When you head outside, you'll want to walk the trail of predators like cougars, wolves and bobcats, oh my! Then enjoy the antics of river otters in their own special habitat (above and below water). In the barns, you may get a close look at baby animals.

NORTH CAROLINA ARBORETUM

Asheville - 100 Frederick Law Olmstead Way (UNC campus, I-26 east to exit 33/ Hwy 191 south Blue Ridge Pkwy, look for signs) 28806. Phone: (828) 665-2492. www.ncarboretum.org. Hours: Grounds open 8:00am-sunset. Visitor Education Center: Monday-Saturday 9:00am-5:00pm, Sunday Noon-5:00pm. Greenhouse: Monday-Friday 8:00am-4:00pm (2:00pm closing on Wednesday). Closed state holidays. Admission: Charge is $6 per personal motor vehicle. Miscellaneous: Café and gift area.

Located at the edge of the Pisgah National Forest, the 424-acre site features a Visitor Education Center, state-of-the-art greenhouse complex, an array of gardens, a loop trail and a variety of ongoing special programs. Stop by the Information Desk to pick up a brochure listing each month's educational programs, tours, garden demonstrations and workshops. Kids will like to visit during the Arbor Day or Bonsai Expo.

GOOMBAY! FESTIVAL

Asheville - YMI Cultural Center and downtown. www.ymicc.org/goombay.html. (828) 252-4614. Goombay emerged during slavery days in Bermuda. Both music and rhythm were brought from Africa and the West Indies. The original dancers used a skin-covered drum that was called "Gombey" meaning rhythm. Goombay dancers wear colorful costumes and high headdresses topped with feathers and, at times, masks. After watching performers, enjoy an authentic Caribbean meal at the Island of Delight Café. Street vendors sell everything from ice cream to third world crafts. Admission. (last weekend in August)

NATIONAL GINGERBREAD HOUSE COMPETITION

Asheville - The Grove Park Inn Resort. (828) 252-2711 or www.groveparkinn.com. See more than 20 gingerbread works of art from all over the country. Houses will be on display throughout the holiday season. This month long event includes over 25 uniquely decorated trees. Enjoy themed areas, garlands, poinsettias, an elves' playhouse and much more. (day after Thanksgiving thru December)

KWANZAA CELEBRATION

Asheville - YMI Cultural Center. Kwanzaa is an African American and Pan-African holiday celebrating family, community and culture through craft, food and fellowship. www.ymicc.org/kwanzaa.html. (December 26 – January 1)

HAMPTON INN TUNNEL ROAD

Asheville - 204 Tunnel Road, (800) 426-7866 or www.ashevillehamptoninns.com, I-240 exit 7. Close to most attractions, this comfortable hotel has a warm indoor pool, whirlpool, expanded continental breakfast, and a fireplace lobby serving tea and cookies nightly.

VANCE BIRTHPLACE STATE HISTORIC SITE

Asheville (Weaverville) - 911 Reems Creek Road (U.S. 19-23 north to New Stock Road or Blue Ridge Pkwy milepost 375/376) 28787. Phone: (828) 645-6706. www.ah.dcr.state.nc.us/sections/hs/Vance/vance.htm. Hours: Tuesday-Saturday 9:00am-5:00pm (April-October); Tuesday-Saturday 10:00am-4:00pm (November-December). Closed weekends (January-March). Admission: FREE.

Historic homestead of North Carolina's Civil War governor, Zebulon B. Vance. The state historic site depicts early pioneer life in the mountains during the 1800s. Also included is the history of Vance's famous political mountain family. As the War Governor of the South, Vance's untiring efforts made on behalf of the soldiers and their families, provided every possible comfort to them during the famine and sadness of war. These actions ensured his place in the minds and hearts of the people he served. Nearby, the visitor center houses exhibits portraying the life of Vance and a 15 minute slide presentation. Best visited during spring and fall living history weekends.

CHRISTMAS CANDLELIGHT TOURS

Asheville (Weaverville) - Vance Birthplace. Candlelight tours with living history. Admission. (mid-December Saturday)

Blowing Rock

BLOWING ROCK

Blowing Rock - PO Box 145 (Hwy 321 South of Blue Ridge Parkway, follow 321 Bypass) 28605. Phone: (828) 295-7111. www.theblowingrock.com. Hours: Daily 9:00am-5:00pm; Open later on weekends in April, May, September, October; Daily 8:30am-7:00pm (May thru Labor Day). Weekends only in January - March. Closed Christmas Eve and Day. Admission: $6.00 adult, $5.00 senior (60+), $1.00 child (4-11). Miscellaneous: Walking the self-guided trail takes an average of 15 to 25 minutes.

The Blowing Rock is an immense cliff 4,000 feet above sea level overhanging Johns River Gorge 3,000 feet below. The phenomenon is so called because

the rocky walls of the gorge form a flume through which the northwest wind sweeps with such force that it returns light objects cast over the cliff. Visible from "The Rock" down the gorge to the southwest are Hawksbill Mountain and Table Rock. To the west are Grandfather Mountain (the highest peak in the Blue Ridge chain) and Mount Mitchell (the highest peak east of the Rockies). The Blowing Rock's mysterious winds cause even the snow to fall upside down. Lookout points have great views of the layers of mountain regions below. Enjoy the scenic views and observation tower, gardens, small garden waterfall and unique gift shop. On a clear day, this is picture taking mecca!

MYSTERY HILL ENTERTAINMENT COMPLEX

Blowing Rock - 129 Mystery Hill Lane (Hwy. 321 between Boone and Blowing Rock. Pkwy exit 291) 28605. Phone: (828) 264-2792. www.mysteryhill-nc.com. Hours: Daily 9:00am-5:00pm. Open until 8:00pm (June - August). Admission: $8.00 adult (13-59), $7.00 senior (60+), $6.00 child (5-12). Includes museums and mystery hill. Miscellaneous: On the premises is the Appalachian Heritage Museum (set up as it might have been in 1910 w/crafters occasionally) and its walls are filled with Native American Relics.

Things that make you wonder. This area attraction defies gravity. In the Mystery House, visitors stand at a 45 degree angle, water flows up hill and anyone can throw a curve. There is a stronger than average pull to the north which causes some of our basic laws of physics to work differently than normal. What causes this unexplained pull? Optical illusions are in the Hall of Mystery but there's also Mystery Rocks, Puzzles and giant Bubbles. Over 40 "experiments" to have fun with - watch, it may tickle your funny bone.

TWEETSIE RAILROAD

Blowing Rock - PO Box 388 (US 321, BRPkwy exit milepost 291, Boone exit) 28605. Phone: (828) 264-9061 or (800) 526-5740. www.tweetsie.com. Hours: Daily

9:00am-6:00pm (Memorial Day week-mid August). Long weekends only (early May, Late August-October). Admission: $30.00 adult, $22.00 child (3-12). Come in between 3:00-6:00pm and get in the next day free. Admission includes railroad, live entertainment, rides and Deer Park.

Be a cowboy, cowgirl, Indian or an engineer. Stroll down Main Street, learn to clog, pan for gold or visit with deer and goats in Deer Park. Be sure to ride the chair lift or hike up Miner's Mountain. Tweetsie also has amusement rides for all ages and venues throughout the park performing live. The main feature, though, is the famous historic train ride. Hop aboard for a fun-filled three-mile Wild West journey through scenic mountains. Funny skits (kids love 'em) abound. If you cooperate, you might even get a souvenir bullet. Of course, you should be on the lookout when you walk around the park because you may meet Calamity Jane or get caught helping the posse look for the gold shipment from Fort Boone. Visitors get involved in most all the "shows" - they know how to keep the family amused and smiling. Plenty of good eatin', too - from hearty western-style meals to their Tweetsie Fudge for dessert.

HELP ! Save the gold from the robbers !!

DAY OUT WITH THOMAS ™

Welcome Thomas the Tank Engine – ride through the scenic Blue Ridge mountains on a vintage, full-size train led by Thomas himself. Meet Sir Topham Hatt, watch Thomas and Friends videos, coloring books, live music and an Imagination Station. Guests will also enjoy all of Tweetsie's famous attractions. (first and second long weekends in June)

4TH OF JULY

Park is open until 8:00pm. Parking $5.00. Be sure to bring a tailgate picnic. Event is for park guests only. Fireworks display.

BLUE RIDGE CELTIC FESTIVAL

Blowing Rock - Chetola Mountain Resort. (800) CHETOLA or www.chetola.com or www.blueridgecelticfestival.com. Top-name Celtic entertainment plus food, crafts and games. Admission. (Saturday before Memorial Day weekend)

Boone

HORN IN THE WEST

Boone - 591 Horn in the West Drive (Powderhorn Theatre) 28607. Phone: (828) 264-2120. www.horninthewest.com. Hours: Nightly except Monday at 8:00pm (late June through mid-August). Admission: ~$15.00-$16.00 adult, child admission is half price. Miscellaneous: Other shows include matinees with young themes throughout the season. See website or brochure.

The Pride of Boone...The Freedom of a Nation. This revolutionary outdoor drama is a tale of tragedy and triumph, happiness and heartbreak, all set in the context of a new wide-open America. Enjoy the three-stage story of Daniel Boone and the courageous settlers in their journey to the west. Specifically, follow the Stuart family as they discover things about themselves and their fellow journeymen. Learn about the Blue Ridge, Appalachia, Moravians, and the Cherokee. It keeps the kids entertained with a simple story-line, action, song and dance. You'll enjoy the lovable characters of the preacher and the widow. Look for the fire dance scene.

Start in the late afternoon with a picnic, then enjoy the HICKORY RIDGE HOMESTEAD LIVING HISTORY MUSEUM. Costumed live interpreters (first person) give visitors a taste of pioneer life. Living history is recreated by docents in traditional costume, working with traditional tools, engaged in hearth baking, candle-making, weaving, tin-smithing and other activities among original mountain cabins. Located on the premises of the Theatre, the cost is included in your price of admission to the drama. Also open weekends each spring and fall.

HICKORY RIDGE HOMESTEAD APPLE FESTIVAL

Boone. (888) 825-6747 or (828) 264-2120. See living history museum cabins and taste all of the apple goodies including: homemade apple butter, pies, cider, and fritters. (last weekend in October)

DAN'L BOONE INN RESTAURANT

Boone - Historic downtown (www.danlbooneinn.com, 828-264-8657) family style dining in a historic property. For over 40 years, Dan'l Boone Inn has been serving Boone and the high country delicious homecooked meals, just like you remember at grandma's house. Family style meals begin with a salad in the summer and soup in the winter. Three meats and five vegetables are served along with biscuits, preserves, dessert and beverage. A full family style breakfast is served on Saturdays and Sundays. Really gets you in the mood to see the outdoor drama. Go hungry, there is tons of food! ($5.00-$15.00).

Bryson City

GREAT SMOKY MOUNTAINS RAILROAD

Bryson City - 226 Everett Street 28713. Phone: (828) 586-8811 or (800) 872-4681. www.gsmr.com. Admission: $29.00-$43.00 adult, $14.00-$22.00 child (3-12). Miscellaneous: Box lunch options can be purchased at time of reservation or eat at restaurants in the gorge during layover. Also, foods can be purchased in the Conductor's Car during the excursion.

Enjoy scenic train journeys across fertile valleys, through tunnels and across river gorges in the Great Smoky Mountains, pulled by diesel-electric and steam locomotives. Over the last several years the trains have played a part in several motion pictures: *The Fugitive* starring Harrison Ford and Tommy Lee Jones; *My Fellow Americans* starring Jack Lemmon, James Garner, and Dan Aykroyd; *Digging to China* with Kevin Bacon; *Paradise Falls* with Sean Bridges and Nick Searcy; and *Forces of Nature* with Sandra Bullock and Ben Affleck. Guests ride in comfortable, reconditioned coaches, crown coaches, club cars, dining cars, and open cars that are ideal for viewing the scenery and taking pictures. Experience the ride of your life with one of their Locomotive Cab Rides. Dillsboro Departures feature a scenic journey along the Tuckasegee River traveling alone side farmland. Bryson City Departures travels into the Nantahala Gorge known for its white water activity. This excursion offers an optional Raft and Rail combination April through October.

THE LITTLE ENGINE THAT COULD™
I THINK I CAN!™ RAIL TOUR

A full-size replica engine of the famous character created in the original book by Watty Piper comes to the GSMR in Bryson City for a wonderful family adventure. Price includes train ride, admission to the event site and also admission to the Smoky Mountain Trains Museum. (long weekends 3rd and 4th weekends in May, including Memorial Day weekend)

DAY OUT WITH THOMAS™

The classic storybook engine chugs into Dillsboro! Enjoy a 25 minute ride with Thomas, meet Sir Topham Hatt™, hear storytelling, live music and much more! Special fare and online reservations in advance. (late July thru early August for ten days)

RAILFEST

Three days of railroad fun! Railroad enthusiasts world wide gather in town to see and ride historic railroad equipment, Motor car display and musical performances. (mid-September long weekend)

PEANUTS™ - THE GREAT PUMPKIN PATCH EXPRESS

Peanuts™ - The Great Pumpkin Patch Express departs Dillsboro Depot at 3:30pm mid-October through late October. Meet Snoopy, Charlie Brown & Lucy, and select your own pumpkin. Enjoy hayrides, live musical entertainment, story telling, hay bale maze, bouncy house, apple cider, peanuts gift shop, face painting and trick or treating! And kids don't forget to wear your costumes. There is also be a petting zoo!

W Area

Great Smoky Mountains Railroad (cont.)

POLAR EXPRESS™, THE

The Polar Express comes to life when the train departs the Bryson City depot for a journey to their "North Pole". Guests on board will enjoy hot chocolate and treats while listening and reading along with the magical story. Experience the joy of watching the children's faces when the train arrives at the "North Pole," where Santa Claus will be waiting. Santa boards The Polar Express and greets each child, presenting them with a special memento. Holiday carols are sung on the return trip to Bryson City. Families will want to make this a holiday tradition! Special fare and online reservations required. (begins long weekends in November, then almost daily in December thru a few days before Christmas)

SMOKY MOUNTAIN TRAINS MUSEUM

Bryson City - 100 Greenlee Street (US 74 exit 67, north on Veterans, east on US 19, north on Greenlee) 28713. www.smokymountaintrains.com. Phone: (866) 914-5200.   Hours: Daily 9:00am-5:00pm. Thursday-Saturday only January and February. Admission: $9.00 adult, $5.00 child (age 3+). Museum admission FREE with all GSMR Regular Train Excursion tickets.

More than 7,000 Lionel locomotives and cars dating back to 1918 are on display. Over a mile of track on three levels with six trains running simultaneously. Visit the freightyard with more than 400 cars, see the five-foot waterfall and 12 animated scenes. There's an operating roundtable with roundhouse and a live cascading five-foot waterfall. There are also various wooden train tables to play with in the activity center and a retail shop. The museum recently added to their vast collection of model trains. What is different is that you (or the kid in you) and the kids can push buttons and operate the trains and over 20 accessory items. If small trains aren't enough for you, walk over to the Bryson City depot of the Great Smoky Mountain Railroad (same owners).

Burnsville

MOUNT MITCHELL STATE PARK

Burnsville - 2388 SR 128 (Blue Ridge Parkway milepost 355) 28714. Phone: (828) 675-4611.   http://ncparks.gov/Visit/parks/momi/main.php   Hours: Visitor Center: Daily 10:00am-6:00pm (May-October).

Mount Mitchell is the highest peak (6,685 feet) in the eastern United States. The park offers easy access from the Blue Ridge Parkway with a restaurant,

W Area

tent camping area, museum and picnic area, as well as hiking trails connecting to the Pisgah National Forest. The Exhibit Hall, located near the mountain's summit, offers visitors insight into the mountain's natural, cultural and historical faces. Exhibits include: An interactive weather station, (punch in your birthday to find out the weather conditions on Mount Mitchell's summit on that date); A life-size wood carving of "Big" Tom Wilson, the mountain guide who led a search for the person who first calculated Mount Mitchell to be the highest peak on the east coast; a replica of "Big" Tom's cabin with historical artifacts and buttons that allow visitors to listen to four different stories about his life; a three-dimensional topographic map of the Black Mountains with interactive buttons; a geology section with a hands-on demonstration of a rock fault and four samples of the different rock types in the state park; and dioramas that depict animal life in the state park.

Cherokee

CHEROKEE BEAR ZOO & EXOTIC ANIMALS

Cherokee - PO Box 1914, 1204 Tsalagi Road (downtown, near Burger King) 28719. Phone: (828) 497-4525. www.cherokeezoo.com. Hours: Open daily 10:00am - early dusk. (March-December) Admission: $5.00 per person age 3 and up. Miscellaneous: Bear Trax Cabin rentals across the street. Snack bar on premises.

As a welcome to the natural Smokies, stop by this open-habitat zoo featuring exotic cats, bears, monkeys, a petting zoo and more. Feed them and watch them stand on their hind legs and beg you for more. They name each animal and they love for you talk to them. Observe and feed the animals at your leisure. Look for cubs and large 800 lb. Grizzlies.

MUSEUM OF THE CHEROKEE INDIAN

Cherokee - (Hwy 441 & Drama Road, center of town) 28719. Phone: (828) 497-3481. www.cherokeemuseum.org. Hours: Opens daily at 9:00am except on Thanksgiving, Christmas and New Year's Day. Museum closes between 5:00-7:00pm. Admission: $9.00 adult, $6.00 child (6-13), FREE pre-schooler (under 6). Educators: A traditional Cherokee story lesson is online.

As the keepers of tradition, Cherokee storytellers played an important role in tribal life. As your guide through thousands of years of the Cherokee experience, the storyteller (shown through holograms and spoken voices) will help the interactive museum come to life. Travel back to a time of mastodons and atlatls - prehistoric time. Step forward where you'll meet a dramatic chieftain, see and hear a medicine man and play the centuries old butter bean game. You'll learn what happened when white men first appeared on their land. Later, you'll pass by the Revolutionary War and the creator of the brilliant Cherokee alphabet, Sequoyah. Finally, travel along the infamous Trail of Tears, and back to the present. Modern, engaging displays work to tell the story in many formats.

OCONALUFTEE INDIAN VILLAGE

Cherokee - PO Box 398, 218 Drama Road (US 19 west to Hwy 441, center of town) 28719. www.cherokee-nc.com/oconaluftee. Phone: (828) 497-2315 or (828)-497-2111 (Off Season). Hours: Daily 9:00am-5:30pm (mid-May to late October). Admission: $14.00 adult, $7.00 child (6-13).

Shiyo! (Hello! In Cherokee) The Oconaluftee Indian Village is an authentic recreation of an 18th century Cherokee Indian village. Here you will see the model of a Cherokee village from over 225 years ago. Cherokee guides in native costume will explain their history, the culture and life-style of their ancestors, and answer your questions. The tours (leaving about every 10 minutes) provide simple, quick explanations of each craft. We especially liked the fact that real Cherokee are crafting. Carefully watch the demos of river cane and mountain cane used to make large and small blow guns or arrows. Then, see men chipping flint creating sharp arrowheads for hunting or fighting. Next, a villager

Observing the making of blow guns from cane

demonstrates the blow gun with a target. Move on to various housing units. The Sweat House was used for a hospital…how? It was so interesting to see how Indians took a giant log and burned a canoe out of it. The Ceremonial Square is where prayer dances were held. Cherokee did not worship idols and nature, just one Creator (God). Cherokee used slow dances to worship or pray. How did they make rattles? Water drums? Why is the number 7 important? Hear Cherokee spoken and interpreted. This Village is highly recommended before attending the drama. You'll learn more than you can imagine about their people. Maybe even learn some Cherokee to impress your friends.

OCONALUFTEE VISITOR CENTER / MOUNTAIN FARM MUSEUM - GREAT SMOKY MOUNTAINS

Cherokee - (2 miles north of town, on US 441 , Great Smoky Mtn. National Park) 28719. Phone: (828) 497-1900. www.nps.gov/grsm. Hours: Open all year during business hours 8:30am-4:30pm. Great Smoky Mountains National Park is open 24 hours a day, 365 days a year. However some secondary roads, campgrounds, and other visitor facilities close in winter. Admission: FREE

The Smokies offer activities for visitors of various ages and interests. Recommended activities include camping, hiking the park's more than 800 miles of trails, picnicking, sightseeing, fishing, auto touring, nature viewing, and photographic opportunities. Guided horseback rides are available in season at four horse stables in the park in Tennessee and North Carolina.

> **Salamander Capital of the World !**
> At least thirty species of salamanders live in the Great Smoky Mountains park.

The Mountain Farm Museum has a collection of southern Appalachian farm buildings assembled from different locations throughout the Park. Visitors can explore a chestnut log farmhouse, barn, hen house, apple house, springhouse, and blacksmith shop. The farmstead even has crops in the field and live farm animals during the summer. Seasonally, park staff and volunteers give demonstrations of some traditional mountain ways like black-smithing, plowing, and syrup making. The Mingus Mill near Oconaluftee (open spring thru fall) exhibits a turbine-powered grist mill and the opportunity to chat with a miller some afternoon.

SANTA'S LAND THEME PARK & ZOO

Cherokee - 571 Wolfetown Rd. (east of downtown on US 19) 28719. Phone: (828) 497-9191. www.santaslandnc.com. Hours: Daily 10:00am-5:00pm (May-October). Admission: Average $17.00 per person (age 2+).

A family Theme Park and Zoo, Santa's Land is a small enchanted Christmas theme park kids will love as a diversion. Enjoy riding the Rudi-Coaster, train, and kiddie rides. Ride the paddle boats to Monkey Island while viewing some of the largest gold fish you've ever seen. Pet domestic animals, visit with Santa, his elves and reindeer, or browse their Christmas shops. Bring a picnic lunch or eat at one of their establishments.

UNTO THESE HILLS OUTDOOR DRAMA

Cherokee - PO Box 398 (off Hwy 441 North, Mountainside Theater) 28719. Phone: (866) 554-4557. www.untothesehills.com. Hours: Nightly, except Sunday at 8:30pm (mid-June to 3rd week of August). Length of Performance - 2hrs 15min. (Pre-show entertainment begins at 7:45 p.m.) Admission: $16.00 adult, Half Price child (6-13). Reserved seats are $18.00 per person (all ages).

> The Cherokee were forcibly removed from their ancestral home in 1838-39. After the Trail of Tears, the few Cherokee who remained formed the Eastern Band of the Cherokee.

"Unto These Hills" is the tragic and triumphant story of the Cherokee. Set against the backdrop of the Great Smoky Mountains, the compelling story opens with the arrival of the Spanish (Hernando DeSoto in 1540), and builds to a climax with the cruel removal of all but a remnant of Cherokee on the infamous "Trail of Tears." This

drama recreates the inspiration of the great Sequoyah and other leaders. Cherokee descendants, whose ancestors were forcefully driven out of the mountains and marched 1,200 miles to Oklahoma, play important roles in the drama and in the many dances, highlighted by the colorful and world-famous Eagle Dance or the Wedding scene (learn where the saying "Tie the Knot" comes from). They mix dramatics with humor and choreographed dance and fighting scenes to keep the play interesting. A great way to study Cherokee history and the events that led to the removal of most Cherokee from this land.

CHEROKEE CORN MAZE

Cherokee - Kituhwa Indian Mound along the Tuckaseigee River. (828) 497-7605 or www.cherokeecornmaze.com. The corn maze covers five acres of bottom land with its giant corn stalks and is cut in a unique Cherokee Indian design. Educational riddles and clues will help you find your way through this extraordinary maze. There is also a smaller Turtle Maze which was designed especially for children. Experience a day of family fun while learning about Cherokee Heritage. Admission. (afternoons and evenings mid-August thru October, daily except Mondays)

HOLIDAY INN OF CHEROKEE

Cherokee - US Highway 19 south. (828) 497-9181 or www.hicherokeenc.com. Located in the Smoky Mountain range. Take a dip in the outdoor or indoor pool. Grab a bite to eat in the Chestnut Tree Restaurant (featuring home-style cooking). Entertainment for the kids includes a cute outdoor playground, pool table, air hockey, and game room.

Chimney Rock

CHIMNEY ROCK PARK

Chimney Rock - PO Box 39 (I-26 east to exit 18A, or just follow US 64 / 74A east towards Lake Lure) 28720. www.chimneyrockpark.com. Phone: (828) 625-9611 or (800) 277-9611. Hours: Daily 8:30am-6:00 or 7:00pm, weather permitting, except Thanksgiving, Christmas, and New Year's Day. Ticket office closes 1 1/2 hours before closing. Admission: $14.00 adult, $6.00 child (4-12). Reduced rates for

very inclement weather (we recommend mid-spring to early fall). Climbing Tower, $5.00 extra. Miscellaneous: Sky Lounge patio accessible to strollers and wheelchairs. Nature Center. Old Rock Café at park entrance. Picnic/grill areas all along the stretch up.

High Atop Chimney Rock...

Prepare to be elevated! Made famous in the movie "The Last of the Mohicans", traverse a cool tunnel and then take the fast elevator up a 26-story shaft blasted through solid granite! You'll get a brief introduction to the Park from the elevator operator on your way up to the Sky Lounge-a gift shop and snack bar with a

75-mile view. Then it's just a short distance across the clear-span bridge to the stairs to the Chimney. Imagine the Indian warriors and early settlers who climbed and explored this same rock (but, with no guard rails!). Hickory Nut Falls, one of the highest waterfalls east of the Mississippi River (404 feet), can be reached by hiking along the Skyline-Cliff Trail Loop (mostly on

Wait 'til a squirrel finds this GIANT acorn...

the edge of cliffs - 90 minutes) to its top or by taking the gentler walk via the Forest Stroll (1.5 mile round trip) to a platform at its bottom. The Great Woodland Adventure is a new, interactive, half-mile trail. Search for clues about creatures that live in the park. Grady the Groundhog shares journal pages with you and offers challenges at each of the 12 discovery stations. Along the way, try to jump as far as spiders, sit on a giant acorn or climb inside a large turtle shell (great photo ops!). Life-size sculptures draw you in. Beware of the mother bear - look for the baby cub nearby! This park is a different adventure for every family member - an experience not to be missed! Promise us you'll plan at least a half day here (especially if you love nature).

EASTER SUNRISE SERVICE

Easter service early morning. FREE. (Easter morning)

Connelly Springs

SOUTH MOUNTAINS STATE PARK

Connelly Springs - 3001 South Mountains State Park Ave. (SR 1904) (from I-40, turn south on NC 18, travel nine miles and make a right turn onto SR 1913 (Sugarloaf Road). Follow signs) 28612. www.ncparks.gov/Visit/parks/somo/main.php. Phone: (828) 433-4772. Hours: Daily 8:00am-dusk. Admission: FREE, fee for camping. Educators: The South Mountains program introduces students to stream and watershed ecology, focusing on the aquatic life, water quality, indicator species, biotic index, watershed and stewardship of Jacob's Fork River. Accompanying the program is a teacher's booklet and workshop, free of charge to educators. Miscellaneous: Trout fishing and camping.

With a variety of trails (over 48 miles) designated for mountain bikes and equestrian or hiking activity, this is trailblazer country. The most popular trail, High Shoals Falls Loop Trail, travels one mile along the Jacob Fork River to the base of High Shoals Falls, a beautiful crystal-clear waterfall. The trail then continues to the top of the falls before looping around and returning to the picnic area. The terrain can be rugged, so be observant of the trail and wear sturdy shoes. An easier trail, originating near the park office, is the Hemlock Nature Trail. This .74-mile wheelchair-accessible loop travels along the Jacob Fork River and through a forest. Eleven display areas along the trail explain the environment of South Mountains State Park and describe its plants and animals.

W Area

Cullowhee

MOUNTAIN HERITAGE DAY

Cullowhee - Western Carolina University campus. www.mountainheritageday.com. (828) 227-7129. Mountain Heritage Day is a combination old-fashioned mountain fair and showcase for authentic Southern Appalachian folk arts. Kids play pioneer games, crafters demonstrate their skill and sell their wares, and there are live dance and music performances all day. FREE. (last Saturday in September)

Dillsboro

EASTER HAT PARADE

Dillsboro - Downtown. (828) 586-2155. Morning festivities with an unpretentious Easter Hat Parade and best hat contest. (Easter Saturday)

LIGHTS & LUMINARIES

Dillsboro - Downtown. (828) 586-2155. Magically, the entire town is transformed into a winter wonderland of lights, candles, laughter and song. (first two Fridays and Saturdays in December, beginning at dusk)

Fletcher

NC MOUNTAIN STATE FAIR

Fletcher - Western North Carolina Agricultural Center, 1301 Fanning Road. (828) 687-1414 or www.mountainfair.org. A 10-day celebration of Western North Carolina heritage blended with fun and games and entertainment. Admission. (weekend after Labor Day for 10 days in September)

Fontana Dam

FONTANA VILLAGE

Fontana Dam - PO Box 68 (Hwy 28 North, off US 129) 28733. Phone: (828) 498-2211 or (800) 849-2258. www.fontanavillage.com.

Historic Fontana Village, set amid this perfect panorama of the Smokies, is a destination resort area. The Village has a wide range of accommodations,

W Area

including inn rooms, suites, cabins, and even RV and tent camping. Other resources include restaurants, outfitters, a bike shop, pools, marina, horseback riding, miles of on-site trails suitable for mountain biking and hiking, ropes course and more. Some of the exciting destinations in the area are the famous Blue Ridge Parkway, Great Smoky Mountains National Park, Nantahala Gorge whitewater rafting, skiing in Maggie Valley, gem mining in Franklin, jet boat rides, or local mountain heritage at Stecoah Valley Center. Fly-fishing and biking on the village trails are favorites for Dads and kids. The Fontana Dam (Visitors Center: 800-470-3790) is 480 feet high, and 2,365 feet long - the highest concrete dam east of the Mississippi. It was constructed in the early 1940s to supply electricity to fuel the war efforts during WWII.

> **"Tail of the Dragon"** with its 318 curves in 11 miles is considered the nation's #1 motorcycle and sports car road - use caution if you're prone to motion sickness.

Franklin

SCOTTISH TARTANS MUSEUM

Franklin - 86 East Main Street　28723. www.scottishtartans.org/museum.html. Phone: (828) 524-7472.　Hours: Monday-Saturday 10:00am-5:00pm.　Admission: $1.00 -$2.00 donation (age 10+).

This museum contains the official registry of all publicly known tartans and is the American extension of the Scottish Tartans Society in Edinburgh, Scotland. See displays on the culture, dress, customs, military, and history of Scotland. The evolution of the kilt can be easily seen from the mannequin displays. Learn the difference between tartan and plaid, kilt and philabeg, pleating to sett and stripe. Watch the kilt transform from a simple woolen blanket to the tailored garment a man can own today. The museum's staff offers help to visitors in locating their family tartans.

TASTE OF SCOTLAND

A Taste of Scotland Festival takes place each June in downtown Franklin, featuring a parade of clans and tartans, Scottish food, crafts, music, children's highland games, and border collie demonstrations. (second weekend in June)

FRANKLIN GEM & MINERAL MUSEUM

Franklin - 25 Phillips Street 28734. Phone: (828) 369-7831. www.fgmm.org.
Hours: Monday-Friday Noon-4:00pm, Saturday 11:00am-3:00pm. (May - October).
Saturday only (rest of year) Admission: FREE.

The museum may provide inspiration to become a rockhound when you see the wealth of gems mined from these mountains in Western NC. It occupies the Historic Old Jail of Macon County that was built in 1850. There are 6 rooms and a couple of hallways that are dedicated to the cataloging and preservation of gem and mineral specimens from around the world as well as those found in North Carolina and of course Macon County - home to the famous Cowee Valley where Rubies and Sapphires have been found for over 100 years. Our favorites were the fluorescent stones and A Replica of Aaron's Breast Plate using the same stones as mentioned in the Bible.

NANTAHALA NATIONAL FOREST / MOUNTAIN WATER SCENIC BYWAY

Franklin - (US 64, SR 1310 - Wayah Road, and US 19) 28734. Phone: (828) 524-6441.
http://ncnatural.com/NCUSFS/Nantahala/scenic.html.

The Mountain Waters Scenic Byway is a 61.3-mile drive that winds through southern Appalachian hardwood forest, two river gorges, and rural countryside. Part of this nationally-recognized byway coincides with two State scenic routes. Much of the byway travels through the Nantahala National Forest. At overlooks and side routes, you may see signs of forest management activities. Here is a sample of attractions along the route:

CLIFFSIDE LAKE & VAN HOOK GLADE: Cliffside Lake Recreation Area is 4.4 miles west of Highlands and then 1.5 miles off U.S. 64. This area offers picnicking, swimming, fishing and hiking. You can camp nearby at Van Hook Glade.

CULLASAJA FALLS: US 64 East. This beautiful waterfall is located on the Cullasaja River at the lower part of the Cullasaja Gorge and cascades for 250 feet over moss-covered stones.

WAYAH BALD: A side trip to Wayah Bald is well worth the effort. From Wayah Gap, journey 1.3 miles up gravel Forest Road (FR) 69 and see the Wilson Lick Ranger Station. Built about 1913, Wilson Lick was the first ranger station in the Nantahala National Forest. Continue another 3.2 miles up FR 69 to Wayah Bald. Take the short, paved trail to the historic Wayah Bald Fire Tower. Built by the Civilian Conservation Corps in the 1930's, the tower provides a great view of the southern Appalachian Mountains in Georgia, Tennessee, and both

Carolinas. You can picnic nearby at the Wayah Bald Picnic Area. Two long-distance trails, the Appalachian Trail and the Bartram Trail, cross the mountain at the tower.

NANTAHALA LAKE: Located about 6 miles west of Wayah Gap, this lake has 29 miles of shoreline and offers fishing and boating. Boat ramps are available.

NANTAHALA RIVER: This mountain river offers great trout fishing in its upper and lower reaches. The stretch of river above the powerhouse has excellent catch-and-release fishing from spring until early summer.

NANTAHALA RIVER GORGE: The river draws more than 250,000 boaters who enjoy whitewater rafting, canoeing, and kayaking. From a wooden walkway, spectators get a thrilling view of the wild ride over the final series of rapids, including Nantahala Falls.

SHEFFIELD MINE

Franklin - 385 Sheffield Farms Rd. (only follow detailed directions on website) 28734. Phone: (828) 369-8383. www.sheffieldmine.com. Hours: Open daily at 10:00am (April-October). Last customer accepted between 2:30-3:00pm. Admission: Buckets range from $3.00-$100.00.

This place uses terminology like Squeakers and Honkers. To find Rubies & Sapphires requires a lot of patience and perseverance and scrubbing and rinsing (and scrubbing and rinsing) the rocks in your tray. Wear old clothes. The average person needs to Scrub-Rinse about 4-5 times per tray load, otherwise you will NOT get the rocks clean enough to discover that some of those rocks are actually RUBIES & SAPPHIRES. They don't look like gems. Instead, look for peeks of colorful rock and purple coloring. Hunting for Rubies and Sapphires takes a minimum of 2 hours - so plan your trip accordingly and don't get here too late. No matter what your age, when it comes to rocks and dirt, we are all kids again.

WILDERNESS TAXIDERMY MUSEUM

Franklin - 5040 Highland Road 28734. www.wildernesstaxidermy.com/index2.html. Phone: (828) 524-3677. Hours: Monday, Tuesday, Thursday, Friday 8:00am-5:00pm, Saturday 8:00am-Noon. Admission: FREE.

A unique facility that features a museum, a wildlife art gallery, and a working studio. Animals are tastefully mounted in dioramas in their natural surroundings. Even see a "stuffed" zebra or lion. You can also watch demonstrations of the process of Taxidermy while at the facility (not for weak stomachs).

Hendersonville

DUPONT STATE FOREST

Hendersonville - DuPont Road (from Asheville/Brevard via US64 and Little River Rd) 28718. Phone: (828) 877-6527. www.dupontforest.com.

The DuPont State Forest is located in the Blue Ridge Mountains. Most first time visitors want to see falling water, and DuPont State Forest probably has as much per square mile as any public land in the Southeast. The large falls are on the Little River - High Falls and Upper Triple Falls - and they are but 20 to 30 minutes from the trail head. The property is presently open to hunting, fishing, hiking, horseback riding and mountain biking. The Forest lies in an upland plateau of the Little River valley, with large sections of gently rolling land bordered by moderately steep hills and mountains. Most all of the ridges have exposed granite slabs and domes.

HOLMES EDUCATIONAL STATE FOREST

Hendersonville - 1299 Crab Creek Road (Rte. 4, southwest of town) 28739. Phone: (828) 692-0100. www.ncesf.org/HESF/home.htm. Hours: Daily daylight hours (mid-March to late November). Admission: FREE

Holmes is located in the Blue Ridge Mountains. With rugged terrain, numerous rock outcroppings, and scenic vistas, it also offers a rich mixture of mountain hardwoods, rhododendron, flame azaleas, and a variety of wildflowers. These features are accessible by a series of well-marked trails which are accented by exhibits and displays (talking trees) depicting the ecology of the managed forest. Picnic areas and hiking trails are available.

HISTORIC JOHNSON FARM

Hendersonville - 3346 Haywood Road 28792. www.johnsonfarm.org. Phone: (828) 891-6585.

The entire structure was handmade from bricks that were fired on site from French Broad River mud. The Johnson Farm was the home of a wealthy tobacco farmer, Oliver Moss. This 1880s brick farmhouse houses a museum. Outside are miniature horses and antique farm equipment displays. Admission charged.

W Area

MINERAL & LAPIDARY MUSEUM

Hendersonville - 400 North Main Street (south of downtown, US 64) 28792. Phone: (828) 698-1977. www.mineralmuseum.org. Hours: Monday-Friday 1:00-5:00pm, Saturday 10:00am-5:00pm. Admission: FREE.

"The Geode Cracking Museum" has a collection of gems, minerals, fossils, and, yes, geodes. They even have two large petrified logs and a fluorescent display. Children can touch a dinosaur egg nest from China for FREE; adults pay a one dollar fee. If you want to find the secret beauty inside the ugly outside rock of your choice - let them crack open a geode for you to purchase as a souvenir.

WESTERN NORTH CAROLINA AIR MUSEUM

Hendersonville - 1340 Gilbert Street (adjacent to Hendersonville airport) 28793. Phone: (828) 698-2482. www.wncairmuseum.com Hours: Wednesday, Saturday and Sunday Noon - 5:00pm. Weather permitting. Admission: FREE.

Home of a collection of airplanes and memorabilia celebrating state aviation history, specifically Western North Carolina air history. Chat with the aircrafts' owners or watch these vintage machines in action in good flying weather. They display at least 12 different airplanes at any one time in their hanger and just outside.

NORTH CAROLINA APPLE FESTIVAL

Hendersonville - Downtown. www.ncapplefestival.org. (828) 697-4557. Apple breakfast, parade, recipe contests, orchard tours, street fair and rides, and local music and dance. FREE. (Labor Day weekend)

CARL SANDBURG HOME NATIONAL HISTORIC SITE

Hendersonville (Flat Rock) - 1928 Little River Road (US 26E to exit 53 south. Upward Rd. turns into Highland Lake Rd. Turn west onto US 25 south, make a right onto Little River) 28731. Phone: (828) 693-4178. www.nps.gov/carl/. Hours: Daily 9:00am-5:00pm, except Christmas Day. Admission: Free for grounds, trails and barn; no park entrance fee. Tours require fee. Miscellaneous: From June until mid-August, live performances of Sandburg's Rootabaga Stories and excerpts from the broadway play, The World of Carl Sandburg, are presented at the park amphitheater. Educators: They offer a seasonal "Something About Sandburg" interactive curriculum program for middle schoolers.

> Carl Sandburg referred to the television as an "idiot box" and "a thief of time."

Home of the famous poet and biographer Carl Sandburg, the site preserves and protects over 260 acres of land (on which the Mrs. raised champion goats), historic structures (check out the goats in the barn - babies in April/May) and over five miles of trails where Sandburg spent the last 22 years of his life. Mr. Sandburg used to take his chair out to some of the rock outcroppings along the trail to sit and write. The house and farm are open to the public for guided tours. Explore the goat barn on your own and meet some of the relatives of Lilian Sandburg's herd. The Sandburg Home was built in 1838 and now houses his collection of 10,000 books, notes and papers. On tour, notice there are books in

Around the curve, past the pond, up the long hill...you'll find inspiration...

every room and hallway! Besides being an author, he was also a folksinger and winner of two Pulitzer Prizes. The collection of walking canes and the guitar are noted by kids in the living room. Famous for biographies about President Lincoln, he provided enduring 20th century insight into the circumstances and spirit of the everyday working person. Are you a night owl? Sandburg always wrote at night.

Note: While the grounds and trails are free to wonder for everyone, families with tweens to teens would best appreciate the house tour. Rangers and volunteers are on hand, outdoors each summer, to share the fascinating story about goats and Mrs. Sandburg's dairy goat operation while others are on the tour.

FLAT ROCK PLAYHOUSE

Hendersonville (Flat Rock) - 2661 Greenville Hwy 28731. Phone: (828) 693-0731. www.flatrockplayhouse.org.

North Carolina's State Theatre presents the best of Broadway and fun productions with YouTheatre. Considered one of the ten best seasonal theater companies in the country, the Vagabond Players perform a variety of hits each summer featuring comedies, American classics, musicals, farces and whodunits. Sit back and enjoy spectacular matinee and evening performances from late May through mid-October. The comfortable atmosphere is ideal for families, vacationers and touring groups.

W Area

FLATROCK - AROUND TOWN

As you enter town, you'll notice The Historic Village of Flat Rock provides some of the finest examples of Southern aristocracy. The community was founded about a century and a half ago. In order to escape the sweltering heat and the epidemic of yellow fever and malaria, affluent Charlestonians, Europeans and prominent plantation owners of the South's Low Country built large summer estates in Flat Rock. The Low Country gentry affectionately called the town "The Little Charleston of the Mountains." With many of these homes still on their original sites, the entire district of Flat Rock is included in the National Register of Historic Places.

Hiddenite

HIDDENITE GEMS

Hiddenite - PO Box 276 28636. www.hiddenitegems.com. Phone: (866) 600-GEMS. Hours: Daily 8:30am-sunset. Only closed on Thanksgiving, Christmas Eve and Day. Admission: General $5.00; Sluicing/Creeking Combo $8.00; Sluicing/Creeking/ Digging Combo $15.00.

The Emerald Hollow Mine is the only emerald mine in the world that is open to the public for prospecting. Try your luck at prospecting for valuable gemstones in one of two large "state of the art" sluiceways where you may wash buckets filled with ore taken directly from the mine. Prospecting in the creek can be very rewarding. It is most productive to work the creek gravels with a screen, although some prefer the easier method of just "eyeing" the thousands of rocks in the creek bed, hoping to catch a glimpse of a nice gemstone. Digging at the mine can be hard work, but many mother lode finds are made chasing veins. For those who prefer easier prospecting, there is also lots of bare ground for surface collecting in the mining area.

Bring a large margarine or Cool Whip container with the child's name on it for their gemstone collection they will find.

Emerald Hollow Mine also conducts popular educational field trips. Field trip program activities include: Earth Science Talk- Lesson w/ rock show & tell; Sluicing; Creeking; and Surface Collecting- Looking for rocks in the mining area. The creekin' activity is everyone's favorite. Here, participants will learn about density, weight and gravity, and how each of these play a role in why gold and gemstones are so often found in the creek. Throughout the program activities, staff offer instruction, identify finds and shed light on the geology, mining and history of this unique area.

Highlands

HIGHLAND AREA WATERFALLS

Highlands - (see below) 28741. Phone: (828) 526-2112.

BRIDAL VEIL FALLS: US 64 West, On the South Side of the Fraser River. Cars can drive under this spectacular 120 foot fall that tumbles over a smooth rock face, creating a veil-like effect. Picnicking and hiking are available in the adjacent, scenic day-use area.

DRY FALLS: US 64, Between Franklin and Highlands. Take an easy walk on a well marked path with a hand rail behind this 75 foot curtain of rushing water that is located on the Cullasaja River, named after the Cherokee word for sugar water.

GLEN FALLS: South of Highland, Highway 106 South. A steep one mile trail leads down to the falls that are composed of three waterfalls that drop approximately 60 feet, each on the east fork of Overflow Creek in the scenic Blue Valley area.

WHITEWATER FALLS: NC 281 at the North Carolina State Line, Approximately 20 miles from Highlands. A very impressive cascade, 411-foot Whitewater Falls – arguably the highest in the eastern United States – is called the "king of waterfalls" No other waterfall in the east has the combination of water volume, height and visibility. The upper falls of this cascading masterpiece falls 411 feet. The lower falls cascade for 400 feet.

Jefferson

NEW RIVER STATE PARK

Jefferson - 1477 Wagoner Access Road (After driving through Jefferson, turn right on NC 88 east. Cross the New River and turn left on Wagoner Access Road (SR 1590) 28640. Phone: (336) 982-2587. http://ncparks.gov/Visit/parks/neri/main.php. Hours: Daily 8:00am-dusk. Admission: FREE, fee for camping. Miscellaneous: Website lists links to watercraft outfitters.

Canoe more than 26 miles of the National Wild and Scenic South Fork of the New River. Easy paddling and spectacular scenery make the New River a natural canoe trail for inexperienced paddlers. Its shallow, gentle waters and mild rapids are perfect for beginners, families and groups. Besides good canoe access, the Wagoner Road entrance features a couple of good, easy hiking trails that allow you to learn about the river environment. The most diverse habitats of the park can be found along the Farm House Loop Trail at

W Area

Alleghany Access Area. Walk through open fields, rhododendron thickets and oak/hickory woodlands for a beautiful view of the cliffs across the river. Our favorite way of enjoying the New River is atop a tube. Local outfitters abound near the parks, so it is easy to rent a tube or canoe. Most offer shuttle service as well. It's hard to beat a lazy float down the scenic New from the Waggoner Road put-in to the US 221 take-out area. So, float this spring and summer in America's oldest river, the New. Three access points, primitive camping, fishing, hiking, mountain scenery and wildlife are other activities.

Lake Lure

LAKE LURE TOURS AND BEACH / WATER WORKS

Lake Lure - PO Box 541 (25 miles southeast of Asheville on Hwy 64/74A. Or, I-26 east to exit 18A) 28746. Phone: (877) FUN-4-ALL. www.lakelure.com. Hours: Beach and the Works: Daily daytime (Memorial Day weekend through Labor Day weekend). Admission: Varies with each activity. Boat Tours: $12.00 adult, $10.00 senior (62+), $6.00 child (4-12). Beach/WaterWorks: $6.00-$8.00 (age 4+). Miscellaneous: Just across the street (separate admission) is the Bottomless Pools (828-625-8324) where admission grants you access to easy hiking trails around three natural whirlpools and waterfalls. Hours: 10:00am-5:00pm (April-September).

Discover why National Geographic named Lake Lure "one of the ten most spectacular man-made lakes in the world." The one-hour lake tour includes a visit to the site of a popular film. Passengers hear the story of Snake Island, view the first home built on the lake, and delight in the legend of the church said to be in the center of the lake...100 feet down. Look for blue heron and fawns along the shore. Do the mountains look like buffalo? Did you know the lake is shaped like a cross? Visitors may rent canoes, kayaks, paddle boats, electric boats and pontoon boats as well. Splash at the beach or play at the Fun Center with family-oriented, interactive games and activities. The Beach Water Works has soaking-wet games, bumper boats, water balloons cannons (what a hoot!), water wars and water slides. A great family spot to have fun getting wet!

RUMBLING BALD RESORT ON LAKE LURE

Lake Lure - I-40 exit 81 south. Stay on Sugar Hill Road, turn right onto Bills Creek Road, then right onto Buffalo Creek Road or follow Rte. 64/74A east past The Beach to the other side of the Lake. http://rumblingbald.com/LakeLure/info/rst.aspx. (800) 419-3854 or (828) 694-3000. Once known as Lake Lure Golf & Beach Resort, the resort is nestled at the base of the majestic 2,800-foot Rumbling Bald Mountain on the north end of beautiful Lake Lure. This resort offers a variety of lodging options. They have everything from studio villas to two and three bedroom condos. Most units have a kitchenette. Weekly summer events include beach cookouts, barbeques, storytellers, live bands and dance nights. The Mountain Kids Program runs weekdays each summer. Everything from Kids Night Out to crafts and outdoor play to nature hikes. Restaurants of all styles are on the property, as is a fitness center, spa, arcade, tennis, bingo, and swimming pools (indoor/outdoor) - one with a floating lazy river.

Lenoir

TUTTLE EDUCATIONAL STATE FOREST

Lenoir - Route 6, Box 417 (I-40 to Hwy. 18-64 north to west on SR 1611) 28645. Phone: (828) 757-5608. www.ncesf.org/TESF/home.htm. Hours: Daily spring thru fall. Closed Mondays. Admission: FREE

Located in the foothills of the Blue Ridge Mountains, Tuttle boasts a wide variety of pines and hardwoods plus rolling terrain and clear streams. These features are accessible by a series of well-marked trails accented by talking tree exhibits and displays which explain the ecology of the managed forest.

Linville

GRANDFATHER MOUNTAIN

Linville - 2050 Blowing Rock Hwy. (US 221 south & Blue Ridge Parkway, near Rte. 105 & Rte. 221) 28646. www.grandfather.com. Phone: (828) 733-4337 or (800)

468-7325. Hours: Daily 9:00am-5:00 to 7:00pm. Closed Thanksgiving and Christmas Days. Open weather permitting in winter. Admission: $14.00 adult, $12.00 senior (60+), $6.00 child (4-12). Miscellaneous: Great gift shop items, restaurant and Outdoor Exploring center. Picnic tables and grills scattered throughout the park. Bicycling is not permitted on the roadways or on the trails. Pets on a leash are welcome on the mountain.

The Mountain features environmental habitats with native wildlife, numerous hiking trails, the famous swinging bridge and an Outdoor Exploring museum and theater. The Mile High Swinging Bridge was built to give visitors easy access to the breath-taking view from Grandfather Mountain's Linville Peak (an adventure mini-hike!). The 228-foot suspension bridge spans an 80-foot chasm at more than one mile in elevation. Exhibits at the Museum include: a North Carolina Amethyst (The 165-pound cluster is considered the finest amethyst ever discovered in North America), Gems & Minerals of North Carolina (see them "before and after" they're polished), North Carolina Gold (including largest gold nugget on public display in NC), and Indians and Daniel Boone at Grandfather

Mountain. When you see the Black Birch Burl Bowl (a 64" x 46" x 34" bowl made from

The "Mile High" marker...

a 3,200 pound piece of black birch), you may think it looks like an "Outdoorsman's bathtub". Outside in the Outdoor Exploring Center Habitat, you'll be most attracted to the river otters and the best "authentic" bear habitat we've ever seen! Along the way

up the mountain look for The Split Rock & Sphinx Rock (two rocks the size of houses). In great weather, plan to spend the day here as there are both indoor and outdoor sites to see and more than 12 miles of maintained trails (some, easy nature walks). Pack a picnic lunch or grab a picnic-to-go from the restaurant. For the best value, pick a nice day in mid-spring through early fall. Otherwise, it's windy and the bears are "sleeping".

On a foggy day, we couldn't see the other side...very creepy !

HIGHLAND GAMES & GATHERING OF SCOTTISH CLAN

Over 120 Scottish clans gather for parades, music and games. This is the New World event with the most variety of Scottish families. Admission. (mid-July Thursday-Sunday)

KIDFEST AT GRANDFATHER MOUNTAIN

A day designed to teach kids about the nature and culture of the North Carolina mountains through fun and entertaining activities. Includes a Junior Ranger project, presentations by our naturalist, tours of the animal habitats, games, face painting, storytelling and mountain music. Park admission. (last Saturday in September)

Linville Falls

LINVILLE GORGE WILDERNESS AREA

Linville Falls - Kistler Memorial Hwy (NC 1238) 28647. Phone: (828) 652-2144. www.cs.unca.edu/nfsnc/recreation/linville.pdf. Hours: Daily during daylight hours. Admission: FREE. Miscellaneous: See their online brochure for trail maps. The gorge trails are for the seasoned rough campers and hikers, folks.

The Grand Canyon of the East – Linville Gorge Wilderness. It covers 12,000 acres and the gorge descends more than 2,000 feet to the Linville River below. Wild and isolated, the Linville Gorge Wilderness offers the primitive camper the ultimate in scenic beauty and tranquility. Pack your fishing rod along with your tent, so you can tangle with smallmouth bass and native trout. Hike or camp near rock formations such as Sitting Bear, Hawksbill, Table Rock, or The Chimneys of the Blue Ridge landscape. At the top of the gorge, and just off the Blue Ridge Parkway is Linville Falls, a spectacular three-tiered waterfall plunging into the wilderness area. This is the most accessible area to vehicles.

Maggie Valley

CAROLINA NIGHTS DINNER SHOW

Maggie Valley - 3714 Soco Road (34 miles from Asheville) 28751. Phone: (888) 622-SHOW. www.carolinanightstheater.com. Hours: Open April-December. Seating begins at 6:15pm. Admission: $27-$29.00 adult, $20.00 military, $19.00 student, FREE child (ages 3-11, if chose the child's meal).

The Carolina Nights Dinner Show combines good food (country fixins) with music along with a comedy act for family entertainment. The dinner is a country meal, consisting of baked herb chicken breast, pulled pork BBQ, baked beans, potato salad, homemade hand dipped hushpuppies, cobbler, with coffee and iced tea. Dinner is followed by an action packed variety show featuring magic, comedy, country, rock'n roll, broadway selections, gospel and it finishes with a patriotic salute to America.

GHOST TOWN IN THE SKY

Maggie Valley - 890 Soco Road 28751. www.ghosttowninthesky.com. Phone: (828) 926-1140. Hours: Daily 10:00am-6:00pm (Memorial Day weekend thru late August), Friday-Sunday only (May, September, October) Admission: Frontier Ticket: Covers all rides, shows & access to Heritage Town Square: $30.00 adult, $22.00 child (3-10), 2 & under free.

Ghost Town In The Sky (cont.)

Re-live life in the Old West, surrounded by the Smoky Mountains. Begin with a ride on the chairlift. Your adventure will continue as you make your way through the park. Stroll the streets, enjoy the shows, ride the rides - all for one admission price. Come re-live the Wild West with hourly shows between good guys and bad guys. Pull up a seat at one of the saloons and watch the Can-Can girls perform or slide down to the next saloon and see live music. Keep your eyes open - you may see authentic Cherokee Indian dancers and musicians. Experience all kinds of rides including a train ride, the Drop Tower, the Scrambler, and Merry-Go-Round. Be sure not to miss the Chance Gunfighter Yo-Yo Swing, a favorite Ghost Town classic. Geronimo!!! The newest addition to the thrill rides at Ghost Town will give you a whole new perspective on just how high you really are. The tower is located at one of the highest points in the park, more than 4,800 feet above sea level. Your heart will drop as you are raised 98 feet up into the sky and then released into a free fall before you are safely stopped by the magnetic brakes.

WHEELS THROUGH TIME MUSEUM

Maggie Valley - 62 Vintage Lane (I-40 West to exit 27 (Maggie Valley). Exit on to U.S. 19/74 North (exit 103 right) 28751. www.wheelsthroughtime.com. Phone: (828) 926-6266. Hours: Daily 9:00am-6:00pm (April-October). Daily, except Wednesday 10:00am-4:00pm (November-March). Admission: $12.00 adult, $10.00 senior (55+), $6.00 child (5-12). Miscellaneous: the new Time Machine online video page offers visitors the opportunity to watch folks magically restore rare machines.

They offer the world's largest collection of rare American motorcycles and cars from each of the 10 decades of America's automobile history. From the early years of 1900 – 1928, motorcycles emerged from a motor powered bicycle to a form of reliable sport and transportation. Over 250 rare antique American Motorcycles unite the "art of the motorcycle" with a new generation of American freedom.

W Area

Marion

CAROLINA EMERALD MINE @ VEIN MOUNTAIN GOLD CAMP

Marion - 1694 Polly Spout Road (I-40 exit 85 to US 221 south 6 miles) 28752. Phone: (828)738-9544. www.veinmountaingoldcamp.com.

North Carolina's newest emerald discovery! The Carolina Emerald Mine is located at the Vein Mountain Gold Camp south of Marion, and is the only native emerald mine open to the public in North Carolina. The material from the emerald vein is transported to the water flume in its natural and unsalted condition. Gem and mineral enthusiasts will appreciate that the ore on this property not only produces native gold, but also 40 different types of crystals and gems, including olivine, moonstone, garnets, aquamarine, tourmaline, several types of quartz, and many more. Gold prospectors will appreciate the 30 acre property with over 4100 feet of river frontage, and a chance to participate in an annual drawing for a large gold nugget. Prospectors can pan in a roofed area, use dredges, set up a high banker, or work from the roofed water flume or sluice. Primitive riverside camping sites are available, as well as sites with power and water. There is also a gift shop, fishing lakes, and handicap bathroom facilities. (Open April -October at 8:30am)

LINVILLE CAVERNS

Marion - PO Box 567 (Hwy. 221 N) 28752. Phone: (828)756-4171 or (800) 419-0540. www.linvillecaverns.com. Hours: Daily 9:00am-4:30pm (November-March, except December, January, February- Weekends Only); Daily 9:00am-5:00pm (April, May, September, October); Daily 9:00am-6:00pm (June-Labor Day). Admission: $6.00 adult, $4.50 senior (62+), $4.00 child (5-12).

Deep inside of Humpback Mountain lie the Linville Caverns, North Carolina's only caverns. These caverns were first explored by the white man over 100 years ago. It is said that in 1822 a fisherman noticed trout swimming in and out of the mountain and he began looking for a way to see where they were going. Linville caverns remain active as mineral deposits continue to form stalactites and stalagmites. The water, produced by this mountain, with its carbon dioxide, created the cavern's natural passageways. A highlight at the end of the tour is the Bottomless Lake, gauged to be 75m deep. A metal bridge allows visitors to gaze deep into the clear water, which is lighted. During the winter and early spring you may get to view an Eastern Pipistrelle Bat, which hibernates here, hanging from the ceiling. The owners approach these formations from a

Creationist's point of view: "Although we do not believe any rock is millions of years old, these formations are still very unique and show the majestic work of an awesome GOD."

LAKE JAMES STATE PARK

Marion (Nebo) - 2785 Hwy 126, Lake James Road (I-40, take the Nebo/Lake James exit (#90) 28761. www.ncparks.gov/Visit/parks/laja/main.php. Phone: (828) 652-5047. Hours: Daily 8:00am-dusk. Admission: FREE. Educators: The Lake James program, Aquatic Critters (an Environmental Educational Learning Experience) introduces students to the lakeshore environment, focusing on the plants and animals that live there. Accompanying the program is a teacher's booklet and workshop, free of charge to educators.**

Tucked away in rolling hills at the base of Linville Gorge is Lake James, a 6,510-acre lake with more than 150 miles of shoreline. Try swimming and sunbathing or enjoy a picnic along the lakeshore. Boat, water ski or fish in cool mountain waters, or take a walk and enjoy an abundance of wildflowers and wildlife along park trails with lake overlooks. Two one-way footpaths travel along the shoreline of Lake James. A half-mile trail leads to Sandy Cliff Overlook, and a 1.5-mile trail leads through the campground to Lake Channel Overlook. Fox Den Loop Trail is the park's longest trail at 2.2 miles. Nature programs presented by rangers.

Old Fort

PIONEER DAY

Old Fort - Mountain Gateway Museum. (828) 668-9259. Visit the state-run museum complex with its two century-old cabins and an excellent collection of early photographs, tools and house wares, that document the region's pioneer days. Nature and history presentations are given throughout the year, many in the museum's outdoor amphitheater. Pioneer music performed. (last Saturday in April)

Pisgah Forest

COLD MOUNTAIN

Pisgah Forest - 1001 Pisgah Highway (from Asheville, drive south along the Parkway past Mt. Pisgah to milepost 411) 28768. Phone: (828) 298-0398 or (828) 877-3265.

Based on Asheville-area native Charles Frazier's best-selling Civil War-era novel *Cold Mountain*, set in the mountains of Western North Carolina. The movie *Cold Mountain* and the actual Cold Mountain have become one of the most famous peaks in America. The easiest place to see it is along the Blue Ridge Parkway just past Wagon Road Gap (mentioned in the book). There, visitors will find a large, weathered, wooden National Park Service sign, not unlike those found at all of the other Parkway overlooks. Visitors can strategically place themselves next to the sign with the now-famous mountain looming in the distance.

CRADLE OF FORESTRY IN AMERICA

Pisgah Forest - 1001 Pisgah Hwy. Ranger Station (I-26E to exit 40, NC280West. When in Pisgah Forest, turn right on Hwy 276 & go 11 miles. Near Parkway milepost 412) 28768. Phone: (828) 877-3130. www.cradleofforestry.org. Hours: Daily 9:00am-5:00pm (mid-April to early November). Admission: $5.00 adult (age 16 and up). FREE for everyone on Tuesdays! *FREE for youth aged 15 and younger. *FREE for Federal Interagency Senior, Access and Eagle passholders. Special events require admission charged for everyone. Educational kits: (Project Learning Tree Trunk and Wilderness and Land Ethics Box). Miscellaneous: Café and gift shop. Nearby is the Pisgah (pronounced Piz-gah) Center for Wildlife

Education (828-877-4423). Events most every weekend promote visiting often.

The Birthplace of the Forestry Service. At this magnificent facility, start with the 18-minute movie *Biltmore's Dream*. Learn how Vanderbilt purchased this land and hired, now famous, foresters. Now, stay indoors for a while to explore the Discovery Center. Walk through re-created scenes from a typical forest with sound effects. Next, crawl through

Learning about the burrows of cottontail rabbits - looks cozy!

a tunnel (parents too!) as you explore where creatures burrow underground. This is also the best area to begin finding clues on your Scavenger Hunt game sheet (prizes awarded for completion). At the edge of the "forest", climb inside a life-size Fire-fighting Helicopter Simulator ride. It's so cool! You actually ride along as the pilots complete a "water drop". Head outside on guided trails to historic cabins with cultural interpreters. Stop at the

Climb aboard a life-size helicopter simulator

original Forestry School, the store and a boarding house. Groups of children get to do some chores (like churning butter or washing clothes) while others watch a toy maker, a weaver, a baker, or a quilter. Another trail leads to the 1915 logging train and antique saw mill. Even though preservation was important here, logging was also part of the mix. We were impressed - very engaging, but make sure you watch the video to better understand the offerings here.

SLIDING ROCK - A NATURAL WATER SLIDE

Pisgah Forest - (US 276, about 7.5 miles south of Blue Ridge Pkwy (or 7 miles north off of US 280) 28768. http://ncnatural.com/NCUSFS/Pisgah/lkglass.html. Phone: (828) 877-3265. Hours: Daily 10:30am-5:00pm (Memorial Day to mid-August) Admission: $1.00 per person upon exiting. Miscellaneous: Lifeguards on duty. Pools of water are very cold, even in the summer. Because rocks are slippery and some are jagged, wear swim socks. The bottom pool water is 8 feet deep. Must be able to swim or be accompanied by an adult. They allow life jackets.

> Wear your old blue jeans or cut-offs to sit and slip down the rock into the pool below, where 60-degree water beats summer heat.

The king of swimming holes in the mountains near Asheville, this 60 foot natural water slide down a well-worn slab of rock was providing summertime entertainment long before water slides became standard fare. What a "hoot & holler" to race down as a family. A worthwhile find in Forest country.

Transylvania County calls itself "Land of Waterfalls" with good reason. Many waterfalls of various sizes are found in the Pisgah Forest Ranger District. On your way into the Forest, take an observation look (or even a dip!) in <u>LOOKING GLASS FALLS</u>...very impressive. Looking Glass Falls is one of the country's most viewed falls. It's 35 feet wide and drops 65 feet! You can view it from the observation deck or you can walk to its base. You might recognize this

Daniel as he completes the fun slide and about to plunge into the 8' pool !

For updates & travel games visit: **www.KidsLoveTravel.com**

waterfall from the movie *Last of the Mohicans*, which was filmed in this and several other beautiful spots in NC. Other falls of note in the area include Turtleback Falls, a favorite swimming spot, Moore Cove Falls, which spills over a tremendous granite shelf, creating a falls you can walk behind, and Twin falls, which features two falls. As a word of caution, always be careful around waterfalls! Mossy covered rocks are VERY slippery and fatalities occur every year on the waterfalls. Particularly stay away from the tops of falls.

BLUE RIDGE CORN MAZE

Pisgah Forest - Blue Ridge Corn Maze, 570 Everitt Road (Hwy 64 east, south on Crab Creek, west on Everitt). (828) 884-4415 or http://blueridgecornmaze.com. The Blue Ridge Mountains are a great backdrop for the corn maze. 6 acre corn maze plus contests, prizes, food, drinks, souvenirs, hay rides, local produce and crafts. Admission. (Friday nights and weekends in September and October)

Roaring Gap

STONE MOUNTAIN STATE PARK

Roaring Gap - 3042 Frank Parkway (I-77, turn west onto US 21. Veer left onto Traphill Road (SR 1002), follow signs) 28668. http://ncparks.gov/Visit/parks/stmo/main.php Phone: (336) 957-8185. Hours: Daily 8:00am-dusk.

It's a strenuous three quarters of a mile hike on the Stone Mountain Loop Trail to the 2,305-foot summit. This magnificent 600-foot granite dome is well worth the wait. Sunlight and shadows dance across a broad tapestry of stone. Gentle streams, trails and the sheer rock face of the mountain have created a haven for anglers, hikers and even climbers. You'll likely see turkey vultures and red-tail hawks wheeling overhead. Wild goats clamber up the hillsides, and wildlife ranging from deer to bobcats may be seen throughout the park. If you are not prepared for the tough climb to the summit, go across the park's meadow and take the more sedate portion of the trail to Stone Mountain Falls. It's also a great place to spread out the blanket. Check out the park's old-time still, loom and other historical artifacts in the Mountain Culture Exhibit in the park office building. Other exhibits include animal pelts and a full-body black bear mount. Walk through one of the park's historic sites, the Hutchinson Homestead. The homestead is complete with a log cabin, barn, blacksmith shop, corncrib, meat house and original furnishings. Visitors can play recordings that explain how different aspects of the farm were run. The park includes camping and views of waterfalls.

Rosman

RIVER ADVENTURES

Rosman - PO Box 145 (intersection of North & West Forks of the French Broad River & Hwys. 64 & 915) 28772. www.headwatersoutfitters.com. Phone: (828) 877-3106. Hours: April-October. Tube Run (mid-May thru mid-September). Weather permitted. Admission: Generally $15.00-$20.00 per person.

They shuttle you to the river, then let the scenic mountain waters gently float you to Lyon Mountain Bridge where you're transported back to the main depot (1-2 hours). Canoe and Kayak trips (3 hours) paddle you down the old river, meandering and twisting thru Outdoor Exploring along the riverbanks.

Rutherfordton

KIDSENSES CHILDREN'S INTERACTIVE MUSEUM

Rutherfordton - 172 N. Main Street 28139. www.kidsenses.com. Phone: (828) 286-2120. Hours: Tuesday-Saturday 9:00am-5:00pm, Sunday 1:00-5:00pm. Admission: $5.00 general.

Imagine the excitement of kids as they create a castle, act as a TV commentator, or explore the streets of a fun city just for them. The layout is bright but not overwhelming. Look around some and then interact in a kid-size Dental Office, Grocery, TV station, Factory, or Stage. Climb the Big Climber or play small in the Alphabet Trail area. Play with Science and Art, too. There's even a room dedicated to Bubbles.

Sapphire

GORGES STATE PARK

Sapphire - Hwy 281 (from I-26, taking exit 9 onto NC 280 and traveling west toward Brevard. Turn west on US 64, follow signs) 28774. Phone: (828) 966-9099. www.ncparks.gov/Visit/parks/gorg/main.php. Hours: Daily 8:00am-dusk.

Rugged river gorges, plunging waterfalls, sheer rock walls and one of the greatest concentrations or rare species in the eastern United States are found within the park. With a 2,000 foot elevation, combined with abundant rainfall, the environ creates a temperate rain forest and supports numerous waterfalls. Being a new park, administration is still planning and building new facilities.

W Area

Sparta

DOUGHTON PARK & PARKWAY HOMESTEADS

Sparta - Blue Ridge Parkway Milepost 241, 28675. Phone: (336) 372-8877.
www.nps.gov/blri/historyculture/index.htm

This landscape of open meadows is a place to view wildlife and get a feel for the lives of those who lived here long ago. Doughton Park is one of the best places along the motor road to view white-tailed deer, raccoons, red and grey foxes, and bobcats, as well as spectacular shows of flame azalea and rhododendron in the late spring. Bluffs Lodge is open during the summer season along with a restaurant and gas station. For reservations at the lodge call (336) 372-4499. There is a campground with ranger talks during the summer season. Hiking opportunities range from a short hike at Fodder Stack Trail to the strenuous 7.5 mile Bluff Mountain Trail. Visit the Brinegar Cabin 1885 (MP 238.5) - the home of Martin Brinegar and his family. Brinegar was a cobbler as well as a farmer. His home is open on summer weekend afternoons. Hand-loom weaving and other craft demonstrations are often given during the summer months. Or, hike into Basin Cove to view the Caudill Family Homestead (MP 241). The Northwest Trading Post at Milepost 258.6 has a wide variety of craft items and souvenirs for sale from this part of North Carolina.

Spruce Pine

GEM MOUNTAIN

Spruce Pine - Hwy 226 (milepost 331 off Blue Ridge Pkwy, just up the road from NC Museum of Minerals) 28777. Phone: (888) 817-5829. www.gemmountain.com. Hours: Daily 9:00am-5:00pm. Closed winter Sundays. Open later in summer. Admission: FREE. Mining Buckets start at $15.00. Miscellaneous: Appalachian General Store & Museum.

Panning. Just place a scoop of rough material on the screen... then rinse with clear water. The Gem Stones, when wet, will reveal colors and crystal shapes. Use the identity chart to compare and name your finds. Larger gems can be cut into jewelry. Gem Mountain gemstone mine has been attracting rock hounds since 1986.

MUSEUM OF NORTH CAROLINA MINERALS

Spruce Pine - Blue Ridge Parkway & Hwy 226 (MP 331 on Parkway at Gillespie Gap) 28777. Phone: (828) 765-2761. Hours: Daily 9:00am-5:00pm. Admission: FREE.

The Museum provides an introduction to the importance of mining in the region and the mineral and gem wealth found here. Exhibits feature more than 300 varieties of minerals and gems found in the state. Many gems are shown in both natural and polished states for comparison (unpolished gem rocks don't look that valuable, do they?). Work is continuing on new interactive displays that will take you deep inside a mountain to see how gems and minerals are formed (or, visit nearby Emerald Village).

EMERALD VILLAGE

Spruce Pine (Little Switzerland) - McKinney Mine Road (off Blue Ridge Pkwy, take exit 334, US 19E northwest) 28749. www.emeraldvillage.com. Phone: (828) ROK-MINE. Hours: Daily 10:00-4:00pm (April-October). Extended hours May-October, especially weekends. Open in the winter by reservation. Admission: Gem mining: $7.50-$10.00 per bucket. Mine & Museums tours: $5.00-$6.00 (age 6+).

In this famous historical mining area, 60 different rocks & minerals have been found including Aquamarine, Emerald, Garnet, Smoky Quartz as well as Uranium and Fluorescent minerals (glow in the night) - all right here in this little village. Historical preservation of these mines and the opportunity to prospect for your own gems, make Emerald Village a center of North Carolina Gem collecting activities. Explore the historic Bon Ami Mine with its authentic mining equipment, mine for gemstones in a fresh water flume, watch artisans cut and mount jewelry and then picnic in indoor or outdoor picnic areas. While here take in the many free displays such as the Antique Music Museum, the Homestead (farm display), Gallery of Minerals, and Crossings of the Blue Ridge Railroad. When gem panning, you are guaranteed a gem find every time and can keep what you find.

ORCHARD AT ALTAPASS

Spruce Pine (Little Switzerland) - 1025 Orchard Rd, 28749. Phone: (888) 765-9531. www.altapassorchard.com.

A Hayride Through the Apples. Guides host the very popular orchard hayride. The 30-minute journey begins by following the path of the Revolutionary War mountain soldiers called the Overmountain Men. The hay wagon swings through the orchard itself, past old and young trees. The scenery is spectacular for the entire route, and the stories are entertaining and educational for all ages. A special storytelling hayride with orchard historian Bill Carson, is offered each season on Saturdays and Sundays at 4:00pm. This ride lasts 45 minutes. Stories are geared to the audience, but cover subjects such as the early settlers, the coming of the railroad, the March of the Overmountain Men in the Revolutionary War, the Flood of 1916, and more delightful tales passed along to Bill by people whose families date back hundreds of years in these parts. A gift shop and entertainment are available each weekend also.

Tryon

FOOTHILLS EQUESTRIAN NATURE CENTER (FENCE)

Tryon - 3381 Hunting Country Road (off I-26, just north of South Carolina state line) 28782. Phone: (828) 859-9021. www.fence.org. Hours: Daylight hours. Admission: FREE.

Five miles of hiking and riding trails thread their way through the property, including a hard-paved trail for the physically challenged. The trails are equipped with information stations and shelters. A nature pond with an observation boardwalk serves as an outdoor classroom for observing wildfowl and native plant species. The Equestrian Center comprises three lighted show rings with all-weather footing, stabling for over 200 horses and spectator seating. The nationally-famous Block House Steeplechase, is run each Spring over an eight-furlong course which encircles the equestrian area. Hunter/ Jumper competitions, cross-country events, dressage and carriage driving are among the equestrian disciplines which make use of the Center.

W Area

Valdese

FROM THIS DAY FORWARD OUTDOOR DRAMA

Valdese - Fred B. Cranford Old Colony Amphitheatre, Church Street. This is the story of the Waldenses, a religious sect that arose in southeast France in the 1100s, and their struggle to survive persecution in their homeland and their eventual arrival in North Carolina to establish a colony in 1893 at Valdese. The show, directed by John Hogan, includes music and dance. http://www.oldcolonyplayers.com/. (800) 635-4778, (828) 874-0176. (8:00pm Friday-Saturday in July and first two weekends in August)

Waynesville

INTERNATIONAL FESTIVAL DAY

Waynesville - Main Street. (828) 456-3517. A day-long extravaganza of music, dance, crafts and food from around the world. (last Saturday in July)

APPLE HARVEST FESTIVAL

Waynesville - Main Street. (828) 456-3517. Live mountain music and dance, craft and demonstrations booths, apples, cider, fresh fried pies and everything apple. (third Saturday in October)

A NIGHT BEFORE CHRISTMAS

Waynesville - (828) 456-3517. Beginning with the Christmas Parade, come share the caroling, handbells, live music, a live nativity, pictures with Santa, old-fashioned wagon rides, storytelling, poetry and streets lined with luminaries. (first three Saturday evenings in December)

West Jefferson

W Area

ASHE COUNTY CHEESE FACTORY

West Jefferson - 106 East Main Street (SR 163 in town) 28694. Phone: (336) 246-2501. www.ashecountycheese.com. Hours: Monday-Saturday 8:30am-5:00pm. Admission: FREE.

Ashe County Cheese is open to visitors year-round who often come in to watch through a viewing room to see just how the cheese is made. The viewing window allows people to watch some of the procedure and see the milk running into the vat along with some of the other things that are done. Ashe County Cheese is the only cheese making plant in the area of its kind and possibly the only one in the state. Around 50,000 pounds of cheese are made a week at the factory. Sample some of the more than 50 varieties of cheese in the gift shop. One of the favorites, cheese curds, are available in the gift shop as well.

Master
Index

For updates & travel games visit: **www.KidsLoveTravel.com**

Activity Index

For updates & travel games visit: **www.KidsLoveTravel.com**

SCIENCE *(cont.)*

SPORTS

SPORTS *(cont.)*

THE ARTS

For updates & travel games visit: **www.KidsLoveTravel.com**